RED RIDING HOOD AND THE WOLF IN BED:
MODERNISM'S FAIRY TALES

From children's books to Christmas pantomimes, and from scholarly anthologies to movies, the many and various adaptations of fairy tales in the late nineteenth and early twentieth centuries speak to the genre's widespread popularity. Narratives whose presence and appeal can be traced through every aspect of modern British and North American culture, fairy tales invite a range of interpretations and applications, as multiple versions of 'Cinderella,' 'Sleeping Beauty,' and 'Little Red Riding Hood' enable multiple and potentially subversive uses of their plots and motifs by writers and readers alike.

By exploring representations of fairy tales in the works of James Joyce, Virginia Woolf, and Djuna Barnes, Ann Martin's *Red Riding Hood and the Wolf in Bed* asserts the significance of the stories as a system of reference for these and other modernists. Allusions to fairy tales in works such as *Ulysses*, *Orlando*, and *Nightwood* signify not only an intersection of popular culture and high modernism, but also an interaction between modern subjects and their social and economic contexts. Drawing on theoretical paradigms from gender and cultural studies, Martin develops a participatory model of modernist literature and culture. The tactical engagements with social normatives that are found in fairy tales and in the modernist texts echo the authors' own challenges to formal and discursive boundaries through intertextuality, just as the readers of the fairy tale allusions become actively engaged in making sense of modernism.

ANN MARTIN is an assistant professor in the Department of English at the University of Saskatchewan.

ANN MARTIN

Red Riding Hood and the Wolf in Bed

Modernism's Fairy Tales

UNIVERSITY OF TORONTO PRESS
Toronto Buffalo London

© University of Toronto Press Incorporated 2006
Toronto Buffalo London
Printed in Canada

Reprinted in paperback 2007

ISBN 978-0-8020-9086-7 (cloth)
ISBN 978-0-8020-9571-8 (paper)

Printed on acid-free paper

Library and Archives Canada Cataloguing in Publication

Martin, Ann, 1970–
    Red Riding Hood and the wolf in bed : modernism's fairy tales / Ann
Martin.

    Includes bibliographical references and index.
    ISBN 978-0-8020-9086-7 (bound). – ISBN 978-0-8020-9571-8 (pbk.)

    1. Joyce, James, 1882–1941 – Criticism and interpretation.   2. Woolf,
Virginia, 1882–1941 – Criticism and interpretation.   3. Barnes,
Djuna – Criticism and interpretation.   4. Fairy tales in literature. I. Title.

PR888.F27M37 2006   823'.9140915   C2006-902209-7

University of Toronto Press acknowledges the financial assistance to
its publishing program of the Canada Council for the Arts and the
Ontario Arts Council.

This book has been published with the help of a grant from the Canadian
Federation for the Humanities and Social Sciences, through the Aid to
Scholarly Publications Programme, using funds provided by the Social
Sciences and Humanities Research Council of Canada.

University of Toronto Press acknowledges the financial support for its
publishing activities of the Government of Canada through the Book
Publishing Industry Development Program (BPIDP).

For Alex and Hazel Munro

Contents

Acknowledgments

I am indebted to many people, without whom this book would not have been possible. Heather Murray's consistently good advice is responsible for the best parts of *Red Riding Hood and the Wolf in Bed*, and I thank her for all the insights and for all of the support that she has provided. Melba Cuddy-Keane has been an invaluable guide, as has Garry Leonard, whose fourth-year James Joyce course set me on this path. I would also like to thank Jo-Ann Wallace; N. John Hall; Russell Brown, who has been a mentor and a friend; Tracy Ware; Ed Lobb; Maggie Berg; Pat Vicari; Andrew Patenall; Michael Tait; John L. Plews for his excellent editorial work for the journal *torquere;* and the English Departments at the University of Toronto, Queen's University, and Dalhousie University. Allan Pero and Marielle Aylen have been instrumental in the development of my work on modernism, as have past members of the Twentieth-Century Reading Group at the University of Toronto, including Dana Draguniou. I am grateful to Jill McConkey and Barb Porter at the University of Toronto Press for their interest, patience, and expertise, and to Charles Stuart for his work on this book.

Thanks also to Alix, Doug, and Jennifer Martin; Pat, Bob, and Marjorie McColl; Estelle Martin and Lillian Voss; and Joanne and Dave Clark. I am extremely appreciative of the assistance of Craig and Barbara Martin, whose home and computers have been a part of the book from the beginning. I must also thank all the friends and family members who have taken the time to talk about fairy tales with me. I find that I'm unable to put into words my gratitude to James, but without him, none of this would mean very much at all.

Material from this book has been published elsewhere: 'Sleeping Beauty in a Green Dress: *Mrs Dalloway* and Fairy Tale Configurations of

Desire' was published in *Virginia Woolf Out of Bounds: Selected Papers from the Tenth Annual Conference on Virginia Woolf* and 'Modernist Transformations' in *Woolf Studies Annual*. I am grateful to Mark Hussey and Pace University Press for their permission to include versions of those papers here. I am also grateful to the Thomas Fisher Rare Book Library, University of Toronto.

Excerpts from 'Burnt Norton' and 'The Cultivation of Christmas Trees' from *Collected Poems 1909–1962* by T.S. Eliot. Reproduced by permission of Faber and Faber Limited. Excerpt from 'The Cultivation of Christmas Trees' from *The Cultivation of Christmas Trees* by T.S. Eliot. Copyright © 1956 by T.S. Eliot. Reprinted by permission of Farrar, Straus and Giroux, LLC. Excerpts from 'Burnt Norton' in *Four Quartets*, copyright 1936 by Harcourt, Inc. and renewed 1964 by T.S. Eliot, reprinted by permission of the publisher. Every effort has been made to obtain permission to reproduce the illustration that appears in this book. Any errors or omissions brought to our attention will be corrected in future printings.

RED RIDING HOOD AND THE WOLF IN BED:
MODERNISM'S FAIRY TALES

Introduction: Modernism's Fairy Tales

Footfalls echo in the memory
Down the passage which we did not take
Towards the door we never opened
Into the rose-garden. My words echo
Thus, in your mind.
But to what purpose
Disturbing the dust on a bowl of rose-leaves
I do not know.
      Other echoes
Inhabit the garden. Shall we follow?
                                   T.S. Eliot, 'Burnt Norton'

In T.S. Eliot's poetry and essays, images of children and images from children's literature are deeply connected to the poet's sense of the past and of interactive community. The garden in 'Burnt Norton,' for example, is an organic space in which youthful innocence can be visited and revisited, and where the sounds of children suggest nostalgic wholeness and plenitude to the experienced modernist. However, the voices and laughter are only echoes of what they once were, and the children themselves are 'invisible' or 'hidden' within the hedges and leaves (T.S. Eliot 1935, 190). Where Mary Lennox has worked her magic on the secret garden and Alice has had her adventures among the Red Queen's roses, Eliot's speaker can only touch dusty petals in a bowl. The modern world is placed in contrast to the 'first world' (190) of childhood here in a reflection of the modern subject's alienation from 'sensuous lived experience' (Nicholls 1995, 256).

The estrangement results from the very experience of modernity; that is, from the immense social and economic changes of the late nineteenth and early twentieth centuries. Accelerating industrialization, the growth of urban centres, shifting gender roles (particularly after the First World War), and the increasing importance of commodity culture would seem to threaten the idyllic pastoral world that is associated with the child. Little wonder that for Eliot, as for others, the children's garden, like the summer of 1914, becomes 'a permanent symbol for anything innocently but irrecoverably lost' (Fussell 1975, 24). Sterility and fragmentation, 'shattered institutions, strained nerves and bankrupt ideals' come to characterize the modern moment, in which 'life no longer seems serious or coherent' (E. Wilson 1931, 106). Only 'brief pure moments of feeling' (106) are possible in this landscape, and meaning is itself fleeting: the speaker can only 'follow' the voices and the birdsong.

The changing dynamics of the first decades of the twentieth century are also the subject of Eliot's essay on Marie Lloyd from 1922, in which the modern subject's disconnection from community and tradition is mirrored in the audience's increasing distance from the artist. Eliot suggests that in the heyday of the music hall, the entertainer and her public participated in a co-operative transmission of oral culture: 'The working man who went to the music-hall and saw Marie Lloyd and joined in the chorus was himself performing part of the act; he was engaged in that collaboration of the audience with the artist which is necessary in all art' (1922a, 174). The threat to this interactive relationship is modern technology, which promises to produce in working-class audiences 'that same listless apathy with which the middle and upper classes regard any entertainment of the nature of art' (174). Instead of the music hall, the spectator 'will now go to the cinema, where his mind is lulled by continuous senseless music and continuous action too rapid for the brain to act upon' (174). Eliot then shifts his focus to the home in order to consider the changes to domestic relationships that may result 'when electrical ingenuity has made it possible for every child to hear its bedtime stories from a loudspeaker' (174). In a scenario that compares the role of Marie Lloyd to the role of the mother, the artist whose greatest strength lies in her 'capacity for expressing the soul of the people' and 'giving expression to the life of that audience' becomes a version of the primal storyteller who passes on an inheritance that is at once familial, social, and cultural (172). Given the importance that Eliot places on images of children in his poetry – the voices in 'Burnt Norton,' for instance, or the redemptive figure of Marina – the challenge posed to the mother-child storytelling dyad is a most disturbing aspect of the rise of information technologies such as film and radio. It is not 'bore-dom' only that Eliot perceives as resulting from electronic mediation (174); he fears that such innovations will lead to a debased culture in which tradition and communal identity have been undercut completely by sterile mediums of expression.

In these references to children and to the literature they read and are read, we see what is often regarded as Eliot's characteristically modern-ist response to 'the immense panorama of futility and anarchy which is contemporary history'.(Eliot 1923, 177). Technology would seem to render audiences passive receivers of transmitted messages instead of active participants in making meaning of texts and shows. Such a sentiment has much to do with visions of the modern city and of the capitalist relations that inform its operation. Georg Simmel in his 1903 study of the divisions that exist within the city, both in the workplace and on its streets, examines, for instance, the sense of anxiety that arises from the individual's anonymity in the midst of the masses (1903, 418). Walter Benjamin contrasts such alienation to the connections implicit in rural communities, particularly where the act of storytelling and the exchange of oral fairy tales make overt the lasting relationships that are at the heart of folk traditions (1936a, 108). Given that 'the technique of reproduction detaches the reproduced object from the domain of tradi-tion,' the printed, staged, and filmed fairy tales that circulate in the modern city would seem to embody the most extreme rupturing or 'liquidation' of this 'cultural heritage' (Benjamin 1936b, 221).

Eliot's 'The Cultivation of Christmas Trees' echoes the oppositional figuration of culture, in which technological alienation and modernity are pitted against communal participation and tradition. In the poem, he suggests that we can dismiss a number of modern approaches to the holy day, including

The social, the torpid, the patently commercial,
The rowdy (the pubs being open till midnight),
And the childish – which is not that of the child
For whom the candle is a star, and the gilded angel
Spreading its wings at the summit of the tree
Is not only a decoration, but an angel.   (1954, 117)

What seems significant here, however, is not Eliot's emphasis on the fragmentation of culture in its commodified state, but rather its flexibil-ity, particularly in relation to the role of the consumer. In Eliot's poem, the sacred and the profane are not necessarily antithetical; rather, because each exists simultaneously within the society and informs the significance or currency of the other, the reader of the image can determine its meaning for him- or herself. The ornament at the top of the tree might be a commodity, but the child's active desire can transform the signifier of capitalism into a signifier of faith. In other words, the reader has the ability to turn the idea of the angel, however much commodified, into the angel itself, and thus to move across the boundaries that divide different visions of the holiday. Though Eliot's concern for a society in which commercialism can so easily displace the 'purity' of culture remains at the forefront of the piece, and though redemption lies still within an idealized vision of innocence and youth, the poem works against its own grain and implies the interpretative possibilities that inhere in the multiple stories of modernity.

The sense of nostalgia that we find in Eliot's allusions to children's literature reflects a common and influential strand of criticism, one that is based upon 'the valorizing of a more authentic, original, or folk culture now eradicated by consumption' (Wicke 1994c, 177). But viewing works of literature according to a strict disjunction between pure and popular or high and mass cultures has become less prevalent in recent studies of Anglo-American modernism, in which scholars examine the intersections of modernist art and the material conditions of the early twentieth century.[1] The fairy tale represents a particularly useful entry point for an exploration of modernism when it is viewed as a response to the varied experiences and discourses of modernity. While Continental fairy tales can be read as remnants of childhood innocence or static folk traditions, they are also narratives with significant connections to adult, urban, commercial societies. The remarkable number of fairy tales that circulate in the late nineteenth and early twentieth centuries does not necessarily speak to their corruption or loss, then, but rather to the continuing process by which the stories have been exchanged and transformed by a range of readers and writers over time. As texts that are present in almost every kind of cultural production from the late seventeenth century and after (if not before), fairy tales are woven into the very fabric of Western culture at the same time that they are adapted to the ideologies and technologies of the day. The range of fairy-tale variants in modernity thus reflects the possibilities of a consumer society in which modern subjects can interact creatively with the inherited narratives of their culture.[2]

It is the dynamic nature of both fairy tales and modernity that James Joyce, Virginia Woolf, and Djuna Barnes capitalize upon, especially in works from the 1920s and 1930s. Their allusions to fairy tales epitomize the complex relationships that have historically linked tradition and the marketplace, and popular entertainment and high art. Their references also suggest the different tactical uses of culture that are possible within capitalist society, whether in terms of individual performances of identity or individual readings of the tales themselves. Instead of juxtaposing fairy tales to their lives and art, Joyce, Woolf, and Barnes use the stories to portray a participatory model of modernity and modernist literature.

A key example of this approach is Nora Flood's epiphanic statement from Barnes's *Nightwood:* 'God, children know something they can't tell; they like Red Riding Hood and the wolf in bed!' (D. Barnes 1937, 79). The quotation suggests the role that the reader plays in interpreting literature, for it is the child's act of reading that undercuts the binary of victim and villain, and that moves the tale in a rather different direction. Just as the characters from the tale become bedfellows, so the tale itself becomes a textual moment at which diverse interpretations of the story can come together. While it conveys its share of innocence, nostalgia, and cultural fragmentation, the allusion to 'Little Red Riding Hood' in *Nightwood* establishes Nora's knowledge of fairy tales and their lasting influence in the adult world, and demonstrates the ability of the reader who can use the stories or their motifs in unscripted ways. As in other works of modernism by Joyce, Woolf, and Barnes, the fairy tale speaks to the individual's ability to interact with the discourses of his or her society.

The sheer variety of fairy tales in modernity suggests that the texts were an almost inescapable source of reference for the writers. Philologists, psychologists, folklorists, and other scholarly types were viewing the stories as repositories of cultural knowledge, or as links to the childhood of the nation, or as representations of an original humanity (see Jung 1948, 239).[3] At the same time, the tales were being firmly entrenched in the popular and not just the academic imagination, especially given the development of increasingly sophisticated modes of mass production and dissemination. Fairy tales are often marketed to children, and many of us first encountered the stories by reading them when we were young, or by having them read to us when we were even younger. That connection between the fairy tale and the child is obvious in the seminal works of Charles Perrault, Madame de Beaumont, and the Brothers Grimm, as well as in the literary fairy stories of the Victorian period by authors such as Oscar Wilde, Jean Ingelow, and George MacDonald. But Continental fairy tales had also been adapted for the stage in the extravaganzas of J.R. Planché and in the wildly popular guise of the Christmas pantomime. The stories continued to be presented in these forms through the twentieth century, as well as in cartoons and in films featuring live actors. Circus acts and advertisements used the same fairy tales as operettas and anthologies, and these variants drew audiences composed of children and adults alike. Appealing to any number of different demographics, the stories were and continue to be adapted, cultivated, and culled according to a range of market forces and political positions.

The process of transmission and reception that led to the multifaceted position of fairy tales in modernity also led to the multiple interpretative possibilities that the texts represented for modernist writers. Instead of a purely literary form, fairy tales are characterized by numerous and productive cultural crossovers. Indeed, it is this characteristic 'interplay between different sectors' of the culture industry (Horrall 2001, 4) that has kept them – especially in their form as popular urban entertainments – malleable and current. They have been produced and reproduced in tremendous numbers, but the key is that any given version of a tale is based upon and accompanied by other versions of the same story. This clustering effect, which we can experience in our own encounters with fairy tales, tends to lead to a comparative and conversational model of textual reception. Multiple versions, multiple contexts, and multiple readerly and writerly perspectives undercut the authority and stability that we might associate with a single source text or writer, and keep the fairy tale a living and adaptable entity.[4]

What the stories represent for modernists, then, is not just a fertile system of reference, made richer by the competing political visions presented in different variants, but a system of reference that is fertile because it has currency across so many social and financial and ideological divides. As narratives whose presence and appeal can be traced through almost every aspect of modern British and North American culture, fairy tales challenge the formal and discursive boundaries that modernists themselves play with in their texts. On the one hand, references to fairy tales are like any other allusion in demanding that the reader engage with both the text and the intertext. On the other, the reader must determine which version out of the dozens of available adaptations of a fairy tale has been made intertextual in the first place, and which interpretation best relates to the work in which it has been used. Allusions to the tales in works such as *Ulysses, Orlando,* and *Nightwood* are thus sites of textual and social interactions, where readers negotiate literary norms just as individuals negotiate social norms.

Perhaps for this reason, the fairy tales that are invoked in the works of the three main authors discussed in this study rarely have single referents or clear metaphorical correlatives; nor do the tales seem to provide 'a master trope, structure, or scaffold' according to which the modernist text can be decoded (Manganaro 2002, 111). Instead of stemming from single, traceable sources, or being grounded in specific and tidy morals, fairy tales occupy a multifaceted place in the writers' cultures and thus in their writing. The references are themselves fragmented and repeated within the works, where different versions and forms of the same tale are evoked at the same moment. This approach to intertextuality leads not to a sense of interpretative stability, then, as much as interpretative slippage, signalling the possibilities of the text and intertext instead of pinning them together through a single or clear meaning. When Rudy Bloom appears at the end of the 'Circe' chapter of *Ulysses,* for example, Joyce draws upon imagery from both pantomime and written versions of 'Cinderella.' In an updating of the props Cinderella uses at the ball, Bloom's longing for his son is expressed through objects associated with money and status, which demonstrate how both his dreams and the fairy tales have been scripted by commodity culture. But the appearance of the 'fairy boy' who symbolizes Bloom's heart's desire and leaves it unfulfilled reflects less ironically the sense of lack and loss at the tale's core, which is only partially redressed by the heroine's marriage to the prince (15.4957).[5] In this sense, the image as well as the invocation of the Principal Boy suggest an interpretation of 'Cinderella' in which class, gender, and desire are not necessarily fixed in place by the 'happy ending.' A similar and similarly rich use of fairy tales is evident in Woolf's *Mrs Dalloway* when Clarissa pieces together different versions of the story 'Sleeping Beauty' as she mends a tear in her green dress. Her shifting interpretations of its heroine in this scene echo Clarissa's shifting sense of her own identity and frustrate Peter's attempts to locate himself according to a stable system of gender. In *Nightwood,* though Barnes uses the very concrete image of Red Riding Hood and the Wolf in bed, it is associated with a moment of intuition and sexual indecipherability that does not lead to a specific reading of the novel, the fairy tale, or the characters of either. Instead of interpretative certainty, such allusions invoke a deferral, a displacement, and even an excess of meaning.

My approach to the process of reading fairy tales in such works is to view the allusion not in relation to a system of metaphoric substitution, but rather – or at the same time – according to a system of metonymic association. This slide along a line of potential meanings seems entirely in keeping with the number of available variants as well as with the sense of ineluctability that often informs the tales themselves. The twisting effects of magic, the transformations of class position, the overwhelming sense of lack that often prompts the action, the happy ending that rarely answers the slippery questions raised elsewhere in the text – these aspects of fairy tales suggest a foreclosed kernel of meaning that invites reinterpretation and retelling. In this sense, the allusion is not just a moment in the modernist work at which the reader derives the message that is prescribed by the author; rather, it is a moment at which the reader is invited to reconcile the range of variants and contradictory associations implied by the reference. Instead of establishing a single correspondence between the novel and the tale, or asserting a hierarchical relationship between guiding author and sub-missive audience, the allusion requires the individual reader to interact with the text and its contexts.

Their emphasis on participation has significance in terms of the con-tent of modernist works as well as their form. Joyce, Woolf, and Barnes feature characters who are able to read their own cultures creatively and to manipulate the social expectations that would appear to con-strain them. Instead of depicting the modern subject's interpellation by market forces, the authors suggest that consumption – whether in the form of purchasing commodities or reading books – can be viewed as an active process (Wicke 1994c, 178). In other words, the consumer, like the reader, has the ability to engage tactically with the demands of the society, where diverse 'modes of use – or rather re-use,' whether of consumer goods, urban spaces, or literary texts, allow individuals to manoeuvre around the official strategies that those cultural forms con-vey (de Certeau 1984, 30). Social structures are not necessarily toppled in these local acts of resistant readings and uses; indeed, despite their subversive potential, even fairy tales may 'remain within the language and forms created and prescribed by patriarchy' (Radway 1984, 147). But the possibilities of the capitalist system are being explored in these works, at least by those subjects who are creative enough to use and not be used by the narratives of consumerism.

Fashion becomes a central means through which such cultural inter-action is demonstrated in fairy tales and modernist texts alike. In both kinds of literature, the protagonists are able to analyse prescribed gender and class roles and to modify their own positions by using fashion creatively. The social system itself enables such resistance. As Judith Butler points out in her discussions of drag, 'sex' as a discursive category 'is both produced and destabilized' by the 'reiteration of norms,' or by the repetition and reinforcement of socially established ideals (1993, 10). Butler argues that acceptable images and behaviours are adopted or cited by individuals in accordance with existing standards. However, there is a gap between the ideal and the ways in which it is adapted by the real body, and the disjunction between the two can lead to unexpected or unconventional results. In other words, if an identity can be approximated or performed by an individual, it can be approximated or performed incongruously or inappropriately. Thus, in what Michel de Certeau might call a tactical use of fashion, an individual can use clothing to 'pass' as something he or she is not, or to draw attention to the constructed nature of the ideal itself. The outcome is an implicit critique of the stability of gendered, sexed, and classed positions, which are revealed to be roles that people play rather than 'natural' states of being.

These kinds of manoeuvrings, and the sexual and social mobility that becomes possible through uses of fashion, are evident in modernist texts as well as in fairy tales. Joyce's Stephen Dedalus, for example, is a modern-day Cinderella: though he rejects the offers of employment that would make his financial status in Dublin secure, the clothes that he borrows from Buck Mulligan allow him to pose as middle class, at least in his job at Deasy's school, despite his real economic standing. In a slightly different example, Mrs Dalloway sews herself into the patriarchal order by mending her green dress, an image through which Woolf makes overt the naturalized status of heterosexuality. The needle, like the spindle in 'Sleeping Beauty,' enables the heroine to put her sexual self to sleep and to repress her desire for Sally Seton and Peter Walsh in order to remain in a more socially comfortable position. Alternately, in *Nightwood*, Matthew O'Connor's drag, like the Wolf's imitation of the Grandmother's role in 'Little Red Riding Hood,' undermines the standard uses of clothing in the larger society. In all three cases, the characters create for themselves a space within the existing order by utilizing its scripts and roles creatively.

Characters are also depicted as overtly interacting with fairy tales in an often productive way. On one level, these embedded references to stories from the Grimms or Perrault are just realistic details that reflect how common the stories were in modernity. On another level, the characters' individual readings of fairy tales enable Joyce, Woolf, and Barnes to demonstrate the forces that both limit and lead to resistant interpretations of the stories. For instance, Gerty MacDowell and Leopold Bloom consciously stage highly sexual versions of 'Beauty and the Beast' during their visual encounter on Sandymount Strand. The reference works in a number of ways in *Ulysses:* while the story is a tale of love that ironically draws attention to Gerty's very limited marital prospects, it is also used by the unmarried Gerty to provide herself with an otherwise prohibited sexual satisfaction. In *Night and Day*, Katharine Hilbery's overt references to 'Cinderella' emphasize her sense of disconnection from the family legacy. Though Mrs Hilbery may be a fairy godmother, restoring this Cinderella to her proper role, the society she represents is based upon a Victorian model of marriage that Katharine must alter. Even though the family unit, like the fairy tale, can be adapted to a modern context, both retain traces of previous uses that cannot be erased. This leads to Katharine's dilemma at the end of the novel, as she remains on the threshold of the family home and of change. A much more disturbing figuration of family dynamics is found in Nora Flood's dream of 'Snow White' from *Nightwood.* The lost maternal figure that haunts Nora's unconscious is both a sleeping Snow White and an evil Queen who threatens the younger woman's sense of authority over her own story. While the characters are interacting with larger structures through the fairy tales, then, like the authors, they encounter the cost of such uses, where the status of their precursors, and not just the potential of the legacy, must be acknowledged.

It is the fairy tale's involvement in multiple contexts that marks its potential as a system of reference in the works of Joyce, Woolf, and Barnes. In their instability and variety, fairy tales open up a space for the reader in the text, not just to interpret the author's intentions or politics, but to engage with the historical and cultural resonances of the story itself. Allusions to fairy tales signal the interactions that take place between the modernist author and the inherited tradition, as well as between the reader, the writer, the text, and its contexts against the backdrop of a rich and constantly changing history. Instead of nostalgic symbols of lost times and traditions; instead of representations of the authentic nation, culture, or folk; instead of archetypal narratives of universal human states, fairy tales are used by Joyce, Woolf, and Barnes as modernist works; that is, as texts that reflect the instability and the variability that is the experience of modernity.

1 Turning Back the Covers: Fairy Tales in the Modern Age

There is considerable resistance to any change to the fairy tale; all right to lose sight of the king and queen, and Prince Charming is not the answer. The emperor is as naked as a jay bird, but woe to the rebel who tries to assert ruthless ambition in Snow White, or lets Bilbo Baggins wander out onto a killing field. The happily-ever-after crowd goes really batty, reports the rebel to the crown, and off with her head.

Beth Follett, *Tell It Slant*

To explore what fairy tales mean in and to modernism, we need to acknowledge the history that has influenced their status. While fairy tales are often read as representations of 'the character of a people' (Hopcke 1997, vii) or of 'collective truths' (Orenstein 2002, 12), individual stories often reflect historically specific visions of gender, class, and sexuality. Interpretations also vary: as Bruno Bettelheim points out, 'the fairy tale's deepest meaning will be different for each person, and different for the same person at various moments in his life' (1975, 12). This combination of factors tends to undercut any final agreement regarding the ultimate significance of a tale. Even the rise of technologies that would seem to signal control over the text, such as the printing press or the movie camera, has led not so much to the reproduction of a given ideology as to the further production of alternate visions of the stories and of their meanings. An example of the possibilities of popular culture, the fairy tale remains open to reinterpretation and debate because of its complicated history.

Definitions of the genre, which differ from critic to critic, exemplify the lack of consensus that characterizes the form. For instance, Iona and

Peter Opie isolate five main traits of a fairy tale: the story is 'unbeliev-able'; it is centred on one person or family who must cope with the supernatural at a time of stress; it involves a young person who is usually 'disowned or abandoned'; it is peopled with stock characters; and it occurs in a distant time with a 'different range of possibilities' (1974, 18–19). Jack Zipes suggests a slightly different definition: the fairy tale occurs in a 'universe where anything can happen at any time' thanks to the presence of 'opportunistic' characters, and it involves a sense of *'wonder'* that 'gives rise to admiration, fear, awe, and reverence' for nature and for life (1999, 5). Following Antti Aarne and Stith Thompson's cataloguing of folktales, some academics have sorted the stories according to their narrative components. In his structuralist analysis of wonder tales in *Morphology of the Folktale*, Vladimir Propp suggests that the stories are based upon thirty-one possible functions, or 'basic elements of the tale' (1968, 71), and seven possible characters. Others, however, suggest twenty possible functions and three narrative roles (Greimas), or even just two (Dundes), marking the rather arbitrary nature of Propp's system (Gilet 1998, 33–5). At the other end of the scale, Marcia Lane's suggestion that the fairy tale is 'a story – literary or folk – that has a sense of the numinous, the feeling or sensation of the supernatural or the mysterious' is a definition that could be applied to any number of texts (1994, 5). Edwin Hartland calls fairy tales by their German name, *märchen,* but also provides a rather loose sense of the stories as being 'untrammelled either by history or probability, [where] the one condition the tale is expected to fulfill is to end happily' (1891, 23). Alison Lurie identifies fairy tales as written versions of folklore, though she does not clarify how the stories differ from other forms of oral literature (1990, 32–9): as André Favat writes, 'A fairy tale, it is generally agreed, is a folk tale, but not all folk tales are fairy tales' (1977, 7). The distinction between fairy tales, folk tales, myths, and legends, depends, it seems, on very subtle shades of difference between uses and sources.[1]

One reason for the definitional difficulties that surround fairy tales is that such descriptions depend upon an existing body of texts whose organization is anything but orderly or systematic. Thus, even when Graham Andersen describes fairy stories as '"short, imaginative, tradi-tional tales with a high moral and magical content," essentially the qualities offered by the German term *Maerchen*,' he admits that 'Such definitions are all too often doomed to admit exceptions' (2000, 1). Marina Warner addresses this problem by identifying the specific anthology that contains the texts upon which most definitions of fairy tales are based: 'Charles Perrault's *Histoires ou contes du temps passé, or Contes de ma Mère l'Oye*' (1994a, xii). Although Warner does define the fairy tale's basic features and indicates its differences from other texts (1994a, xii), her emphasis on the importance of the existing canon indicates a central fact about the study of fairy tales: we cannot help but *know* what a fairy-tale is before we know *what* a fairy tale is. In other words, we seem to know *avant la lettre* which stories can be considered fairy tales. We do not always arrive at this knowledge by the same route, a point that speaks to our highly contextual experience of the stories and their variants. But the fact that our seemingly intuitive cultural knowledge allows us to discuss certain stories as fairy tales testifies to their continuing currency.

Fairy tales have become integral to Britain and North American societies, part of their everyday functioning. Indeed, the history of fairy tales can be viewed as the history of popular culture, and particularly the history of popular culture in the modern era. Fairy tales are present in almost every textual form imaginable: chapbooks, bound collections, scholarly anthologies, novels, paintings, pantomimes, scripts, libretti, jokes, and popular metaphors: 'a wicked stepmother'; 'a Cinderella story'; 'a fairy-tale ending.' These versions are augmented in the late nineteenth and twentieth centuries by films, cartoons, comics, mass-produced books, and advertisements. As a result, it is often difficult to establish not only the specific source material of literary allusions to fairy tales, something that will become more evident in subsequent chapters, but also the 'authentic' or original version of a story we might identify as a fairy tale. Instead of a clear-cut, stable, and regulated body of knowledge, bound and defined by an elite group, fairy tales are individual stories that permeate any number of discourses and social strata, that move in and out of anthologies and canons, and that fluctuate in number and increase in variety as time goes by.

Perhaps for these reasons, I have chosen only a few tales to discuss in my readings of the works of Joyce, Woolf, and Barnes, and they represent some of the most accessible stories from the most mainstream of sources. 'Sleeping Beauty,' 'Little Red Riding Hood,' and 'Cinderella' are included in Charles Perrault's collection of 1697. 'Beauty and the Beast' comes from a story written by Madame Leprince de Beaumont, first published in French in 1756. 'The Fisherman and His Wife' and 'Snow White' appear in the Grimms' collections, first translated and published in English in 1823, but further refined in subsequent editions.

These are stories that were used consistently through the nineteenth century in fairy-tale extravaganzas, pantomimes, and children's books, and which continued to be popular in decades that followed.

There are, however, other kinds of fairy stories and works of children's literature that, unfortunately, I do not address in any detail though they are alluded to by the modernists I discuss. *Arabian Nights' Entertainments,* for example, was first circulated in France by Antoine Galland in the early 1700s and translated into English in the 1880s by Sir Richard Francis Burton. The collection became a mainstay of the nursery, the pantomime stage, and, as Zack Bowen has argued, James Joyce's novels (1998). Nursery rhymes are also part of the authors' cultures, as are English tales, such as 'Dick Whittington and His Cat,' and American folklore, such as the stories adapted and created by Washington Irving. I pay almost no attention to the native fairy stories of the British Isles, which tend to centre on small fantastic beings, like pixies, sprites, and leprechauns. Nor do I explore the late-nineteenth-century vogue for fairies themselves, which comes to a climax in the 1920 Christmas issue of the *Strand Magazine* when an article by Sir Arthur Conan Doyle and Edward Gardner featured photographs of the Cottingley fairies taken by two girls in Yorkshire. Though the pictures were later debunked, the immense popularity of the photos at the time speaks to the influence of nineteenth-century figurations of childhood innocence and imagination (Carpenter and Prichard 1984, 175).

Other books that have become associated with children and that have a significant influence on modernism include *Alice's Adventures in Wonderland* and *Through the Looking-Glass* by Lewis Carroll, which are important references for Virginia Woolf (see Dusinberre 1987), Djuna Barnes (see Martin 2000, 115–18), and Dorothy L. Sayers (1935). But my focus is not children's literature or literature that grants the adult access to an otherworldly realm associated with the child or with supernatural creatures. Nor is it folklore, where readers often hope to find the oral roots of a culture. Rather, the fairy tales that I identify in the works of Joyce, Woolf, and Barnes are texts that explore the individual's role in a modern urban society. They are predicated upon the dynamics of consumerism and the subject's performance of a gendered, classed identity. Fairy tales are not primarily escapist fictions or flights of fancy in this view; while these are valid ways of reading the tales, it is the stories' connections to social pressures that I explore. The magic that the stories feature can easily be read as the twin forces of money and patronage, especially in Perrault's worldly morals. Obviously their ties to children's literature and folk culture and the imagination influence the ways in which the tales are used by the three authors. But in this study, I read the Continental fairy tales published by and derived from Perrault, de Beaumont, and the Grimms as texts that reflect and convey modern attitudes towards sexuality, social mobility, urbanity, and commodity culture.

Despite the marketing of fairy tales as creative and fanciful texts for children, written variants have their roots in adult literature and are very much involved in the material systems that affect younger and older readers alike. The history of the stories, especially in the seventeenth and eighteenth centuries, indicates how deeply fairy tales are implicated in the politics of gender, education, and class, where the status of the teller is tied to perceptions of the morality of the tale. The cultural anxieties that continue to influence the stories' significance in nineteenth-century England have much to do with their commercialization, as tensions arise from conflicting views of the fairy tale's cultural purity and of its mass appeal. The presence of fairy tales in the metanarratives of modernity stems in part from these debates, which certainly influence a number of modernist authors. What makes Joyce, Woolf, and Barnes unique is their foregrounding of the productive as well as delimiting uses of the tales in their culture. Their references signal the possibilities of the present, rather than an investment in a mythic past, and thus reflect the relationships that have historically existed between a range of texts, contexts, and readers.

A Brief History of the Fairy Tale

Fairy-stories are by no means the rocky matrices out of which the fossils cannot be prised except by an expert geologist. The ancient elements can be knocked out, or forgotten and dropped out, or replaced by other ingredients with the greatest ease: as any comparison of a story with closely related variants will show.

J.R.R. Tolkien, *Tree and Leaf*

The first literary fairy tale may be 'Psyche and Cupid' from Apuleius's *The Golden Ass*, which appears in the second century AD (Zipes 1999, 8; Tatar 1992, 141). The sexual encounter in Book Five between Psyche and Cupid is a more explicit version of the children's version of 'Beauty and the Beast,' indicating that the text was intended to be read by adults (Apuleius 1996, 69–70). Many of the stories that have been viewed in hindsight as fairy tales were written to appeal to a grown-up audience, including the *Gesta Romanorum* manuscript from about 1300 AD, Giovanni Francesco Straparola's *Le piacevoli notti,* or *The Pleasant Nights,* from the sixteenth century, and Giambattista Basile's five-volume *Lo Cunto de li Cunti* or *The Tale of Tales,* from 1634.

During the English Renaissance, William Shakespeare alludes to supernatural entities in a number of his plays. References to folkloric figures such as Puck seem to fade from English literature, however, as the rise of Puritanism in seventeenth-century Britain discourages the development, or at least the publication, of literary fairy tales (Townsend 1974, 47). The fairy story returns officially to Britain in the eighteenth century from France, where, in the last years of the ancien régime, the court of Louis XIV, with its passion for pastoral rusticity, produces most of the literary fairy tales in circulation today (Darton 1932, 85–6). Between 1690 and 1714, aristocratic French literary salons, and the fairy tales and storytelling that occurred within them, enable women as well as some men to demonstrate their wit. Stories derived from and inspired by folk tales become the conduits for veiled critiques of the court, of contemporary manners, and of the patriarchal social system (Warner 1994a, 24). When published, these fairy tales appeal, again, to adult, upper-class audiences and often appear in larger prose works and multivolume sets, such as Madame Marie-Catherine d'Aulnoy's *Les Contes des Fées* of 1696, Mlle de la Force's *Les Contes des Contes* of 1697, and Mme de Murat's *Contes de Fées* of 1698 (Warner 1994a, 420). The most recognizable collection, however, is Charles Perrault's *Histoires ou contes du temps passé; avec des Moralitez,* known also according to its frontispiece as *Contes de ma Mère l'Oye,* which is published in verse in 1695 but more famously in prose in 1697 (Perrault 1989).

Perrault's collection is a bit of an anomaly in the French tradition, since, using his son's name as a pseudonym, he wrote the volume expressly for children (A. Lang 1888, xxvii). On one level, Perrault is speaking through his hat: by asserting a native folkloric tradition rather than a classical literary one, he participates in the adult academic debate between the Ancients and the Moderns. However, in the prefaces to his collections, he emphasizes his intent to please and to teach, and subsequent editions of his book are identified almost entirely with a younger audience. While the morals themselves are pragmatic commentaries on social and sexual politicking, they pave the way for subsequent adaptations that modify Perrault's rather Machiavellian touch.

When the texts are translated by Richard Samber in 1729 as *Histories, or Tales of Past Times. Told by Mother Goose,* the volume is advertised specifically for children. In contrast, when d'Aulnoy's work is translated into English in 1699 as *Tales of the Fairys,* and again in 1721–2 as *A Collection of Novels and Tales, Written by that Celebrated Wit of France, the Comtesse D'Anois,* the length and price of the collection indicate that it is probably published for adults (Opie and Opie 1974, 30).

In England, these tales encounter a force mostly antithetical to fantasy: enlightened reason. The Puritans had reacted against the stories' preoccupation with earthly and supernatural rather than spiritual matters. With the Enlightenment and its emphasis on rationality and education, the frivolity of the tales is again the focus of condemnation, particularly in relation to the stories' effects on children (Summerfield 1984, xiv). However, they become important texts within the mainstream or the middle-class world as early as the 1730s thanks in part to the belated influence of John Locke. In *Some Thoughts Concerning Education,* he emphasizes the importance of play in pedagogy: 'If his *Aesop has pictures* in it, it will entertain him much the better, and encourage him to read' (1693, 212). Like Aesop's *Fables,* collections of fairy tales are often published as primers in the eighteenth century, where French rather than Latin accompanies an English version of the text on the facing page. Indeed, John Newbery's sixth edition of Perrault's tales is the first to be published in English only (Kinnell 1995, 28–9). By the middle of the century, fairy tales had become further refined and 'mobilized to serve the purpose of moral education' (Tatar 1992, 49). Sarah Fielding's *The Governess, or Little Female Academy* of 1749, for example, demonstrates how 'Mistress Teachum and Her Nine Scholars' use a variety of narratives – fables, letters, and fairy tales – to teach proper feminine behaviour. Though 'The Princess Hebe: A Fairy Tale' is fantastic and therefore suspect, Mrs Teachum tells her students that, if interpreted appropriately, the story contains important lessons:

> I would have you consider seriously enough of what you read, to draw such Morals from your Books, as may influence your future Practice; and as to Fairy Tales in general, remember, that the Fairies, as I told Miss *Jenny* before of Giants and Magic, are only introduced by the Writers of those Tales, by way of Amusement to the Reader. For if the Story is well written, the common Course of Things would produce the same Incidents without the Help of Fairies. (1749, 178–9)

Perhaps guided by Mrs Teachum, a number of writers embrace the pedagogical potential of fairy tales. One is Madame Jeanne-Marie Leprince de Beaumont, who publishes her *Magasin des Enfans, ou Dialogues entre une sage GOUVERNANTE et plusiers de ses élèves*[2] in 1756. The work, which is translated into English in 1760, contains several fairy tales, including Madame Leprince de Beaumont's 'Beauty and the Beast' (Warner 1994a, 292). The didacticism of the work is directed towards its female readers, apparently to further the cause of arranged marriages, but in a pleasing and relatively subtle way.

One of the most significant factors in the popularity of fairy tales and related texts for children is this kind of soft sell. Publishers such as John Newbery, Mary Cooper, Thomas Boreman, and Andrew Millar produce in the 1730s and 1740s 'literature for children's entertainment, even if entertainment was sometimes alloyed by instruction' (MacDonald 1982, 127). Focused on mainly secular issues, and published with profit as the goal, the texts cater to the tastes of a youthful audience and attempt to make the act of reading a pleasurable experience (Carpenter and Prichard 1984, 375). Though Roger Sale suggests that publishers like Newbery 'were attempting to extricate children from the clutches of fairy tales and the French fantastic' (1978, 58), fairy tales have a significant influence on the kinds of books the publishers issue. For example, Newbery's *The History of Little Goody Two-Shoes: Otherwise called Mrs. Margery Two-Shoes* from 1765 is clearly inspired by 'Cinderella,' though the themes of Perrault and d'Aulnoy – marriage, sexual politics, courtly manner – are replaced by values such as 'thrift' and 'hard work,' which the largely middle-class audience would be more eager to have their children read (Kinnell 1995, 37). The emphasis on social mobility within the stories leads, however, to another kind of anxiety regarding fairy tales and their influence on children's expectations. Though Perrault's Cinderella is already a member of the aristocracy who regains her position (Yolen 1982, 296), the heroine of Samuel Richardson's *Pamela*, a text that Ian Watt identifies as 'a modern variant of the age-old Cinderella theme' (1957, 204), rises above her initial position, as does Margery Two-Shoes. There are thus two ways in which fairy tales could be condemned as fantastic: where one relates to the magical elements of the stories, the other relates to the fantasy of class ascension in the rags-to-riches plot.

The fairy tale's status as a form of popular culture, and a fairly cheap one at that, also threatens the status quo. The published stories are relatively inexpensive, which means that children could conceivably purchase the tales on their own, away from the watchful eye of their guardian. These books are in fact marketed with such an audience in mind. Along with illustrations and a playful tone, Newbery's books come with 'tops, pincushions, and games,' though as Sheila Egoff points out, Newbery is selling more than just books: in *Goody Two-Shoes*, the father figure dies 'from a want of Dr James's fever powder – a patent medicine sold by Newbery' (1980, 407). Even so, these literary or published fairy tales represent only one aspect of the market. The chapbook also plays a major role in the history of fairy tales. As Victor Neuberg points out, 'The rich tradition of English fairy mythology survived in the eighteenth century almost entirely because of chapbooks' (1968, 15). These small, very inexpensive, paper-covered books contain a range of material: ballads, recipes, jokes, prophecies, riddles, hagiographies, political sketches, devotional tracts, criminal stories, fabliaux, and, of course, fairy tales. Accompanied by some rough woodcut illustrations, the chapbooks do not necessarily represent good literature, but they do indicate popular tastes and trends. The penny histories contain material from 'the folk,' such as cures and weather predictions, but also literature associated with the aristocracy, such as medieval romances like *Guy of Warwick,* and of the middle-classes, such as novels like *Moll Flanders.* The source texts are often truncated and altered, but the chapbook itself represents an almost democratic dissemination of the dominant cultural productions of the day.

Like many fairy tales, chapbook stories tend to present 'fantasies of power and wealth' (Summerfield 1984, 31), which are certain to appeal to the wide audience for which they are produced: children, 'the lower-middle class and the poor in London,' and 'people in every major provincial town and every village and hamlet to which the chapmen [...] wandered' (M. Jackson 1989, 68). The chapmen (also known as running stationers, hackmen, and peddlers) had operated in Britain since the advent of the printing press. But the rise of the chapbook, stemming in large part from a decision in 1693 to repeal an act of 1662 that had limited printing, gives them renewed life (Neuberg 1968, 34; Summerfield 1984, 33). Another significant influence is a rise in literacy levels in the eighteenth century, especially in the rural populations (Neuberg 1968, 46). Even so, the key to the chapbook's popularity is its universal appeal. Though chapbooks begin to be oriented towards children starting in the 1730s, these younger readers had already been consuming texts designed for an adult audience. Especially before the rise of more mainstream children's publishers and publications, chapbooks represent a publishing subculture that enabled the preservation of 'the old folk materials' previously considered 'appropriate only for those who did not matter, that is, the working classes' (C. Silver 1994, 328).

Perhaps because of the connection between chapbooks and the lower echelons of society, the fairy tale becomes associated not just with the threat posed by the rural poor but by the working classes in general. Locke, for instance, warns parents against the influence of servants: 'Children (nay, and Men too) do most by Example. We are all a sort of Camelions, that still take a Tincture from things near us' (1693, 126). The staff could infect the child's imagination and mould the tabula rasa inappropriately. Locke thus advises the tutor or parent to 'preserve his [the child's] tender Mind from all impressions and Notions of *Sprites* and *Goblins,* or any fearful Apprehensions in the dark. This he will be in danger of from the indiscretion of Servants' (196). In *Émile,* Jean-Jacques Rousseau shares the same concerns regarding 'the babble of his [the child's] nurse' and the 'superstitious' lower classes (1762, 37, 98). For Rousseau, surveillance is necessary in order to trace 'the how and the why of the entrance of every vice' back to its source (56), as well as to ensure that the children follow the intended lesson: 'Watch children learning their fables and you will see that when they have a chance of applying them they almost always use them exactly contrary to the author's meaning' (79). The child must be guarded against his or her own wayward desires as well as the values and beliefs of the working class.

Within the official history of the fairy tale, then, lurk the subversive figures of publishers, peddlers, and the working classes, who produce texts of fantasy that cause children to run amok by secretly buying books and reading them improperly. Against such socioeconomic and generational revolt, Anna Barbauld, Sarah Trimmer, and Maria Edgeworth assert a considerable moral authority. Though the popularity of fairy tales in the eighteenth century is evident from the number of texts that are published, including Charles Mayer's forty-one-volume collection, *Le Cabinet des Fées* (1785–9), attitudes begin to change, especially towards the turn of the nineteenth century, when Sarah Trimmer replaces the fictional Mrs Teachum as an arbiter of taste. Trimmer's magazine, *The Guardian of Education* (1802–6), sets the ground rules for children's literature in accordance with strict Christian standards, and the fairy tale is firmly excluded from the canon. Harvey Darton states that 'All Mother Goose's and Mother Bunch's tales' are, according to

Trimmer, '"only fit to fill the heads of children with confused notions of wonderful and supernatural events, brought about by the agency of imaginary beings"' (1932, 97). Ironically, Trimmer had initially embraced Sarah Fielding's novel in the June 1802 issue of *The Guardian of Education* for the lessons it presented through fairy tales (Grey 1968, 72–3). By 1820, however, Mrs Sherwood has published a revised version of *The Governess,* which includes no fairy tales whatsoever (74).

Along with Trimmer's right reading and reason come Hannah More's *Cheap Repository Tracts,* which are issued between 1795 and 1797, and which are intended as alternatives 'to bawdy and violent chapbooks' (Avery and Kinnell 1995, 48). Nevertheless, chapbook versions of fairy tales hold their ground in early-nineteenth-century mass culture, 'even if the middle classes (ostensibly) concentrated upon more improving literature' (Butts 1995, 88). Indeed, in the 1800s, publishers such as James Catnach, John Pitts, and Solomon King bring chapbook fairy tales into mainstream bourgeois culture by publishing them primarily as 'literature for children,' rather than as stories for a mixed audience (Neuberg 1982, 51). The sheer number of tales in circulation in the first years of the nineteenth century indicates the extent of the revolt against Trimmer and, as Charles Lamb called them in a letter to Samuel Coleridge, 'the cursed Barbauld crew' (Salway 1976, 109). Publishers are joined by writers and by academics, whose recuperations of fairy stories and folklore lead to a refiguration of the child, the folk, and the value of imagination in the modern era.

But if the overt didacticism of the Sunday School movement and its adherents is challenged in the Golden Age of Children's Literature, equally restrictive though more subtle standards are brought to bear upon the tales and their youthful readers. As Walter Benjamin puts it, the official texts of both 'the edifying, moral Age of Enlightenment' and 'the sentimental period of the nineteenth century' that followed it are 'characterized by a sterile mediocrity,' which rests upon an idealized vision of childhood (1929, 252). The Victorian era represents a resurgence of fairy tales and fantasy, and a proliferation of written variants; but its investment in the cultural and moral value of the stories, and in the purity of children themselves, seems at odds with the fairy tale's increasingly important role in commodity culture. The tensions that result from this dynamic, and from the different visions of class, gender, and morality that the tales represent in the nineteenth century, set the stage for modernist reactions to and refigurations of fairy tales.

The Politics of Authentication

Mr Best eagerquietly lifted his book to say:
– That's very interesting because that brother motive, don't you know, we find also in the old Irish myths. Just what you say. The three brothers Shakespeare. In Grimm too, don't you know, the fairytales. The third brother that always marries the sleeping beauty and wins the best prize.
    Best of Best brothers. Good, better, best.

James Joyce, *Ulysses*

The nineteenth century sees a shift away from the unease surrounding the tellers of fairy tales. Where the traditional roots of the stories in rural communities or in women's working circles had been obscured in previous literary adaptations or reviled by theorists of children's education, these origins become in the 1800s a significant factor in the tales' mainstream recuperation. The hierarchy of middle-class reader and uneducated peasant is not, of course, altered in this movement, but the image of 'the folk' is reinvested with value. 'The folk' become the signifier of cultural purity: because they are uneducated, 'the folk' are seen to be untainted by the changing values and technologies of the Industrial Revolution. 'The folk' are a link to the past of the nation as well as to past stages of human development. As James Orchard Halliwell-Phillipps writes in 1849, fairy tales and nursery rhymes told to children 'are not the modern nonsense some folks may pronounce them to be. They illustrate the history and manners of the people for centuries' (9). A central opposition emerges from the social and political contexts of this time, then, with the corrupting forces of modernity on one side and the folk history of the people on the other.
    Increased interest in fairy tales as representations of an originary culture can be traced back to a number of different impulses that connect 'the folk,' the child, the countryside, and the nation. Rousseau's portrayal in *Émile* of the rural population and their healthy 'natural' lifestyle is one influence; another is the growing reevaluation of the rural landscape in light of dramatic technological advances. According to Raymond Williams, the aesthetics of English Romanticism stem in no small part from the industrial development of the countryside: 'It is significant and understandable that in the course of a century of reclamation, drainage and clearing there should have developed, as a by-product, a feeling for unaltered nature, for wild land: the feeling that was known at the time as "picturesque"' (1973, 128). The works and

philosophies of the Romantics can thus be traced to the writers' 'recognition of what the Industrial Revolution had done to England's natural and human landscape' (C. Silver 1994, 328). The city, with its economic systems and technological innovations, is seen to undermine the integrity of the country and its traditions even though that rural ground is necessary for the health of the metropolis. William Wordsworth's 'London' poems of 1802, for example, present an urban reality so far removed from country ideals that 'Plain living and high thinking are no more' (1965). In William Blake's 'The Ecchoing Green,' imagination and the countryside are the necessary alternatives to the divisive structures of the city, for rural space is where citizens and generations are brought together in a vibrant, communal relationship (1789).

Partly as a response to urbanization and industrialization, the child is also redefined in the 1800s, becoming increasingly associated with the purity of the countryside. The works of Blake, Wordsworth, and other writers demonstrate how important the figure of the child becomes in representing a privileged site of natural innocence or 'visionary simplicity' (Carpenter 1985, 7), and in acting as 'a corrective for adult presuppositions about the constitution of reality, value, and meaning' (Knoepflmacher 1998, 7). However, this idealized vision of youth is also modified according to theories derived from Darwinian and eugenical discourses. Towards the end of the Victorian period, popular views of phylogeny lead to a vision of the child and of the literature the child read as representing a stage in the development of human civilization. Children, women, 'savages,' and the working classes – the tellers and listeners of fairy tales – are grouped together under the sign of the 'primitive.' Edwin Hartland in *The Science of Fairy Tales* makes this link overt: 'The incidents of which they [fairy tales] are composed are based upon ideas not peculiar to any one people, ideas familiar to savages everywhere, and only slowly modified and transformed as savagery gives way to barbarism, and barbarism to modern civilization and scientific knowledge of the material phenomena of the universe' (1891, 24–5).

Sir James Frazer's *The Golden Bough* also situates fairy stories and folklore in this way: 'folk-tales are a faithful reflection of the world as it appeared to the primitive mind' (1922, 774). Karl Pearson makes a similar connection: 'the customs and feelings of *Märchenland* are merely reflexes of a long past stage of social development – of the childhood of human culture' (1897, 54). In 1899, Percy Green argues that 'the only light shed on the memorials of Northern Europe's early youth comes from the contributory and dimly illuminative rays of folk-lore' (22).

Henry Bett echoes this position: 'children are as tenacious of their rhymes and stories as they are of their games. There is the same uncanny persistence of tradition, age after age [...] It is precisely the same with savages' (1924, 3). In 1931, John Buchan states that fairy tales 'come out of the most distant deeps of human experience and human fancy. They belong to a people themselves, not to a specially gifted or privileged class, and they are full of traces of their homely origin' (6). Carl Jung's readings of fairy tales reflect the same approach: 'Being a spontaneous, naïve, and uncontrived product of the psyche, the fairytale cannot very well express anything except what the psyche actually is' (1948, 239). Whether the stories and their influence on modern society are praised or condemned, they remain the site of the Other: the child, the savage, the woman, the folk, or the unconscious.

One of the results of these discourses was a bifurcation of the tales' place in the culture, as the middle-class adult and academic recipients of stories taken from folk sources are differentiated from the politically 'naïve' audiences of children and rustics. This demographic division is reflected in the presentation and marketing of the texts themselves. For instance, in England, T.W. Croker issues the multivolume *Fairy Legends and Traditions of the South of Ireland* (1825–8) for a mature and scholarly audience (Butts 1995, 86), where William Godwin edits and Benjamin Tabart publishes *Popular Fairy Tales* in 1809 for young people (Townsend 1974, 53). The folktale is thus distinguished from the literary fairy tale, even though the same stories are referenced in both academic anthologies and collections for children.

That said, the consumers of fairy tales do not seem to be much affected by such strategies. Washington Irving's collection of 1819, *Sketch Book of Geoffrey Crayon, Gent,* includes 'sketches of British life' as well as adult-oriented folklore that is taken from both American and German sources, but the miscellany appeals to a range of audiences, both younger and older (Carpenter and Prichard 1984, 272). In a similar demographic bridging, Hans Christian Andersen's 1835 collection of Danish and literary fairy tales, *Eventyr, fortalte for Børn,* or *Tales Told for Children,* is intended for a younger audience, but the book's success and the author's 'reputation both in Europe and America came not only from children but from the numbers of men and women who had read and savoured the tales' (N. Lewis 1984, vii). The reception of these texts depends not only on the writer or publisher but also on the reader or consumer.

When Andersen's volume is translated into English in 1846, its popularity cements the less pedantic or the 'implicitly moral' direction that much literature for children would take in the Victorian era (Egoff 1980, 412). His narratives are politically conservative, religiously oriented, and highly sentimental without seeming overtly didactic. While the stories appear to critique social flaws, they do not pose a significant challenge to the system that creates the problems. In 'The Little Match Girl,' for instance, readers experience sorrow and pain and fear, but are encouraged to celebrate 'the virtue of the obedient, non-complaining poverty-stricken' protagonist (Rush 1980, 108). Political change is replaced by an otherworldly system of punishment and reward: 'there was no more cold and no more hunger and no more fear – they were with God' (H. Andersen 1998, 277). The stories are appealing for this very reason. Andersen criticizes without critiquing and thus allows the status quo to continue to offer its (somewhat questionable) rewards to the patient, persevering, and passive recipient of ideology. In a notable exception, 'The Snow Queen' emphasizes the active role that children can play, where a little girl rectifies the situation, rescues the victimized boy, and grows into his partner within an asexual but companionate marriage: 'There they sat together, grown up, yet children still, children at heart' (272). This nostalgic figuration of childhood-in-adulthood suggests, however, a return to a state of political and social innocence that is at odds with the contemporary realities Andersen presents in his texts.

While Andersen's stories remain popular today, the most influential tales of the early 1800s are those from the collections of the Brothers Grimm. Wilhelm and Jakob Grimm publish the first edition of *Kinder- und Hausmärchen* in 1812, complete with scholarly annotations. The Grimms are hailed as heroes for rescuing their nation's past and culture, and celebrated for their dedication to folkloric studies. According to Bett, 'Their work might be described as the real beginning of the science of folk-lore' (1924, 14). Recent studies have, however, been more critical of the Grimms. The tales are not, in fact, collected by the brothers from peasant sources, but often stem from middle-class friends of the family, like Dorothea Wild, the Hassenpflug sisters, Dorothea Viehmann, and the land-owning von Haxthausens (Warner 1994a, 20). While these men and women may have originally learned the stories from sources closer to the folk – Karen Rowe points to the 'movement of tales into upper class or bourgeois kitchens and parlors, where old servants or nurses might tell tales *en famille*' (1986, 65) – the process of hearing, telling, and collecting the tales is accompanied by editorializing and filtering. As Warner writes, 'Though the stories are unquestionably traditional, they are not quite as homespun – or as rustically lowborn – as the brothers claimed' (1994a, 192). The nationality of the stories that the Brothers Grimm select and edit has also been called into question, even though the project is part of the brothers' lifelong study of German language, laws, and culture. The Hassenpflugs are descended from Huguenots, as is Dorothea Viehmann, and the tales themselves often stem from French sources (Zipes 1999, 70).

The Grimms' already mediated source material undergoes a series of further alterations, especially in editions published after 1819, when the brothers begin to add tales gleaned from literary sources (see Zipes 1992, 728). These are adapted, like the oral variants the Grimms collect, for the audience that would be reading them. The stories are altered to reflect the bourgeois Christianity of the brothers and to provide a strong backbone of moral didacticism, which is not always present in the source texts. Maria Tatar suggests that where spoken versions of 'Little Red Riding Hood' contain 'bawdy episodes, violent scenes, and scatological humour,' versions published by the Grimms stress 'the importance of restraining natural instincts and adhering to social norms set by adults' (1992, 37, 38). Jack Zipes catalogues specific changes between editions to indicate the ideological nature of the Grimms' project. In the 1812 version of 'Rapunzel,' for example, Mother Gothel discovers Rapunzel's sexual dalliances with the Prince when the pregnant girl asks, 'why do you think my clothes have become too tight for me and no longer fit?' In the 1857 edition, Rapunzel's question has been sanitized, as, upon pulling Mother Gothel up to the tower room, she asks, 'how is it that you're much heavier than the prince?' (1999, 73). Feminist critics have also pointed to the Grimms' conscious choice of tales featuring passive heroines and active heroes: 'In each subsequent edition of the tales, for instance, women [are] given less to say and do' (Lurie 1990, 36).

The Grimms publish seven German editions of their tales by 1857, as well as numerous English translations and reprintings (Zipes 1999, 72). But theirs are not the only anthologies. The variety of fairy tales available to children and adults in the Victorian era is evident in the number of collections that are in circulation. Henry Cole begins to issue his *Felix Summerly's Home Treasury* in 1841; in 1849, J.O. Halliwell-Phillipps publishes *Popular Rhymes and Nursery Tales*; in 1858 J.R. Planché translates *Four and Twenty Fairy Tales (from Madame d'Aulnoy)*; in 1863 Mrs Craik edits *The Fairy Book*; in 1890 Joseph Jacobs publishes *English Fairy Tales*. Literary fairy tales, or fairy tales written by specific authors, also become popular. John Ruskin's *The King of the Golden River* from 1851, Jean Ingelow's *Mopsa the Fairy* from 1869, George MacDonald's *The Princess and the Goblin* from 1872, and Oscar Wilde's *The Happy Prince* from 1888 are only a few of the stories that appear in what becomes known as the Golden Age of Children's Literature (R. Green 1946, 302–3; Hunt 1995, 552–5; Townsend 1974, 53; Zipes 1999, 125).

Despite the apparent popularity of the genre, however, there are still debates regarding the status of fairy tales in the nineteenth century, particularly in relation to the values that the tales present to children. In some quarters, fairy tales are viewed as escapist and thus suspect texts. In others, the commodification of fairy tales is seen as a degradation of an authentic and vulnerable link to the past. While the mass reproduction of fairy tales may be excused by the morality of the lessons they contained, the tales are used both to reinforce and to challenge Victorian expectations of gender and class. In either case, the fairy tale maintains its centrality in British culture, as its circulation through competing discourses carries it into the late nineteenth and early twentieth centuries.

The Perils of Commodification

Everyone's heart palpitated as Leo Dillon handed up the paper and everyone assumed an innocent face. Father Butler turned over the pages, frowning.
– What is this rubbish? he said. *The Apache Chief!* Is this what you read instead of studying your Roman History? Let me not find any more of this wretched stuff in this college. The man who wrote it, I suppose, was some wretched scribbler that writes these things for a drink. I'm surprised at boys like you, educated, reading such stuff. I could understand it if you were ... National School boys. Now, Dillon, I advise you strongly, get at your work or ...

James Joyce, 'An Encounter'

In his 1853 essay 'Frauds on the Fairies,' Charles Dickens defends fairy tales' emphasis on fancy by emphasizing the importance of the imagination 'In a utilitarian age' (111). Drawing upon the virtues of the past in his critique of the modern world, Dickens praises the stories for their latent educational content: 'It would be hard to estimate the amount of gentleness and mercy that has made its way among us through these slight channels' (111). In a similar vein, John Ruskin finds value in their subtle presentation of Victorian morality, 'a teaching for which no other can be substituted' (1868, 129). Andrew Lang in 1892 echoes this sensibility: 'The old fairy tales, which a silly sort of people disparage as too wicked and ferocious for the modern nursery, are really "full of matter," and unobtrusively teach the true lessons of our wayfaring in a world of perplexities and obstructions' (133). In these essays, the confusion of modern society is contrasted with the constancy of the virtues presented in the fairy tale.

As Dickens indicates in what became a coincidental commentary on George Cruikshank's teetotaller version of 'Cinderella,' it is the value of the traditional stories that is under attack: 'With seven Blue Beards in the field, each coming at a gallop from his own platform mounted on a foaming hobby, a generation or two hence would not know which was which, and the great original Blue Beard would be confounded with counterfeits' (1853, 112). The 'Bluebeard' that is contained in Perrault's collection becomes the gold standard here, and any version of it is an inferior copy or a 'counterfeit' that leads to fraudulent exchange. Dickens's monetary metaphor suggests his own investment in the stories of his childhood, but by placing the stories as commodities in order to illustrate their worth, he points to a central paradox that characterizes the fairy tale's position in modernity.

This is the dilemma: on one hand, the fairy tale reflects the purity of the child and of the culture. On the other hand, it reflects the views of the writers and editors who would adapt it to the present day. Despite the fact that literary fairy tales would seem to have always been tied to their contemporary moment, whether as commodities or as political commentaries, Dickens's concerns are echoed well into the twentieth century. For instance, Roger Sale argues in 1978 that 'whenever a tradition fades so it can be recovered only imperfectly, and only by isolated individuals, damage is inevitable' (25). It is difficult to establish what would be more distasteful: the exchange of fairy tales by the masses who contaminate the originals, or the isolation of the tradition to the point at which only a precious few can recognize the genuine article. Either way, fairy tales are positioned in an economy that situates mass-produced texts as inauthentic or valueless.[3]

Andrew Lang's twelve colour-coded Fairy Books, which first began to appear in 1889, provide an interesting example of how the fairy tale's cultural currency could be used to the editor's advantage (R. Green 1946, 82). Lang publishes his books to instruct children and to preserve existing cultural traditions. A journalist, anthropologist, folklorist, historian, translator, and writer (Demoor 1989, 6), Lang had ties to prominent academics and access to folklore from a range of different nations, which lend credibility to his work. But his reproduction of this lore for monetary gain suggests his complicity with the modern market forces that ostensibly threaten the very values and traditions embodied by the tales. Indeed, the stories 'were adapted and re-written so as to make them suitable for children' by Lang, his wife, and other translators (R. Green 1946, 81). Like the Grimms, what Lang is able to do is bridge the academic world and the world of children's literature, appealing to parents and children alike. Also like the Grimms, who publish their first edition of *Kinder- und Hausmärchen* in December 1812 (Rush 1980, 109), Lang issues a Fairy Book every two or three years in the strategically chosen Christmas season (Langstaff 1978, 138).

If Victorian book-sellers recognize the potent combination of Christmas and fairy tales, they have nothing on the producers of the British pantomime. These theatrical creations add another facet to the debate surrounding the authenticity of fairy tales, particularly in terms of their diverse formal influences. Many of the conventions of the English pantomime come from the Italian *commedia dell'arte* of the sixteenth century, though the main plots are adapted from the literary fairy tales of Perrault and the Grimms, as well as from nursery rhymes. The pantomime is also inspired by James Robinson Planché's fairy-tale extravaganzas of the early 1800s, by burlesque and music-hall routines from the late 1800s, by fairy-tale operettas such as Engelbert Humperdinck's *Hansel and Gretel* of 1893, and by the parodic works by Gilbert and Sullivan, such as *Princess Ida* of 1884.[4] Just as importantly, they are influenced by contemporary consumer realities, being not only staged and marketed in the major commercial centres of Britain, but often depicting the experience of the modern metropolis and its stores.

The popularity of the pantomime has persisted into the twenty-first century, as the productions continue to capitalize upon the connection between children, fairy tales, and the Christmas season.[5] The pantomime, according to Peter Holland, was and still is 'the cornerstone of the British theatrical economy' (1997, 195). In December of 1897, for instance, at least twenty-five fairy tales, including 'Cinderella,' 'Beauty and the Beast,' and 'Red Riding Hood,' are staged in London and its suburbs (Archer 1898, 424–5). In the late Victorian era, pantomimes are an industry unto themselves, and each show 'employed many people for the best part of the year' (Mander and Mitchenson 1973, 25). The elaborate sets, costumes, and stage machinery, particularly of the transformation scene, represent significant investments for the theatre (see Booth 1976, 6; Herr 1986, 115–16). The harlequinade section of the pantomime, in which the lovers are transformed into the commedic figures of Harlequin and Columbine, is particularly materialistic in content, as the scene showcases the most popular products of the holiday season. Towards the 1870s, the harlequinade is usually set on 'a street showing a long row of shops gaudily decorated' (A. Wilson 1949, 35). The producers of later pantos go even further in their presentation of commodity culture: 'In the *Cinderella* of 1895 the heroine rides to the ball in an electric motorcar; automobiles also make an appearance – baffling and enraging the principals – in *The Sleeping Beauty and the Beast* and in the 1902 *Mother Goose*' (Booth 1976, 61).

The props of the pantomime mirror the concern of the plots, which are based consistently on narratives in which an advantageous marriage involves wealth and not just love. Two lovers from different classes encounter a stumbling block relating to money. At the end of the show, vice is punished and the reward for virtue 'is always material: an inheritance, a wealthy marriage, a business success' (Bailey 1966, 31). As Cheryl Herr suggests, the pantomime 'appealed in no uncertain terms to the bourgeois audience which was its principal economic support' (1986, 107). The staged presentations of magical solutions to financial and social obstacles pose little threat to the world offstage and tend not to reflect the actual hurdles faced by economically marginalized members of the audience (165). While the harlequinade 'satirically and crazily reflected [the] real world and simultaneously laughed at it' (Booth 1976, 6), the panto ends comically with a reassertion of community and of society, containing the critique within the space of the theatre.

The fantasy of class mobility is accompanied by a much less conservative vision of gender mobility, which reflects some of the challenges and changes to sexual roles that were taking place at the time. The part of the Principal Boy is taken by a woman, who plays the hero of both the fairy tale and the harlequinade. The Dame role is played more comically by male actors, such as the famous Dan Leno, who appears in drag as the Wicked Stepmother, an Ugly Stepsister, the Queen of Hearts, or Mother Goose (see Booth 1976, 59; Garber 1992, 176). The Dame figure, a parody of femininity, draws attention to the fact that the part is played by a man, just as the Principal Boy is traditionally played by women who are 'ample of figure' and whose 'considerable embonpoint' belies the gender of the character (Garber 1992, 176, 177). In the 1880s and 1890s, the male lead is taken over by music-hall entertainers such as Hetty King and the male impersonator Vesta Tilley. By the twentieth century, the harlequinade has largely disappeared from pantomimes, and the Principal Boys is 'slimmer, more "boyish"' (176). Though the Dame remains the same in contemporary pantomime, the male lead is now usually played by a man, with the exception of some performances of *Peter Pan.*

The rise of cinematic versions of fairy tales may have played a part in reducing the gender trouble of pantos. The realistic nature of the medium of film encourages a more 'authentic' – that is, strictly heterosexual – presentation of romantic love. Even so, filmed versions of the tales draw heavily upon theatrical traditions and popular stage business, especially in the early years of the cinema. *Barbe Bleue* (1901), for instance, filmed by and starring Georges Méliès, features the theatrical trick of 'a friendly goblin [who] appears in a puff of smoke,' and the lens of the camera recapitulates the frame of the proscenium arch of the Victorian stage (Warner 1994a, 242). A popular film of the modernist era, Walt Disney's *Snow White and the Seven Dwarfs* (1937) also involves aspects of the pantomime stage, especially in the comic figures of the dwarves. The more striking formal influences on Disney's film are, however, storybook illustrations by artists such as Arthur Rackham, Edmund Dulac, and W. Heath Robinson (Holliss and Sibley 1987, 10). As important is Disney's exploration of the possibilities of film itself. The depiction of Snow White's movements through the sinister-looking trees and the shifting, shadowy spaces of the forest capitalizes upon a psychological projection of fear that is only hinted at in Rackham's suggestive illustrations. As Jean Cocteau's surrealist *La Belle et La Bête* (1946) demonstrates, cinematic versions of fairy tales could depict the fluidity of the psyche as well as the elements of magic that appear in the stories. The intensity of the experience arises not just from the tale being brought to life, but from the sensory impact of visuals and sounds that push the boundaries of the technology and reflect a modern medium of expression.

With films, and especially Disney films, which continue to occupy a central position in the fairy-tale market, the stories are an increasingly important part of commodity culture, whether at the cinema or at home through spin-off products. But fairy tales are not just commodities in themselves; they are used, and continue to be used, by advertisers in order to sell other goods. An example is the advertisement for Fry's Cocoa from 1891 that Peter and Iona Opie include in their collection of fairy tales, which depicts Red Riding Hood bringing hot chocolate to the Wolf-as-Grandmother. The caption – 'A Charming Drink for Young

& Old; Tis Almost Worth Its Weight in Gold' (1974, 120) – plays upon the multigenerational appeal of the story. The tale's figuration of familial responsibility is the key to the advertisement, where the dutiful granddaughter emphasizes Fry's Cocoa's association with 'family values.' The advertisement addresses the child who knows the story and who is encouraged to think of Fry's Cocoa when she or he reads the tale next. It is oriented towards the adult too, who buys the product for the sake of a demanding offspring, if not for its nostalgic value. Significantly, the Wolf's teeth are pulled in the ad, for the text is suspended at the moment just before Little Red Riding Hood – and the reader – realize that the Grandmother is not all that she seems. It is a rather dangerous image in this sense, and yet the recognizability of the scene and the ironic twist that is implicit in the visual itself somehow carry it off, where the appropriate consumption of the advertised product would seem to prevent the inappropriate consumption of the little girl.

That an advertisement would feature a scene from 'Little Red Riding Hood' indicates the widespread knowledge of fairy tales in turn-of-the-century Anglo-American societies. In their status as both commodities and objects of scholarly research, in their publication for children and in their production for adults, in their presentation on film and in their circulation as oral narratives, fairy tales represent a vast reservoir of cultural reference. Just as importantly, they are manipulated to include 'topical and local allusions,' whether in film, on the panto stage, or in the halls where travelling lecturers would retell and alter the tales using slides and lanterns (Horrall 2001, 22). But the fairy tale is also the screen onto which cultural anxiety continued to be projected. Reactions to increased industrialization, urbanization, and destabilized classed and gendered roles inform the stories' circulation in the twentieth century. Not just an object of scholarly evaluation but a vehicle for social critique, the fairy tale is awarded a position in the most important theoretical paradigms to emerge in modernity.

The Possibilities of Transformation

Go, said the bird, for the leaves were full of children,
Hidden excitedly, containing laughter.
Go, go, go, said the bird: human kind
Cannot bear very much reality.   T.S. Eliot, 'Burnt Norton'

It is not surprising that fairy tales are key texts in the early twentieth century, since, as cornerstones of the Golden Age of Children's Literature, the stories are embedded in the childhoods of so many modern theorists and artists. The rise of folklore studies is, in this sense, a symptom of the popularity of fairy tales. Antti Aarne's catalogue of folktale patterns from 1910, revised by Stith Thompson in 1928 to become the Aarne-Thompson tale type index, confirms the stories as valuable objects of scholarly inquiry.[6] Vladimir Propp's *Morphology of the Folktale*, first published in 1928, echoes this emphasis on classification and categorization. Propp's mapping of the structure of wonder tales and of the multiple possibilities of the folktale's plot is an attempt to stabilize the fairy tale within a larger body of knowledge, and to grant it an official place in the Western literary and cultural tradition. While the drawbacks of defining fairy tales through structuralist analysis become quickly apparent – the complexity of different social and historical contexts, and the political ramifications of variants can, for example, be potentially ignored – such studies reflect the fairy tale's place in the larger drive towards recognizing, systematizing, and thus formalizing the experience of modernity.

Fairy tales are integral facets of revolutionary views of the history and the psychology of modern 'man.' Indeed, the plots, characters, and images of the stories are used to elucidate and illustrate some of the most important metanarratives of modernism. Sigmund Freud alludes to fairy tales in a range of his studies. Generalized motifs such as the choice between three caskets (1958b, 291), literary tales such as E.T.A. Hoffmann's 'Der Sandmann' (1973, 227), and variants from the Brothers Grimm (1958a, 281) are used to illustrate psychoanalytical concepts. In the case of the 'Wolf-man,' for instance, Freud draws upon 'Little Red Riding Hood' and 'The Seven Little Goats' (1959, 493). Another key figure for modernity, Sir James Frazer, uses the stories in *The Golden Bough* to suggest the link between fairy tales and the primitive past of contemporary civilization: 'any idea which commonly occurs in them, however absurd it may seem to us, must once have been an ordinary article of belief' (1922, 774). That both Freud and Frazer use fairy tales as a system of reference testifies to the stories' pervasive cultural status in the nineteenth century, as well as to the subsequent consolidation of the tales in the modernist imagination.

Certainly the connections between social theory and artistic innovation are evident in modernist works that respond to fairy tales as well as to the dominant modes of modern thought. While Karl Marx does not address folklore overtly in *Capital*, aside from comparing capital to a 'vampire' (1995, 149), his depiction of the inequities of social classes is echoed in Oscar Wilde's fairy tale 'The Happy Prince,' in which the forces of nineteenth-century industrialization and utilitarianism are countered by the Happy Prince's nascent socialist gestures (1888). In *Beasts and Super-Beasts*, Saki takes aim at the sentimentality of texts like Wilde's by invoking Darwinism in his depictions of the bloodthirsty, survival-of-the-fittest attitudes of young, rebellious readers. In 'The Story-Teller,' for example, a 'horribly good' little girl is eaten by the Wolf to the delight of the three unruly children who are being told the thoroughly 'improper story' (1914, 123, 126). Boris Vian's 'Blue Fairy Tale' from 1949 is an example of the influence of psychoanalytic thought, as his surrealist take on 'Puss in Boots' set in wartime France is informed by theories of the subconscious as well as by the trauma of the Occupation (Vian 1992).

James Whitcomb Riley, Walter de la Mare, and Randall Jarrell write poems based on fairy tales (1993; 1927; 1956). Robert Graves's poetry indicates the influence of the nursery and of childhood stories (1965). Max Beerbohm's *The Happy Hypocrite* combines fairy tales with classical references and Christian motifs (1915), as does Sylvia Townsend Warner's collection *The Cat's Cradle-Book* (1940). Ford Madox Ford's fairy tales of the 1890s, such as *The Queen Who Flew*, and Ronald Firbank's *Odette: A Fairy Tale for Weary People* use established stories to express the concerns of a modern world (1894; 1916). In Jean Rhys's *Good Morning, Midnight*, Sasha Jansen is employed for a short and unhappy time as a writer of fairy tales (1939). Edith Sitwell in the 1920s was engaged in rewriting 'Sleeping Beauty' and 'Cinderella,' and invokes figures from the pantomime in *Façade* (1987). Katharine Mansfield's 'The Little Governess' is a retelling of 'Little Red Riding Hood' (1945).[7] Henry James, Willa Cather, James Stephens, and Stevie Smith also refer to fairy tales, which represent a potent system of reference for a range of authors (Callander 1989; see Tintner 1989; Montefiore 1994, 43; Stephens 1912).

In many of these works, the fairy tale speaks to a nostalgia for the coherence of a pre-war era or for childhood innocence. In this sense, the rewriting of the stories rests upon the juxtaposition of times and mores, which can be read as an attempt to make sense of a rapidly changing world. In *The Four Quartets*, for instance, T.S. Eliot's references to the rose gardens of *Alice's Adventures in Wonderland* (Carroll 1988) and *The Secret Garden* (Burnett 1911) are joined to the vision of the celestial rose from Dante's *Divine Comedy* of the fourteenth century (Briggs 1995, 167–8; Dusinberre 1987, 180). This multilayered allusion connects different national and literary traditions in order to establish a sense of stability or continuity. Dante's medieval Catholic vision is joined to the modern time and space that is 'Now and in England' (T.S. Eliot 1942, 215), and his paradisal rose becomes aligned with the Victorian ideal of the natural child, as the garden becomes a space in which the poet rediscovers a timeless or atemporal identity that joins the individual to a continuum of spiritual and cultural significance.

Like Rudyard Kipling's rural Sussex in *Puck of Pook's Hill*, the land is a conduit for the rediscovery of value, where the subject renews his (or her) connection to the culture and its traditions in the modern present. The countryside plays a prominent role in other works as well, as a return to rural space comes to represent an appealing 'escape to the natural, the apolitical, [and] the imaginary' (Murray 1985, 41). This world is often embodied by a supernatural being, an animal or bird, or more often, a rustic (preferably old or mad). In *The Secret Garden*, for instance, Mary Lennox is helped first by a robin and then by Dickon, the working-class brother of her maid. In both cases, healthy rusticity, which has bred in Dickon both compassion and patience, allows Mary and the invalid Colin to be rejuvenated by the power of nature. As Colin says to his father after being healed, 'It was the garden that did it – and Mary and Dickon and the creatures – and the Magic' (Burnett 1911, 264). In *Puck of Pook's Hill*, the rustic intermediary is 'old Hobden the hedger' (Kipling 1906, 61), as well as 'his son, the Bee-Boy who is not quite right in his head' (149). These representatives of rural England are supplemented by the magical figure of Puck, Kipling's symbol of Shakespeare's Britain, who comes to life for Dan and Una (herself a nod to Spenser's *Faerie Queene*). The literary and cultural traditions of the country are given new life in Kipling's text. Puck and his leaves of ash, oak, and thorn represent a natural corrective for a corrupted view of the nation, and his imaginative representation of history instructs the children on what being English 'really' means.

For the protagonists of many of these texts, the pastoral British countryside is experienced in comfort thanks to the labour of the working classes or to the privilege of inherited position. In Kenneth Grahame's *The Wind in the Willows*, for example, Toad Hall and the various houses owned by the upper-middle-class male animals of the story form a homosocial community that is based upon highly traditional class and gender divisions.[8] Property is the factor that enables this idyllic vision. As Mole states upon returning to Mole End with the Water-Rat, 'it was good to think he had this to come back to, this place which was all his own, these things which were so glad to see him again and could always be counted upon for the same simple welcome' (1908, 107). The 'simple' creature comforts that Mole, Ratty, and Badger cherish and are able to afford – the family estate, good food and drink, and holidays and meals at friends' houses – prefigure the largely bourgeois preoccupations of J.R.R. Tolkien's Bilbo Baggins in *The Hobbit*. Like Mole End, Bag End in Hobbiton represents the Bagginses' traditional place in their society. With its 'panelled walls, and floors tiled and carpeted,' the hobbit-hole speaks to wealth and security, especially for Frodo, who benefits from Bilbo's speculation on Smaug (1937, 13). The Shire and the Hill are images of hobbitness and the conservative values upon which it is based. As we see in the *Lord of the Rings* trilogy, however, Sam Gamgee is the necessary lower-class anchor for Frodo's success. It is Sam's willingness to be exploited out of his love for his master that enables 'The Scouring of the Shire' in *The Return of the King* (1955, 336), and the shift from an industrial society replete with mills 'full o' wheels and outlandish contraptions' (356) back to a stable, feudal system. The 'Hundred Acre Wood' of A.A. Milne's *Winnie-the-Pooh* from 1926 represents a similar kind of English rural community, where the reassuring roles played by the animals have been created by their squire, Christopher Robin, and narrated his father (1971, 204). J.M. Barrie's play *Peter Pan*, first staged in 1904 and subsequently adapted, involves another rural utopia, in which the Never Land community of Lost Boys is run by a largely benign dictator and where housework is carried out by women.

Though the scenes of domesticity and hierarchy that such stories present may be reassuring, they are haunted by the threat of disorder and division. The uprising of the stoats and weasels who take over Toad Hall, the temporary nature of Christopher Robin's dominion, the incursion of the forces of darkness into the Shire, even the largely absurd figures of Captain Hook and the lower-class adult pirates – these reminders of the fragility of the community in question represent the inevitable passing of childhood. Peter Pan thus lives out a dream by defying the end of the game and by not growing up or going home. Significantly, the threat that is implied in Barrie's text is not just the everyday world, where grown men must go to the office, but the more specific danger symbolized by Peter's original home and the Darlings' current residence: London. The Never Land is Barrie's alternative to Bloomsbury, just as Burnt Norton is Eliot's response to the 'Unreal City' (1922b, 65). Nostalgic visions of the pastoral world can be seen, then, as reactions to urban modernity, and to the technological changes and demographic shifts that alter British and North American societies in the 1900s. Though Raymond Williams points out that the modernist response to the city through representations of the country is diverse, and extends well beyond 'Eliot's pessimistic recoil' (1989, 43), the green world still signals a sense of authenticity and value in early-twentieth-century children's literature. It is the vegetation of Misselthwaite Manor that provides Mary Lennox with an alternative to her city-like solitude in the dry and sterile Indian landscape; it is the farm at Green Gables that allows Anne Shirley to have a social place (Montgomery 1997); and though it is the Emerald City in which Dorothy Gale is sheltered after her journeys through the Land of Oz, the metropolis is merely a stepping stone to her real home, the Kansas prairie farm (Baum 1900). These traditional, rural communities, threatened by the fragmentation and division that modernity represents, are also its antidotes.

Specific fairy tales are used to depict the fragmentation of early-twentieth-century life, especially in relation to the modern city and its gendered, classed spaces. Katherine Mansfield's 'The Little Governess' from 1920 is a significant example of the politicized appropriation of a fairy tale, as she sets 'Little Red Riding Hood' in the metropolis. The motifs of the story are reworked in this updating: the Wolf is still a sexual predator but in the guise of a Grandfather figure who takes advantage of a naïve, young governess. In Mansfield's depiction of how women must deal with unfamiliar geographical and social territory, the main focus of critique is the double standard, in which men's and women's sexual conducts are judged differently and inequitably. This is the cause of Red's victimization, for the governess's reputation is ruined despite her innocence and ignorance of any misdoing. She has been taken advantage of, not just by her employer and Grandfather Wolf, but by the society as a whole. If there is irony in Mansfield's story, it arises from the recognition that the Grimms' patronizing moral still applies: girls who stray from the path of acceptable behaviour will not survive.

Anaïs Nin's *A Spy in the House of Love* from 1954 is an equally unsettling portrayal of modern gender relations. Sabina's promiscuity seems to undermine a patriarchal control over her identity, as she becomes the Cinderella whose continual escape from the Prince and towards other men mocks his authority. Using the tricks of the fairy godmother – make-up, clothes, classed behaviour – Sabina can attract men, but she can also evade them by virtue of the chaotic space that is the city. She is caught only by the Lie Detector, who asks her to make of herself 'a competent actress' rather than one who would 'continue to play

Cinderella for amateur theatres only' (1954, 162). The result is a 'complete dissolution' of her identity (166), where the role of the fairy-tale protagonist seems more real than Sabina herself. In contrast, 'Bluebeard's Daughter' from Sylvia Townsend Warner's *The Cat's Cradle-Book* (1940) shows characters who learn from the fairy tale and move forward. Rather than a female protagonist who is punished by Bluebeard for her curiosity, Djamileh (Bluebeard's daughter) is joined by her husband Kayel, and both sublimate the destructive potential of their shared curiosity by studying astronomy instead of opening locked doors.

Interpretations of these modernist adaptations of fairy tales would seem to depend upon the reader's recognition not just of the source text but of the way in which it has been interpreted by the author. Thus, Little Red Riding Hood remains a victim in Mansfield's figuration of the story, and though the setting is contemporary, the lesson is the same. Nin's Cinderella also remains trapped by her narrative and must learn the role of woman again and more effectively if she is to remain afloat. Bluebeard's daughter may change her family's story, but she does so according to her knowledge of the fairy tale and thus confirms the cautionary message of the intertext. While all three comment upon women's social roles and critique a patriarchal order, they also use fairy tales as the 'straight men' to their variations. This is precisely where the authors differ from Joyce, Woolf, and Barnes, whose references to fairy tales are not predicated upon a stable and single source text, or upon linear narratives of climax and resolution. Though their allusions signal the presence of ideologies of previous generations, they use the stories to invoke not just the past but the present, and to present not just struggles but productive interactions with narratives of gender and class. As cultural common ground, the tales traverse the same kinds of social and literary boundaries that Joyce, Woolf, and Barnes cross in their works. Fairy tales come to reflect, then, the fluctuating experience of modernity for these authors, and most importantly, the agency of the subject in a modern consumer society.

2 James Joyce: The Fashionable Fairy Tale

ARCHIE: Will you tell me a fairy story, Mr. Hand?
ROBERT: A fairy story? Why not? I am your fairy godfather.

James Joyce, *Exiles*

In 'An Analysis of the Mind of James Joyce' from *Time and Western Man*, Wyndham Lewis dismisses Joyce's subject matter as the naturalistic rubbish of a Victorian curio cabinet. He labels Joyce '*the craftsman*, pure and simple' (1927, 88), reserving the accolade of creator for himself, and calls Stephen Dedalus a 'small, pointless, and oppressive character' (96) and a 'frigid prig' (97). Why, then, begin this section on Joyce with a discussion of Lewis, the scapegoat of modernism? Perhaps because it is a tradition, and one followed by such illustrious critics as Frank Budgen (1934), Hugh Kenner (1955), and Bonnie Kime Scott (1987), to name just a few. The problem with this tradition, however, is that Lewis's insights and analyses are often rather convincing. Stephen *is* a bit of an 'irritating, principal figure' (W. Lewis 1927, 97), and Joyce *does* seem to be obsessed with 'the sewage of a Past twenty years old' (89), or, as Jennifer Wicke terms it, 'a material world awash in the detritus of consumer objects' (1994c, 175). As germane to this chapter, and to my exploration of fairy tales, fashion, and consumer culture in Joyce's writing, is Lewis's suggestive comparison of Joyce and W.B. Yeats in relation to their treatments of the past and of the present.

There are crucial distinctions to be made between Yeats's work with Irish legends, sagas, and stories, and Joyce's references to Continental fairy tales in his essays, plays, and novels. Though critics have noted that Joyce does indeed allude to Irish folklore in his texts,[1] others see the writer as rejecting the stuff of the Revival altogether: 'he could not adjust himself to the popular taste of Dublin, not even to the more precious taste of the Yeats-A.E.-Gregory inner circle' (Gorman 1940, 112). In such readings, the modernist chooses modernity over 'a time-less mythic past' (Kearney 1988, 31) and embraces reality rather than 'the dulling, paralysing charms of a legendary, unreal past, haunted by fairies and primitive heroes of superstition' (Cixous 1972, 165). The satire of the 'Cyclops' chapter of *Ulysses* thus indicates Joyce's critique of Revivalist agendas that take their inspiration from ancient traditions, as the author and his views represent 'the antithesis of the value-system and imaginative world of O'Grady, Yeats, and Lady Gregory' (Gibson 1991, 68).

In *Time and Western Man*, Lewis relates these differences between Joyce and the author of *The Celtic Twilight* to their presentations of Ireland and the Irish:

> Yeats is the chivalrous embodiment of 'celtic' romance, more of St. Bran-don than of Ossian, with all the grand manners of a spiritual Past that cannot be obliterated, though it wear thin, and of a dispossessed and persecuted people. Joyce is the cold and stagnant reality at which that people had at last arrived in its civilized Reservation, with all the snobbish pathos of such a condition, the intense desire to keep-up-appearances at all costs, to be ladylike and gentlemanly, in spite of a beggared position – above which that yeatsian emanation floats. (1927, 75)

But for all that Yeats embraces the folk and nostalgic romance here, and Joyce depicts the grimy reality of the fallen bourgeoisie, Lewis asserts their essential ideological connection: they both remain writers of the 'exhausted [...] Past' rather than of the present (81). The point Lewis makes is that, although these writers share neither a literary nor a nationalist agenda, a 'time-fanaticism' underwrites the attitudes of both (83) and undercuts a distinction based upon the imagery of their work.

Significantly, Lewis invokes fairy tales in his discussion of the 'wild-goose chase' after 'the sphinx of the Past' upon which both Yeats and Joyce embark (1927, 80). In critiquing Joyce, he focuses on the author's choice of time as his métier instead of space, and of history instead of the present. The temporal and lost world of *Ulysses* becomes 'as unsub-stantial as a mist on a Never-Never landscape' (81). The narrative method Joyce uses – '"telling from the inside"' – is also the stuff of fantasy: 'it lands the reader inside an Aladdin's cave of incredible bric-à-brac in which a dense mass of dead stuff is collected, from 1901 toothpaste, a bar or two of Sweet Rosie O'Grady, to pre-nordic architecture' (89). The fairy story, whether in the form of Barrie's *Peter Pan* (81) or the *Arabian Nights* (89, 101), represents an escape from everyday life into the 'compensating principle' (81) of the Past.

In arguing against Lewis's 'brilliant but negative essay,' Frank Budgen defends the reasons behind Joyce's presentation of 'the vast amount of local time detail in *Ulysses*': 'if the artist is not to be the abstract and brief mirror of his own time, of what time is he to be mirror and abstract? [...] Only the fairy story begins, "Once upon a time" with people dressed in timeless garments going on from one adventure to another in unsurveyed places.' (1934, 128). But note here how Budgen remains within the dichotomous framework of Lewis's argument regarding reality and romance, where fairy tales are escapist fictions rather than narratives that speak to the socioeconomic systems of modernity or to the material conditions of Joyce's Dublin. To paraphrase Lewis, so long as *fairy tales are fantastic* is the capital truth of your world it matters very little if you deny the fairy tale's relevance to Joyce's work, like the Budgenian, or say there is nothing else at all, like Lewisian (1927, 109).

The irony here is that Lewis undercuts his own argument that fairy tales are remnants of the Past rather than exemplars of the Present. When he invokes fairy tales as metaphors of Joyce's escape from modernity, Lewis shows their very timeliness by using them in his own argument. Indeed, not only does he use the language of fairy tales in his piece, demonstrating their cultural currency, he also makes overt the connection between fairy tales and commodity culture, particularly in his references to stories that were popular sources for British pantomimes. While he criticizes Joyce for not examining the ideology that informs his subject – 'it matters very little to him *what* he writes, or what idea or world-view he expresses, so long as he is trying his hand at this matter and that, and displaying his enjoyable virtuosity' (1927, 88) – Lewis tacitly identifies the role that Joyce assigns fairy tales by using them himself to critique representations of a modern, urban world.

By drawing upon a tradition of European fairy tales, including those popularized by Perrault and the Grimms, Joyce places such stories not as nationalist texts, escapist fantasies, or chronicles of an essential humanity, but as powerful and pervasive narratives of turn-of-the-century capitalism. Identity is linked consistently to performance in Joyce's works, and fashion plays a significant role in both his own texts and in the fairy tales he cites. As we see in 'Cinderella,' which has particular relevance to Stephen's identity in *Ulysses,* clothes can hide the individual's actual social status. But as we see from the mirror in 'Snow White,' which is used in the 'Nausicaa' section, there is a fine line between imitating the ideals of a culture and being trapped by social expectations. The anxiety and the pleasure that arise from this balancing act is what Joyce explores in his allusions to fairy tales, which act as a corrective to the sense of nostalgia and timelessness that surround the lore of the Revival. In *Ulysses,* the matter of fairy tales reflects the material conditions according to which Joyce's characters live their lives.

Joyce and the Celtic Revival

There was an artificial, pseudo-historical air about the Rebellion, as there was inevitably about the movement of 'celtic' revival; it seemed to be forced and vamped up long after its poignant occasion had passed.

Wyndham Lewis, *Time and Western Man*

In the ninth section of *Ulysses,* Stephen Dedalus feels that he must elude the slings and arrows of outrageous scholars and by opposing, end their threat to his identity. Scylla and Charybdis can be viewed as the twin forces of Buck Mulligan and Haines, here, or as dear dirty Dublin and imperial England. They also symbolize the various writers, theorists, and thinkers of the Celtic Revival that attempt to ensnare the 'lover of the true or the good' who 'abhors the multitude' to which those Revivalists address themselves (Joyce 1901, 69). A significant number of artists involved in Irish literary and language movements are mentioned in the chapter, including John Eglinton (William Kirkpatrick Magee), W.B. Yeats, Oliver St John Gogarty, A.E. (George Russell), Richard I. Best, Douglas Hyde, George Moore, Padraic Colum, Susan Mitchell, George Sigerson, Seumas O'Sullivan (James S. Starkey), Edward Martyn, James Stephens, and John Millington Synge (Gifford 1989, 192–256). The figures attest to the cultural importance of Dublin, to the strong sense of nationalism in 1904 Ireland, and to the range of different perspectives that the Celtic Revival comprised. They also draw attention to Stephen's Bloom-like exclusion from the inner circles of the Hibernian mysteries:

– They say we are to have a literary surprise, the quaker librarian said, friendly and earnest. Mr Russell, rumour has it, is gathering together a sheaf of our younger poets' verses. We are all looking forward anxiously.

Anxiously he glanced in the cone of lamplight where three faces, lighted, shone.

See this. Remember. (9.289–94)

Stephen's distance from A.E. et alia is a hazy mirror image of Joyce's real–life situation: similar but distorted along the tit-for-tattish lines of 'The Holy Office': 'And though they spurn me from their door / My soul shall spurn them evermore' (1904, 106). In fact, Joyce was connected to the members of the Celtic Revival on a number of levels. He took language lessons for a time with Padraic Pearse and was friends with George Clancy, Francis Sheehy-Skeffington, and John Francis Byrne (the fictional Madden, MacCann, and Cranly), who were deeply involved with Irish political reform (Ellmann 1982, 61). While he was consistently dismissed by Moore (135), A.E., Yeats, and Lady Gregory were strong supporters, and through them he came to know Synge and Arthur Symons (111, 124). Nevertheless, the Irish Nationalists were generally wary of Joyce's apparently apolitical and amoral Continental views, just as Joyce was highly suspicious of the politics and aesthetics of the Revival.

Hélène Cixous argues that 'there is in Joyce a current of anti-Celtic racialism opposed to the Celtophilia so in favour with his contemporaries, that of Yeats and A.E., of Griffith and the Sinn Fein' (1972, xiii). The reason seems to be that Joyce regarded Irish nationalism as leading to a kind of propaganda in art (Ellmann 1982, 55). The tendency to present in literature a specific vision of national identity was as distasteful to Joyce as the demand on Yeats to constrict Cathleen to a Catholic vision of Irish womanhood. Indeed, Joyce's refusal to sign a letter to the *Freeman's Journal* condemning *The Countess Cathleen* in 1899 (Ellmann 1982, 67) indicates the connections between the two positions, though his stance had less to do with the object of the debate – the 'obscene' portrayal of Irish women – and more to do with his concern for the freedom of the writer. In 'Day of the Rabblement,' for example, Joyce distinguishes the artist from his or her audience and reacts against the impulse that places the creator among the masses who sully the creative impulse with their demands: 'If an artist courts the favour of the multitude he cannot escape the contagion of its fetichism [sic] and deliberate self-deception, and if he joins in a popular movement he does so at his own risk. Therefore, the Irish Literary Theatre by its surrender to the trolls has cut itself adrift from the line of advancement' (1901, 71). Joyce's concern over the censorship in Ireland that Yeats, Martyn, and Lady Augusta Gregory were dealing with is obvious. He is sympathetic with their struggle, acknowledging the fact that 'directors are shy of presenting Ibsen, Tolstoy or Hauptmann, where even *Countess Cathleen* is pronounced vicious and damnable' (70). But at the same time, Joyce criticizes the directors' inattention to European works: an artistic attitude that cannot expand its cultural horizons comes dangerously close to the Citizen's reductive vision of Irish identity.

Joyce had stated his opposition to dogma in literature a year earlier in 'Drama and Life' when he argued that 'Art is marred by such mistaken insistence on its religious, its moral, its beautiful, its idealizing tendencies' (1900, 44). Instead of idealism, he asserts his own vision of realism: 'Life we must accept as we see it before our eyes, men and women as we meet them in the real world, not as we apprehend them in the world of faery' (45). In the context of the Celtic Revival, Joyce's reference to the 'world of faery' is not necessarily a condemnation of the tales of the Brothers Grimm; rather, it indicates his suspicion of how folk tales were being used by Yeats, Lady Gregory, Russell, Hyde, and others. The 'world of faery' is that almost-forgotten rural past that was perceived and celebrated in its most 'authentic' state as Irish folklore.

Obviously, the revival of Celtic history and Gaelic oral literature was both aesthetically and politically motivated. In a nation inundated by the narratives of a foreign state, there was a real need to rescue and reassert those traditions that had, as W.R. Wilde pointed out in 1852, 'gradually vanished before the spread of education, and the rapid growth of towns and manufactories' (v). As an alternative to the threat of industrialization, 'folktales seemed to offer safely indigenous models to link the increasingly Anglicized present with the pristine Gaelic past' (O'Leary 1994, 102). Yeats's collections, for instance, are intended to retain a disappearing oral tradition. As he asserts in his *Autobiographies*, the '*Grimm's Fairy-Tales* that [he] read at Sligo, and all of Hans Andersen except *The Ugly Duckling*' are stories that have paled for him in comparison to 'the knights and dragons and beautiful ladies' of Irish sagas and legends (1955, 47). Yeats's appreciation for native lore and for its folk roots is thus posited in opposition to a European influence, which is dominating the domestic scene.

The Revival partook, then, in what Regina Bendix suggests is a common nationalist enterprise, where the use of 'folklore in the guise of native cultural discovery and rediscovery' anchors the nation's reconstituted worth (1997, 7). Revivalists deconstructed British and European figurations of Ireland only to reconstruct, often with reference to an idealized vision of 'a rural and primitive West,' its people and stories (Cheng 2000, 249). In 'The Celtic Element in Literature,' for example, Yeats responds explicitly to 'On the Study of Celtic Literature' by Matthew Arnold, which presents an interpretation of 'the Celt's genius and history' (1898, 39). In his essay, Arnold outlines first the heroic and manly qualities of the English and Germanic 'races,' which display respectively *energy with honesty* and *steadiness with honesty* (1866, 80, 81). He then outlines the traits of the Celt: 'timidity,' 'shyness,' 'delicacy,' and sentimentality (82). Emotion, not intellect or integrity, is the dominant and lamentable characteristic of the Irish, whose 'want of sanity and steadfastness' restrains the nation from reaching 'the highest success' (86). Taking Arnold and Ernest Renan as the starting point for his defence of the Irish people and their culture, Yeats emphasizes instead the intensity and continuing influence of Celtic tradition, in which emotion becomes the passion that 'has again and again brought "the vivifying spirit" "of excess" into the arts of Europe' (1898, 198).

The political significance of Yeats's arguments on behalf of Irish culture was, however, partially overshadowed by their aura of mystical zeal. As Max Beerbohm's circa 1904 caricature of Yeats and George Moore shows, those outside Revivalist and theosophical circles regarded the collection of Irish folklore as a somewhat dubious pursuit. In 'Mr W.B. Yeats presenting Mr George Moore to the Queen of the Fairies,' Beerbohm satirizes not only Yeats's nationalism but also its associations with spirituality and the occult (1997, 49). A map of Ireland on the wall to Yeats's left is paired with a bookshelf on his right, which contains such texts as *Realism: Its Cause & Cure, Half Hours with the Symbols, Life of Kathleen Mavourneen, Erse Without Tears, Songs of Innocence, Murray's Guide to Ireland,* and *Short Cuts to Mysticism.* The very formality of the 'meeting' – Yeats at his sepulchrally genteel best, and Moore standing hat in hand, his head bowed before the tiny, floating fairy as well as before his literary successor – suggests the tension between the romantic and the prosaic that Yeats must overcome in order to bring folklore back to Irish literature.

Beerbohm's depiction of the Queen of the Fairies also signals the disjunction between the Celtic Revival's notion of the supernatural and the European versions of fairyland. The British Tinkerbell in the picture

'Mr W.B. Yeats presenting Mr George Moore to the Queen of the Fairies,' plate 35 in *The Poet's Corner* by Max Beerbohm (W. Heinemann, 1904). The Thomas Fisher Rare Book Library, University of Toronto.

stands in direct opposition to the figures from saga, legend, and folklore to which Yeats refers. As the poet states, 'The personages of English fairy literature are merely, in most cases, mortals beautifully masquerading. Nobody ever believed in such fairies. They are romantic bubbles from Provence. Nobody ever laid new milk on their doorstep for them' (1888, 6). By pointing to the French literary roots of English fairy tales, Yeats emphasizes the ethnic purity of Irish oral folklore, as well as its continuing and living presence in the life of the nation.[2] In 1927, however, Wyndham Lewis points out the irony of this vision of the folk and their tales:

> The romantic persons who go picking about in the Arran Islands, Shetlands, the Basque Provinces, or elsewhere, for genuine human 'antiques,' are today on a wild-goose chase; because the sphinx of the Past, in the person of some elder dug out of such remote neighbourhoods, will at length, when he has found his tongue, probably commence addressing them in the vernacular of the *Daily Mail*. For better or for worse, local colour is now a thin mixture; it does not inhere in what it embellishes, but is painted on, often with a clumsy insolence. (80–1)

Virginia Woolf puts forth a similar sentiment in 1934: 'I dont [sic] believe in the songs of the Aran islanders, or in old men who cant [sic] read – that is, theyre [sic] not of necessity Homer' (1982a, 216). The issue here is the authenticity of the folklore, which is revealed by Beerbohm to be, at least in part, a construction. Though Yeats's fairies are ostensibly part of the everyday workings of the Irish nation, it is Yeats who must reintroduce these figures and beliefs – 'the very voice of the people, the very pulse of life' (Yeats 1888, 5) – to the current generation of writers and thinkers. And where John Eglinton states that 'it is from the peasantry that he [the Anglo-Irishman] derives nationality,' what Beerbohm's caricature and the Revival's anxieties over the purity of folklore prove is that the rural peasantry are given or attributed national significance by the urban scholar (1916, 9).

Though their aims were dissimilar, Vincent Cheng suggests that both Irish Nationalism and British Imperialism 'engaged in defining Irishness as distinctively "other" and different' (2000, 243). Obviously, the definition of the Irish citizen as a noble Celt instead of a drunken Mick was an enabling change. But in the reappropriation and re-creation of national pride, the plural identities that make up any culture collide with the desire for a representative voice or image. What results is precisely what Beerbohm points out: a re-education of the populace so they 'know' what being Irish 'really' means. As Standish O'Grady acknowledges in 1879, 'the author of a work on Irish history has to labour simultaneously at a two-fold task – he has to create the interest to which he intends to address himself' (12). In this doubled movement, the folk are the guarantors of a historic Irish identity and of a political discourse that 'founds its narrative authority in a tradition of the people'; but they are also the subjects whose status needs to be reformed by and according to the new nationalist agenda (Bhabha 1990, 299). Again, the central issue is the difference between 'real men and women' and the 'world of faery,' where the same people who tell the stories that are collected by scholars become a kind of story themselves when they are represented as 'the folk.' The tension that results has particular relevance for Stephen Dedalus, who attempts to avoid being exploited according to his class, religion, and nationality. It is by interacting with the various narratives of his culture on a personal rather than an official level that Stephen is able to resist the forces that would place him as an object rather than a subject.

Objecting and Subjecting to Irish Nationalism

Although entertaining the most studied contempt for his compatriots – individually and in the mass – whom he did not regard at all as exceptionally brilliant and sympathetic creatures (in a green historical costume, with a fairy hovering near), but as average human cattle with an irish accent instead of a scotch or welsh, it will yet be insisted on that his irishness is an important feature of his talent; and he certainly also does exploit his irishness and theirs.

Wyndham Lewis, *Time and Western Man*

Joyce's work reflects the national, political, and religious debates of his day, but social status is an issue that often anchors his depictions of modern identity. It is in relation to class and to the division between the economies of the city and the country, for example, that the protagonist of *Stephen Hero* openly criticizes the Revivalist idealization of the folk:

> – One would imagine the country was inhabited by cherubim. Damme if I
> see much difference in peasants: they all seem to me as like one another as
> a peascod is like another peascod. The Yorkshireman is perhaps better
> fed.[3] (1944, 54)

Stephen's dismissal of a romanticized view of the peasantry is traditionally identified as urban prejudice. Madden's opinion in this scene –

'Of course you despise the peasant because you live in the city' (54) – is in fact echoed by G.J. Watson, who argues that 'Joyce was a totally urban man who had a contempt for the idiocy of rural life, in part natural, in part no doubt a product of Irish sensitiveness to the *Punch*–like view of Paddy-with-the-Pig-in-his-kitchen' (1994, 158). Cixous makes a similar argument regarding *A Portrait of the Artist as a Young Man*: 'The peasant becomes a devilish being, whom a note in Stephen's journal (14 April) describes as his deadly enemy, the mythical ancestor of his race, the anti-Dedalus who cannot even imagine the world around him but who has not yet progressed beyond a vaguely Ptolemaic conception of it' (1972, 467). But Joyce's attitudes, expressed in his fiction at least, seem to be more complicated than these rural/urban, illiterate/sophisticate, or philistine/snob dichotomies suggest.

In *A Portrait of the Artist as a Young Man*, for instance, Stephen Dedalus's response to the old man that John Alphonsus Mulrennan meets in the west of Ireland is notable for its ambivalence:

Old man had red eyes and short pipe. Old man spoke Irish. Mulrennan spoke Irish. Then old man and Mulrennan spoke English. Mulrennan spoke to him about universe and stars. Old man sat, listened, smoked, spat. Then said:
– Ah, there must be some terrible queer creatures at the latter end of the world.

I fear him. I fear his redrimmed horny eyes. It is with him I must struggle all through this night till day come, till he or I lie dead, gripping him by the sinewy throat till ... Till what? Till he yield to me? No. I mean him no harm. (1916, 216–17).

Stephen's imagined struggle with the old man stems not from his scorn for the storyteller at the peat-hearth of the Irish hovel – as Stephen says, 'I mean *him* no harm' (emphasis mine) – but from the peasant's place as the guarantor of Irish nationalism. Declan Kiberd suggests that the Irish-speaking peasant and the English-speaking scholar reflect the cultural dichotomy that leads to Stephen's 'split-mindedness,' for they represent the two languages and systems that he must choose between in his postcolonial position (1995, 333). Stephen's identification with the old man is not just about language, but about the roles that they share, and this is what causes much of the young man's anxiety. On one level, the old man embodies the class position from which Stephen attempts to distance himself in *A Portrait of the Artist as a Young Man* and *Ulysses*. But he also embodies the paradox of Irish-Catholic identity that Stephen himself experiences. The old man is both an object (the rural peasant upon whom the Celtic Revival depends) and a speaking subject (the storyteller whose voice is appropriated by the nationalist agenda). These are the very positions that Stephen occupies and that threaten his sense of artistic autonomy, especially in *Ulysses*.

The woman who brings the milk to the Martello Tower in 'Telemachus' prompts a similar process of identification and anxiety. The female figure is even more fraught in terms of referential depth than Mulrennan's storyteller. She is Irish identity incarnate: the goddess Dana, Cathleen ni Houlihan, the sow who eats her young. Significantly, however, she does not inhabit fully the identity that is created for and expected of her; as Cheng points out, 'the milkwoman does not pass muster, is not sufficiently and authentically Irish' (2000, 240). Joyce emphasizes this point when Haines speaks to her in Gaelic:

> – Do you understand what he says? Stephen asked her.
> – Is it French you are talking, sir? the old woman said to Haines. Haines spoke to her again a longer speech, confidently.
> – Irish, Buck Mulligan said. Is there Gaelic on you?
> – I thought it was Irish, she said, by the sound of it. Are you from the west, sir?
> – I am an Englishman, Haines answered.
> – He's English, Buck Mulligan said, and he thinks we ought to speak Irish in Ireland.
> – Sure we ought to, the old woman said, and I'm ashamed I don't speak the language myself. I'm told it's a grand language by them that knows. (1.424–34)

Like George Moore in Max Beerbohm's caricature, this is an Irish subject who needs to be re-educated; unlike Moore, she is the object upon which the nationalist discourse depends: the elder, the old woman, the peasant, the rural figure who brings milk to the urban sophisticates and grounds their flights of fancy in her wisdom. Joyce turns this 'faery' figure into a 'real' woman, emphasizing her position as a person rather than a stereotype and undercutting the expectations of the folklorists who have constructed this identity for her.

Interestingly, before he cleanses the doors of perception for his companions by revealing the woman's ignorance of her 'own' tongue, Stephen indulges in a flight of fancy, in which the woman becomes a character from Irish folklore:

Crouching by a patient cow at daybreak in the lush field, a witch on her toadstool, her wrinkled fingers quick at the squirting dugs. They lowed about her whom they knew, dewsilky cattle. Silk of the kine and poor old woman, names given her in old times. A wandering crone, lowly form of an immortal serving her conqueror and her gay betrayer, their common cuckquean, a messenger from the secret morning. To serve or to upbraid, whether he could not tell: but he scorned to beg her favour. (1.400–7)

The passage demonstrates Joyce's ability to match the mysticism of the best of the Celtic will-o'-the-wispers, but it also depicts the conundrum Stephen faces. The old woman is never just an old woman, never just a speaking subject; she is, like the old man, tied inevitably to metaphors relating to her class, gender, and nationality. The question for Stephen is how to escape the representations that threaten to capture him as well.

Despite his urbanity and education, Stephen is expected to play a part in sustaining the culture industry that the Irish folk represents. As F.L. Radford points out, he 'is not a colleague in these researches; he is a subject' (1987, 256); or rather, he is the object who is scrutinized by Haines and the actor who is encouraged to perform by Mulligan. Wyndham Lewis argues that the chapter involves caricatured national identities, in which Haines the Über-Brit and Buck the Wildean wit represent 'the conventional reality of one satisfied with the excessive, unusual and ready-made' (1927, 95). But Joyce critiques and historicizes these stereotypes in order to emphasize the centrality of such caricatures in nationalist ideologies. He also suggests how the constructed nature of the images can be used in potentially unscripted ways. For instance, Buck Mulligan plays 'the jolly, attractive, Wild Irishman' (W. Lewis 1927, 94) and participates in Haines's snobbery, but he also satirizes the Englishman's desire for sanitized homely sayings by pointing to the disjunction between romantic and realistic visions of the folk:

– When I makes tea I makes tea, as old mother Grogan said. And when I makes water I makes water. [...]
– So do I, Mrs Cahill, says she. Begob, ma'am, says Mrs Cahill, God send you don't make them in the one pot.
   He lunged towards his messmates in turn a thick slice of bread, impaled on his knife.
– That's folk, he said very earnestly, for your book, Haines. Five lines of text and ten pages of notes about the folk and the fishgods of Dundrum. Printed by the weird sisters in the year of the big wind. (1.357–67)

Mulligan parodies the Irish working class in his joke, and in doing so distances himself from an undesirable connection to the Dublin peasantry. But he also criticizes, 'very earnestly,' the Revival and Haines for not collecting the bawdy or 'real' stories of the folk. In fact, his over-the-top performance implicitly challenges the hierarchical relationship between the ignorant storyteller and the authoritative scholar, or between the speaker of the five lines of text and the editor who adds the ten pages of notes. Haines is identified here not as a highbrow scholar but as an English tourist who is being exploited by his Irish hosts because he has internalized the fiction of the authentic, noble, Celtic peasant.

No wonder Ellmann suggests that 'Joyce had the same contempt for both the ignorant peasantry and the snobbish aristocracy that Yeats idealized' (1982, 100). In *Ulysses,* however, we might acknowledge that this contempt arises from anxiety, since the peasant and the aristocrat represent Stephen's alternatives in Dublin society. Perhaps as a result, Stephen refuses to play a scripted role in this scene: he does not provide Haines with Irish wisdom, nor does he join Buck in an ironic enactment of stage-Irishness. Instead he attempts to break down the boundaries that constrain both Irish and English subjects. He refuses to identify Mulrennan's old man solely as a rival storyteller or a symbol of the limits of Irish art: 'No. I mean him no harm.' He refuses to place the milkwoman in an equally idealized role: where Haines identifies her as 'that poor old creature' (1.489), Stephen sees her as the contemporary Irish audience whose influence he withstands by refusing 'to beg her favour.' Most significantly, he refuses to view Haines as only an Imperialist and meets the Englishman's clinical detachment with an attempt at understanding: 'Stephen turned and saw that the cold gaze which had measured him was not all unkind' (1.634–5). Stephen's emphasis on the real men and women rather than on their discursive status undermines the social divisions that would otherwise place the individuals.

A.E., or George Russell, represents Haines's Irish counterpart in *Ulysses,* by mining folklore for his own purposes, and Joyce parodies Russell's selective view of Irish culture in much the same way as Buck Mulligan parodies Haines's selective scholarship. In a restaging of the library scene from 'Scylla and Charybdis,' the 'cone of lamplight' that has excluded Stephen from Russell's friends and favourites becomes in 'Circe' the spotlight that illuminates A.E.'s pedantry:

(*In the cone of the searchlight behind the coalscuttle, ollave, holyeyed, the bearded figure of Mananaun MacLir broods, chin on knees. He rises slowly. A cold*

*seawind blows from his druid mouth. About his head writhe eels and elvers. He is
encrusted with weeds and shells. His right hand holds a bicycle pump. His left
hand grasps a huge crayfish by its two talons.*)
MANANAUN MACLIR
(*with a voice of waves*) Aum! Hek! Wal! Ak! Lub! Mor! Ma! White yoghin of
the gods. Occult pimander of Hermes Trismegistos. (*with a voice of whis-
tling seawind*) Punarjanam patsypunjaub! I won't have my leg pulled. It
has been said by one: beware the left, the cult of Shakti. (*with a cry of
stormbirds*) Shakti Shiva, darkhidden Father! (*He smites with his bicycle
pump the crayfish in his left hand. On its cooperative dial glow the twelve signs of
the zodiac. He wails with the vehemence of the ocean.*) Aum! Baum! Pyjaum! I
am the light of the homestead! I am the dreamery creamery butter. (15.2261–
76)

This passage operates on many levels, as Joyce spoofs A.E.'s involvement with the practical applications of nationalism in his references to
the *Irish Homestead,* which Joyce apparently called '"the pigs' paper"'
(Ellmann 1982, 164), and to the 'dairy cooperatives,' with which Russell
was involved (Paterakis 1972, 35). But a primary point of reference is
the performance of A.E.'s play *Deirdre,* in which Russell appeared 'as
the head of Mananaan' (Paterakis 1972, 35). Though the Irish folk figure
of Mananann gives 'the secret of language to mankind' (Radford 1987,
265), here that language is reduced to a jumble of syllables – 'Aum!
Hek! Wal! Ak! Lub!' – and incantory noises – 'Aum! Baum! Pyjaum!'
The bicycle pump with which MacLir smites the crayfish refers directly
to Bloom's sighting of A.E. with Susan Mitchell in the eighth section of
Ulysses: 'Beard and bicycle. Young woman' (8.523–4). However, Russell's
jargon causes some confusion for Bloom in that scene: 'the eminent
poet, Mr Geo. Russell. That might be Lizzie Twigg with him. A.E.: what
does that mean? [...] What was he saying? The ends of the world with a
Scotch accent. Tentacles: octopus. Something occult: symbolism' (8.523–
30). Bloom, the man on the street, does not quite grasp the terms of
Russell's mysticism, which is so far removed from the citizen's reality
that it has become incomprehensible.

One of the more pointed targets in Joyce's parody of A.E. is Russell's
view of the superiority of rural folklore and the inferiority of urban
popular culture. In 'Scylla and Charybdis,' Russell argues that significant political change arises from 'the dreams and visions in a peasant's
heart on the hillside' (9.105–6). In contrast, 'the academy and the
arena produce the sixshilling novel, the musichall song' (9.107–8), and

other apparently irrelevant forms. Joyce's response is not just to parody A.E.'s folklore play, *Deirdre,* but to set it as a piece of popular theatre. By placing the author not on the hillside but instead in the very music hall that he disdains, Joyce reduces the lofty aims of A.E.'s text and compares his declamations to the stage antics of any other entertainer. Indeed, A.E. becomes a figure of ridicule in the scene: it is no coincidence that his speech is followed by the 'Pooah! Pfuiiiiiii!' of the gasjet, which acts as his derisive audience and echo (15.2280). *Deirdre* becomes a pantomime in this satire of the Revival, albeit with a nationalist twist, since it is based upon Irish rather than French or German fairy tales.

Joyce's presentation of A.E. in 'Circe' obscures the novelist's very real debt to Russell and the Celtic Revivalists. However, it also illuminates the difference between Joyce's view of fairy tales and A.E.'s view of folklore. Irish legends at this time are tied almost inextricably to the past of the nation. In contrast to these stories of the Irish countryside, the fairy tales to which Joyce consistently alludes had been disseminated throughout Europe and not always in the service of nationalism or spiritualism. The diffusion of the tales and the different ways in which they had been adapted made them markers not just of an archaic past but of a realistic present. The result is that fairy tales from Perrault, de Beaumont, and the Grimms reflect consistently the issues of the world in which and of which Joyce writes.

Mirrored Identities

CYRIL: [...] I can quite understand your objection to Art being treated as a mirror. You think it would reduce genius to the position of a cracked looking glass. But you don't mean to say that you seriously believe that Life imitates Art, that Life in fact is the mirror, and Art the reality?
VIVIAN: Certainly I do. Paradox though it may seem – and paradoxes are always dangerous things – it is none the less true that Life imitates Art far more than Art imitates Life [...] A great artist invents a type, and Life tries to copy it, to reproduce it in a popular form, like an enterprising publisher.

Oscar Wilde, *The Decay of Lying*

Stephen's observation to Buck Mulligan that Irish art is 'the cracked lookingglass of a servant' (1.146) places an excerpt from Oscar Wilde's *The Decay of Lying* into a postcolonial context. The line speaks to the disparity between the master or Imperialist who embodies the ideal and the servant or native who emulates him.[4] Irish Nationalism would seem to lead to a similar split in subjectivity, where the literary and political ideals of the Celtic Revival are to be reflected by the supposedly authentic Irish subject. The crack in the looking glass corresponds to the gap that inevitably divides the ideal image and its flawed imitation. This frustrating split accompanies the individual's attempt to perform not only national but gendered, sexed, and classed identities. As Wilde points out, Art does not arise from Nature as much as our perception of Nature arises from Art: 'Things are because we see them, and what we see, and how we see it, depends on the Arts that have influenced us' (1902, 58). Characters in Joyce's works, as well as in the fairy tales to which he alludes, must become artful consumers of cultural ideals in order to reflect the identities that will allow them to circulate most effectively in their societies.

By reversing the hierarchy of Art and Nature, Wilde does not undercut the binary relationship of the two terms as much as he explores the interactive nature of modern culture, where artists and audiences are involved in a complicated web of inspiration and appropriation. Wilde uses the example of fashionable womanliness to exemplify his point: 'We have all seen in our own day in England how a certain curious and fascinating type of beauty, invented and emphasised by two imaginative painters, has so influenced Life that whenever one goes to a private view or to an artistic salon one sees, here the mystic eyes of Rossetti's dream, the long ivory throat, the strange square-cut jaw, the loosened shadowy hair that he so ardently loved' (1902, 45). The image from the painting is not only an idealized vision of a real woman, but an ideal that is in turn emulated by real women, whose imitations are 'Equivalent, [...] but not identical' to the ideal to which they aspire (Barthes 1967, 4). This view of fashion is based upon the idea of 'fit,' or the extent to which the real (body) inhabits the space of the ideal (cultural image). Of course, the ideal can never be inhabited fully, something Wilde signals by depicting only parts of the woman: the eyes, the throat, the jaw, the hair. While these aspects of the body become fetish-objects in their own right, the ideal composite can be realized only in art.

Wilde's Pre-Raphaelite model of femininity is a reference, perhaps, to Lizzie Siddal and her relationship with Dante Gabriel Rossetti. Siddal is the model for the iconic painted image, which becomes itself an object of imitation. Like Wilde's allusion to 'Rossetti's Dream,' Christina Rossetti's 'In an Artist's Studio' invokes the tension between the real woman and the painted ideal:

One face looks out from all his canvases,
　　One selfsame figure sits or walks or leans:
　　We found her hidden just behind those screens,
That mirror gave back all her loveliness. (1861, 264)

The artist is both the consumer of the real woman and the producer of an idealized image. In a sense, Dante Gabriel Rossetti patents Lizzie Siddal by replacing the woman herself – 'wan with waiting' (264) – with her simulacrum. His sister indicates that it is this artistic product that holds his attention: 'And she with true kind eyes looks back on him, / [...] / Not as she is, but as she fills his dream' (264). Siddal is increasingly viewed as an object rather than as a subject, where the image presented in the work of art takes on a life of its own.[5]

The process results in a radical disconnection between the image and its original, as well as between the image and its imitation. The dynamic echoes Lacan's formulation of the mirror stage, in which the child's view of his or her reflected self results in the central division at the heart of subjectivity. The 'I' that perceives the image in the mirror is divided from the 'I' that is perceived in the mirror. The result is that the 'coherent identity' that the child sees in the looking glass 'only has meaning in relation to the presence and the look of the mother who guarantees its reality for the child' (Rose 1985, 30). In other words, the 'ideal that organizes and orients the self' (Gallop 1985, 79) must be placed into a larger system in order to have significance. To use Lacan's theory of the mirror stage as a metaphor for Wilde's reading of Pre-Raphaelite beauty, the woman who poses for the painting, as well as the women who try to become that painted ideal, are like images in the looking glass: they depend upon the eye of an Other for meaning and value.

The performances of femininity gain significance, then, not just when they are seen by an audience, but when they are compared. This is the dynamic that we find in the fairy tale 'Snow White,' where the Queen compares herself constantly to her stepdaughter. The status of each woman depends upon that comparison, and the results are proclaimed by the mirror: 'Thou art fairer than all who are here, Lady Queen. / But more beautiful still is Snow-white, as I ween' (Grimms 1972, 250). It is only when Snow White is no longer in the picture or within the frame of reference that the Queen can be called 'fairest of all' (256). The same comparative model of beauty and status is evident in 'Cinderella,' but in this story it is the Prince who measures the various women at the ball against the image of the titular heroine, and ultimately against the foot that fits the glass slipper.

The relational nature of such judgments, which depend on a comparison of women who attempt to 'be' the ideal, betrays the provisionality of social identity itself. In 'Cinderella,' for example, the slippery nature of fashion as a signifier of class enables the Wicked Stepmother to marginalize the heroine and alter the ways in which her own daughters will be viewed. Her attempts to 'reterritorializ[e]' the terms of reference that have been used to 'abject' her less beautiful offspring fail (Butler 1993, 231), but only because Cinderella's shoe is the magical embodiment of the ideal upon which the system is based. The Queen in the Snow White story experiences a similar amount of success when she too alters the context according to which she is judged. She revises the established hierarchy of femininity for a time by eliminating one of its terms from the competition, and thus consolidates her position as the main focus of the (internalized, law-enforcing, mirror-represented) King's eye. However, this strategy is not sustainable: there is always a younger and more desirable figure coming into view. In the Walt Disney film version of the tale, the Queen, figured first as a *homme manqué*, and second, as an old peddler-hag (see Warner 1994a, 222), is no match for the young, nubile, and innocent girl. Unlike Snow White, who is perfection, the Queen overreaches her 'true' gender position in this society. In her Faustian descent, she is crushed by the weight of the social pressures that the mountain represents in the animated feature.

Ulysses is full of characters who attempt to imitate certain gendered and classed identities. In this sense, it is a novel that is haunted not just by the image of a cracked looking glass, which suggests the partial success that those individuals experience in reproducing popular fashions and images, but more specifically by the figure of Oscar Wilde. Wilde knew the power of style and the fact that clothes can make the man: as Garry Leonard suggests, Wilde once 'defined "masculinity"' (1999, 10). However, clothes can also make the man 'too much' of a woman, and as Joseph Valente points out, 'Wilde played a large part in conflating male homosexuality and effeminacy in the public mind' (1999, 131). These different readings of Wilde's dandyism demonstrate how the significance of clothing shifts according to the frames or spaces in which the body appears. For instance, while Blazes Boylan's clothes inform his peacockish display of masculinity, they also connect him to the less masculine man, 'Mr Denis J Maginni, professor of dancing &c, in silk hat, slate frockcoat with silk facings, white kerchief tie, tight lavender trousers, canary gloves and pointed patent boots' (10:56–8). The sky blue clocks on Boylan's socks align him with the Seaside Girls who show their stockings while bicycling in order to attract attention

(Leonard 1998, 162). These flashy displays of fashion connect both stylish men to Buck Mulligan, who wants 'puce gloves and green boots' (1.516) and wears a 'primrose waistcoat' (1.550), and whom Stephen connects with Wilde and homosexuality. All of these men signal the mercurial nature of the gender of clothing where, like language, garments depend upon contiguity and context for meaning.

Clothes are integral to the performance of gender and sexuality, but given that fashion is also 'a synecdoche of consumption' (Wicke 1994a, 25), or an indicator of disposable income, clothes also signify class. The desirability of the woman whom Bloom sees on the street in the 'Lotus Eaters,' for instance, arises in large part from the hose that she can afford to buy: 'Silk flash rich stockings white' (5.130). Bloom's appreciative view of her hosiery, however, also depends upon the effect of the cheaper stockings worn by the less wealthy women whom he has sighted throughout the day (4.171–9; 8.542). What results is a depiction of fashion that challenges its atemporal or naturalized position in the society. The significance of clothing depends upon the moment, space, and economy in which it is used, viewed, and compared.

Joyce's focus on the everyday history of clothing extends to his examination of the labour that is involved in the production, marketing, and maintenance of the fashionable image. As Kimberly Devlin points out, Maggy, Boody, Katey, and Dilly Dedalus 'run an unofficial laundry service for others out of their kitchen' just as their mother did (1999, 83), and their poverty is established in contrast to the people who form their client base. In the 'Wandering Rocks' episode, Katey's 'stained skirt' (10.275) shows up the contrastingly 'gay apparel of Mr Denis J Maginni' (10.600). Similarly, though the blouses that the Misses Kennedy and Douce wear in the 'Sirens' episode are 'both of black satin,' the two women are ranked 'gold and bronze' according to the cost of the fabric they have purchased and used: 'two and nine a yard [...] and two and seven,' (11.110–11). A little farther down the socioeconomic ladder, Gerty MacDowell has created a hat from cloth that she has bought on sale. Despite being home made, however, the finished product takes on a value of its own, and may move her up the scale of classed femininity: 'she knew that that would take the shine out of some people she knew' (13.163–4).

Jennifer Wicke points out that 'fashion is a language of class, and its nuances map out the border territories of class overlap and conflict' (1994c, 188). This is especially true in early twentieth-century Dublin, where, according to Desmond Clarke, 'grinding poverty was clearly evident in the number of ragged men, women, and children thronging the streets. A cynic remarked that half the population of Dublin was clothed in the cast-off garments of the other half' (1977, 162). If fashion is a classed discourse, then clothes, second-hand or otherwise, indicate the tension between citation and plagiarism (as demonstrated by the cases of Oscar Wilde, Snow White's Evil Stepmother, and Cinderella). In other words, clothes are the means by which individuals walk the fine line between posing and imposturing, where social mobility can lead upwards or downwards depending on how convincingly the role has been played. In *Ulysses*, clothes are most obviously joined to class and to fairy tales through the figures of Stephen Dedalus and Gerty MacDowell. The two characters differ in terms of their individual histories, but they share an equally unstable place in the modern economy of Dublin that both invites and limits their creative uses of fashion.

Cinderella and Stephen Dedalus

– The mockery of it, he said contentedly. Secondleg they should be. God knows what poxy bowsy left them off. I have a lovely pair with a hair stripe, grey. You'll look spiffing in them. I'm not joking, Kinch. You look damn well when you're dressed.
– Thanks, Stephen said. I can't wear them if they are grey.
– He can't wear them, Buck Mulligan told his face in the mirror. Etiquette is etiquette. He kills his mother but can't wear grey trousers.

James Joyce, *Ulysses*

In one of the most poignant images of *Ulysses*, Rudy Bloom appears at the end of 'Circe': 'Against the dark wall a figure appears slowly, a fairy boy of eleven, a changeling, kidnapped, dressed in an Eton suit with glass shoes and a little bronze helmet, holding a book in his hand. He reads from right to left inaudibly, smiling, kissing the page' (15.4956–60). David Galef suggests that Leopold Bloom's vision represents 'true warping of reality to suit unconscious wish. The glass shoes themselves betray the Cinderella-like fantasy behind the father's desire to see his son transformed' (1991, 423). Rudy-as-Cinderella is fully in keeping with the pantomime feel of the chapter, not only in terms of the gender confusion that recalls the parts of the Principal Boy and the Dame, but also in terms of the transformation scene, the 'hallmark' of the panto tradition (Bowen 1998, 301). In an echo of that topsy-turvy world, Rudy's clothing represents a collage of incompatible identities: he is not just a dead son brought magically back to life by his father's longing, but a Judaic scholar educated at Eton, an ad canvasser's child wearing jewels, and a Hermes whose mythic status is at odds with the Dublin streets in which he appears (see Gifford 1989, 529). Rudy has become what he wears: a glass shoe, an unattainable ideal through which Bloom's conflicting dreams and identities are magically sutured together. Rudy's position in Nighttown, that site of the most basic of exchanges, and his finery – 'diamond and ruby buttons,' a 'slim ivory cane' (15.4965–6) – link Bloom's hallucination to the script of consumer culture. The object of desire is Rudy, who becomes the ultimate commodity: wanted, even needed, but tantalizingly out of reach.

The glass shoes connect the haunting image of Rudy in 'Circe' to the haunted figure of Stephen in 'Telemachus,' and make overt Joyce's emphasis on 'Cinderella' as a text that has tremendous resonance in the context of modern consumer culture. The fairy tale underscores in large part the uncertain nature of class performance in *Ulysses*. The compensatory image of Rudy, for example, signals the frustrating reality of Bloom's position as an outsider in Dublin regardless of his attempts to integrate or move up the social ladder. For Stephen, Buck's second-hand clothing and its reflection of a certain class position enable him to be employed in Dublin, but the loan indicates the collective loss that the Dedalus family has experienced. Through references to 'Cinderella,' Joyce explores the possibilities and costs of the economic system, where fashion represents not just the social role that can be played, but the underlying lack that prompts the performance itself.

In Joyce's uses of the fairy tale, Perrault's emphasis on the financial trials and successes of the heroine is coupled with the Grimms' focus on the trauma that results from the death of Cinderella's mother. But these source texts are themselves fragmented and their plots and characters refigured at different moments in the novel. Stephen and Rudy both demonstrate the heroine's slide through class identities but in different ways, just as Buck Mulligan, May Dedalus, and Leopold Bloom play the roles of Fairy Godmother, mother, Stepmother, and Prince to different ends. The formal aspects of the fairy tale – the loss of the mother, the intervention of a benevolent figure, the restoration of social position – are further undercut by Joyce's alterations to the stable ending of most versions. As a result, 'Cinderella' becomes a shifting reference in *Ulysses* that leads to ambiguity more often than to certainty.

Central to Joyce's use of the tale is Cinderella's exchange value, which is, like Rudy's, signalled by the clothes she wears. Her shift from lady to scullery maid and back to lady again is conveyed through changes in her dress: Cinderella's 'wretched clothes' (Perrault 1969, 68), or 'old grey bedgown' and 'wooden shoes' (Grimms 1972, 121), indicate her poverty. In contrast, her 'gold and silver dress' and 'slippers' attract the Prince and fool her stepfamily, who do not 'know her' (124). More importantly, Cinderella's 'glass slippers' and 'gold and silver' garments 'bedecked with jewels' – not to mention the coach, the coachman, the six horses, and the six lackeys who accompany her – cause the guests at the ball to think of her as 'a princess' (Perrault 1969, 70–2). Indeed, most versions of 'Cinderella' emphasize not just the dress but the *cost* of the dress: her beauty means nothing without this display of wealth. The shoe-fitting scene at the end of the fairy tale makes the connection between clothes and position overt: the slipper's perfect fit fixes Cinderella in her aristocratic role. The shoe enables the Prince to determine her authenticity and Cinderella's real body is acknowledged as the ideal. In fact, her body becomes iconical: 'All the ladies were eager to scrutinize her clothes and the dressing of her hair, being determined to copy them on the morrow, provided they could find materials so fine, and tailors so clever' (Perrault 1969, 71). At the end of the Grimms' version, her stepfamily's misrecognition of her value is punished when birds fly at the sisters and peck out the eyes that do not see according to the rest of society (1972, 128).

The clothes are, however, only the outward display of her perfection. What becomes obvious in the scenes at the ball is that Cinderella's grace (learned) and beauty (enhanced by the right dress) are the keys to her success and enable her to embody the models of femininity that are themselves 'set by upper-class French society' at the time in which Perrault recorded his version of the tale (Zipes 1983, 26). Imitating these ideals involves labour and, as Perrault suggests in his second moral to the tale, the finished product is not necessarily as important as its marketing:

Godmothers are useful things
Even when without the wings.
Wisdom may be yours and wit,
Courage, industry, and grit –
What's the use of these at all,
If you lack a friend at call? (1969, 78)

The tale's depiction of Cinderella's reformation is thus pedagogical; it serves as a handbook for women who want to advertise their worth.

But where Jack Zipes sees Cinderella's adherence to civilized behaviour as submissive – 'Only because she minds her manners is she rescued by a fairy godmother and a prince' (1983, 30) – her cunning use of packaging and her politically astute arrangement of wealthy husbands for her sisters indicate a tactical engagement with the culture. Though the result does little to change the hierarchy that has caused Cinderella's initial marginalization, she can at least take advantage of the gaps in the system and move herself into a position of more power.

Cinderella's story ends on a positive note, but Stephen Dedalus's raises the question of the cost that the happy ending entails, where Joyce emphasizes the anxiety that accompanies Stephen's shifts in class standing. The similarities between Stephen and Cinderella are evident in 'Telemachus.' He begins as Cinderella-in-the-ashes: the death of his mother has left him drifting, and the social privilege that was once his has been lost through his father's irresponsibility. These losses are emphasized in *Ulysses* by the series of Fairy Godmothers who offer him employment throughout the day. Haines, Deasy, Crawford, and Russell would return him to the position of a bourgeois subject, but they would also transform the artist into a commodity in a capitalist system towards which he feels most ambivalent.

The Martello Tower in 'Telemachus' is the concrete representation of Stephen's cultural context, and this opening section of *Ulysses* is dominated by images of exchange: Stephen lends Buck his handkerchief; Haines pays for Irish folklore; Stephen pays for the milk. The most important transaction, though, concerns Buck's clothes, which Stephen needs in order to have a place in Dublin. Like his family and his social status, his garments have virtually disintegrated: 'Stephen [...] leaned his palm against his brow and gazed at the fraying edge of his shiny black coatsleeve' (1.100–1). The loan of clothing is, however, vaguely threatening. Valente observes that in 'Proteus,' and again in 'Scylla and Charybdis,' Stephen's unease regarding Buck coalesces in his thoughts of footwear (1999, 128–9). In Valente's first example, Stephen remembers trying on women's shoes in Paris: 'But you were delighted when Esther Osvalt's shoe went on you: girl I knew in Paris. *Tiens, quel petit pied!* Staunch friend, a brother soul: Wilde's love that dare not speak its name. His arm: Cranly's arm. He now will leave me' (3.449–52). Buck, Cranly, and Wilde represent a nexus of emotional and physical attachment tinged by homoeroticism that leaves Stephen unsettled. In the second passage Valente presents, set in the library, Stephen thinks of the footwear he has borrowed from Buck in terms of the Oedipus legend:

'His boots are spoiling the shape of my feet' (9.947–8). Valente suggests that, 'As a site of feminine identification (small-footed Stephen as Cinderella) and incestuous desire / castration (spoiled-footed Stephen as Oedipus), Stephen's feet reveal both his gender involution and his homosexual anxiety to be unconsciously grounded in his maternal attachment and abjection' (1999, 129–30). The significance of 'Cinderella' relates most obviously, then, to Stephen's concerns regarding his gender and the loss of the mother. But the images of sexual anxiety are connected also to economic lack, and to the master/slave relationship figured in the cracked looking glass. The young artificer aligns himself with the Other in these scenes: woman (Esther Osvalt), homosexual (Wilde), child or exile (Oedipus), and above all, financial dependent. Indeed, his insolvency is what necessitates Stephen's reliance on Buck and his goods in the first place, and what signals the fairy tale's continuing resonance in *Ulysses* as a marker of class-based tensions.

In this sense, the relationship between Buck and Stephen echoes the relationship between Cinderella and the Fairy Godmother of Perrault's tale. Buck plays the benevolent maternal figure that rescues Cinderella from her impoverished and emotionally bereft life. Like the Fairy Godmother, he provides not just footwear but clothes: 'Ah, poor dogsbody! he said in a kind voice. I must give you a shirt and a few noserags. How are the secondhand breeks?' (1.112–13). Buck also presents Stephen to an eligible literary *parti*, as Haines offers the financial and social possibilities of a Prince Charming: 'Cracked lookingglass of a servant! Tell that to the oxy chap downstairs and touch him for a guinea. He's stinking with money and thinks you're not a gentleman' (1.154–6). Buck situates himself as a mentor figure, the only person of means who can recognize, rescue, and restore the impoverished hero to his original state: 'And to think of your having to beg from these swine. I'm the only one that knows what you are. Why don't you trust me more?' (1.160–1).

In acting as the Fairy Godmother, however, Buck is the surrogate for May Dedalus, and this is a dangerous role. For both Cinderella and Stephen, it is the absence of the mother that causes emotional upheaval and socioeconomic marginalization: 'Cinderella is a child in mourning for her mother, as her name tells us; her penitential garb is ash, dirty and low as a donkeyskin or a coat of grasses, but more particularly the sign of loss, the symbol of mortality, which the priest uses to mark the foreheads of the faithful on Ash Wednesday, saying "Dust thou art, and to dust thou shalt return"' (Warner 1994a, 206). Stephen reflects this kind of abasement, especially in terms of his mourning clothes: as Buck notes, 'he can't wear grey trousers' (1.122). But May Dedalus is not necessarily the positive maternal figure that is presented in the Grimms' version of the tale, where Cinderella's movement up the social ladder is enabled by her prayers at the mother's grave. Instead of the redemptive nurturer (see Cashdan 1999, 94; Lüthi 1970, 60–1), the lost mother is seen as a threatening ghost: 'Ghoul! Chewer of corpses! / No, mother! Let me be and let me live' (1.278–9). She haunts Stephen in dreams and in hallucinations, her breath smelling of the 'ashes' of the funeral service and of the fairy tale (1.105; 1.272; 15:4182). This sense of maternal threat is usually projected onto the Wicked Stepmother, and in *Ulysses* it is Buck who plays a version of that role. Buck's *'beastly'* comment regarding May Dedalus (1.198), his criticism of Stephen's reaction to his mother's death, and his use of Stephen's tower result in a sense of betrayal: 'Usurper' (1.744). Just as importantly, while Buck's generosity allows Stephen to gain a foothold in Dublin, it indicates consistently the conditions for both the Evil Stepmother's intervention and the Fairy Godmother's benevolence: Buck's clothes, like the ashes of the mother's breath or the signs of Cinderella's abjection, become not just gifts but symbols of Stephen's lack.

The ambivalence that Stephen experiences regarding his mother and the irony that attends Buck's performance of the Fairy Godmother role indicate the underside of class mobility, where identity is not consolidated but is instead under attack even as the subject plays according to the script. Stephen's moving encounter with his sister in 'The Wandering Rocks' emphasizes the precarious nature of his status regardless of the message that his clothes present. Dilly's 'shabby dress' (10.855) and 'broken boots' (10.859) compare unfavourably to Stephen's borrowed outfit. She becomes the foil to Stephen's class 'success,' but also represents that station to which he could easily slide. If Stephen has been rescued to a certain extent by his Fairy Godmother, Dilly has taken over the role of the abjected Cinderella. She is another cracked looking glass that shows Stephen the divisions in his own identity, as his assumed clothes and class are challenged by the reality of the family's disintegration. Moreover, her poverty emphasizes Stephen's reliance upon and debt to Buck. Buck Mulligan becomes not just a Fairy Godmother or Evil Stepmother, then, but another Prince Charming who has rescued Stephen from Dilly's fate. In contrast, and in an echo of his mother, Dilly haunts Stephen's present by signifying his past. Stephen's guilt over his sister and anxiety regarding his mother's death indicate 'the cost of articulating a coherent identity-position if that coherence is produced through the production, exclusion and repudiation of abjected spectres that threaten those very subject-positions' (Butler 1993, 113). Though Stephen experiences the 'agenbite of inwit' (10.879) both in this scene and elsewhere in *Ulysses*, perhaps because of his class consciousness he maintains his distance from the Dedalus family. What he repudiates here is not just his sisters or his father or their demands on his emotions and finances, but also a version of himself, one that threatens his role in the class hierarchy of Dublin.

At the same time, however, Stephen refuses to re-establish his position as a bourgeois subject in this society and rejects the financial opportunities that are made available to him. Buck's attempt 'to package Stephen's performance as "authentic Irish genius"' (Leonard 1999, 5) and sell his 'symbol of Irish art' (1.290) to Haines in 'Telemachus,' prefigures the variety of job offers that Stephen receives and declines. The two most significant proposals, at least in terms of their place in the first and last of Stephen's chapters, come from Mulligan and Bloom. In both cases, Stephen refuses the economic and emotional dependence that these surrogate mother/father/lover figures offer, and chooses exile instead: 'I will not sleep here tonight. Home also I cannot go' (1.739–40); 'Was the proposal of asylum accepted? / Promptly, inexplicably, with amicability, gratefully it was declined' (17.954–5). For Stephen, it is his exchange value that underwrites these financial transactions and his reluctance to package himself as a commodity that results in their failures.

Stephen also declines to encounter the dangers implicit in the larger social system that is implied by these two offers. In both cases, his labour would be marketed by a middleman. Buck's request to Stephen – 'Touch him for a quid, will you? A guinea, I mean' (1.290–1) – involves a share in the profits, just as Bloom's plans to manage Stephen's singing career are based on a cut of the proceeds. Significantly, clothes are involved in both propositions, particularly in Bloom's vision of Stephen's circulation:

an *entrée* in the near future into fashionable houses in the best residential quarters of financial magnates in a large way of business and titled people where with his university degree of B.A. (a huge ad in its way) and gentlemanly bearing to all the more influence the good impression he would infallibly score a distinct success, being blessed with brains which also could be utilised for the purpose and other requisites, if his clothes were properly attended to so as to the better worm his way into their good

graces as he, a youthful tyro in society's sartorial niceties, hardly under-
stood how a little thing like that could militate against you. (16.1825–33)

Bloom seeks to advertise Stephen as he has advertised Molly, where
Stephen's manners and 'bearing' would, like Cinderella's, become significant by virtue of the clothing provided by his new Fairy Godmother.
   Obviously, Stephen's view of this transformation of the subject into
an object differs from Bloom's, and is foreshadowed by his business
dealings with Mr Deasy in 'Nestor':

> – Thank you, sir, Stephen said, gathering the money together with shy
> haste and putting it all in a pocket of his trousers.
> – No thanks at all, Mr Deasy said. You have earned it.
>   Stephen's hand, free again, went back to the hollow shells. Symbols too
> of beauty and of power. A lump in my pocket: symbols soiled by greed
> and misery. (2.223–8)

Where Deasy's fetishization of the money invests it with social value –
it has been 'earned' – Stephen's alienation from the money emphasizes
its physical reality – a 'lump' in the material of his borrowed trousers.
Stephen's treatment of the notes and coins indicates that currency, like
fashion, depends on context for significance. Just as symbols of wealth
can be transformed into symbols of misery, so any exchange involves
the possibility of a slippage in value. If, as Bloom suggests, Stephen's
performance would be signified by 'filthy lucre' (16.1842), the value of
Stephen as a singer and as a middle-class subject is about as stable as
the value of money. Thus, in 'Ithaca,' Bloom returns (or refunds)
Stephen's money and signals the artist's withdrawal from the market.
   Stephen withstands the pressure exerted by individuals who would
turn him into Cinderella at the ball: a commodity dressed and marketed
to the masses; an object circulated within larger economic systems; a
subject to be controlled by the cultural expectations that Buck and
Bloom represent. Stephen's refusal to participate in these transforma-
tional schemes parallels the refusal of the (untried) artist to prostitute
himself for money, where the temptations of the schoolroom or of the
Revival movement or of the stage or of the newspaper are the nets that
threaten to catch him before he realizes his calling. But what seems
significant in Stephen's response is not the purity of the artist's mind
and soul that enables him to transcend debased financial dealings;
rather, it is the fact that the opportunities represent real temptations.

Butler points out that 'a radical refusal to identify with a given position suggests that on some level an identification has already taken place, an identification that is made and disavowed' (1993, 113). To change the context of this observation from gender politics to class politics, Stephen identifies very much with the positions he is offered by Mulligan, Haines, Deasy, Crawford, and Bloom. His disavowal is prompted, however, by his recognition of the fluidity of the social system itself. The anxiety that compels his resentment of Buck's double-edged generosity is the anxiety that accompanies the assumption of a class position that cannot be authenticated by the test of the glass slipper. Here, whomever the shoe fits can wear it – but not for long. The instability implied by the sliding on and off of the slipper relates not just to gender, as Valente emphasizes, then, but to socioeconomic status, where the presence of his mother's ghost and his sister's rags indicate the potential of his own failure to pass. In this sense, the references to 'Cinderella' that cluster around Stephen do not ground his character according to a stable intertext but instead emphasize the shifting nature of identity itself.

The contradictions of the class system that promises social mobility and threatens social abjection take us back to the image of Rudy glimpsed at the end of 'Circe.' Where Stephen's experiences suggest the uncertainties and inequities of Dublin's economy, Bloom's vision of his son suggests its possibilities. The liminality of Nighttown allows for a suspension of literary and social laws, which is reflected by the overdetermined figure of Rudy. As Cheryl Herr points out, 'Rudy is both silent harlequin and the hero of the twentieth-century panto' (1986, 176), and his costume and his very presence reflect the overturning of logic and the law that characterizes the traditions of the pantomime. But more than a theatrical figure that arises from the apparently 'settled, not to say exploited, domain of popular culture' (Herr 1986, 177), Rudy is a 'changeling' (15.4957). In his Eton suit, he passes as an Imperial subject, part of the British ascendancy, as does Bella Cohen's 'son in Oxford' (15.1289). Ironically, it is Bella's work as the madam of a Nighttown brothel that enables her son to aspire to a higher class position. In other words, the mystification of money in the capitalist system allows for the mystification of paternity, and thus for social mobility. Similarly, Bloom's borrowing of fairy-tale imagery from narratives associated with commodity culture enables him to imagine a highly personal and meaningful image.

At the same time, however, the fictions can be recognized as such, which is what happens when Bloom tries to prevent Bella from calling the police: '(*urgently*) And if it were your own son in Oxford? (*warningly*) I know' (15.4306). Bella's response – '(*almost speechless*) Who are. Incog!' (15.4308) – is a melodramatic exaggeration that is fully in keeping with the stagy feel of 'Circe.' But her shock and fear exemplify the anxiety that is involved in this kind of social 'passing.' Bella's son, Rudy, and even Stephen are 'Incog': not just incognito – hidden or in disguise – but incomplete, or '"partial" presence[s]' (Bhabha 1983, 381). They may have the right manners, the right look, and the right clothes, but even as they perform their identities, they gesture to their own lack of authenticity. The dream of class ascension is still potent, but, as Cinderella shows, the reality involves both labour and luck.

Snow White and Gerty MacDowell

Her very soul is in her eyes and she would give worlds to be in the privacy of her own familiar chamber where, giving way to tears, she could have a good cry and relieve her pentup feelings though not too much because she knew how to cry nicely before the mirror. You are lovely, Gerty, it said.

James Joyce, *Ulysses*

Bloom's dreams in 'Circe' are prefigured in 'Nausicaa,' where desire and commodity culture are connected to the performance of class and gender roles. Like Rudy, Gerty MacDowell appears to many critics as a kind of commodity that Bloom consumes visually. And like Bloom, at least in Herr's reading, Gerty has apparently internalized the messages of capitalism. Indeed, the chapter has been read consistently as Joyce's ironic portrayal of a woman whose mind and appearance have been manufactured by advertisements and by popular culture. As Herr states, Gerty MacDowell 'has bought all of the culture's prescriptions for the care and feeding of the lower- and middle-class female [...] her lameness thus extends into a psychological crippling or entrapment by cultural mores that cause her to yearn for a state – utter conformity to the physical ideal of her society and wedded bliss in a vine-covered cottage – that is impossible for Gerty to attain' (1986, 193). In this kind of approach, the encounter on Sandymount Strand is seen to represent the reified gender relations of capitalism, where, according to Thomas Richards, as an advertiser, 'Bloom produces the seaside girl, Gerty identifies with it, and Bloom consumes the product of that identification' (1990, 246). What seems obvious, however, is that there is much more going on. First, Gerty is not just an object that has been interpellated to the point of passivity; indeed, as Philip Sicker suggests, Bloom in the scene has to 'suppress [...] his sense of Gerty as a gazing subject' in order to sustain his role as cinematic voyeur (1999, 831). Second, capitalism is the system that enables both these individuals to express their desire in socially subversive ways. Gerty and Bloom are both active agents in this spectacular sexual encounter, where both engage with a range of narratives and discourses and use them for their own ends.

Gerty's familiarity with mass-produced images and narratives, such as the seaside girl and titbit stories, is the focus of many readings of 'Nausicaa.' The chapter's famously "namby-pamby jammy marmalady drawersy" style (Ellmann 1982, 473) echoes that of the texts she reads: advertisements, lady's magazines, sentimental novels. The multiple references to fairy tales such as 'Snow White,' 'Cinderella,' and 'Beauty and the Beast' in the section are often linked by critics to the romantic narratives that Gerty is seen to consume unthinkingly and to recapitulate unsuccessfully. But her readings of fairy tales and popular culture are more thoughtful and productive than critics generally give her credit for. Gerty uses a number of different fairy tales to create, stage, and narrate an enjoyable sexual experience for herself on Sandymount Strand. Her fantasies of Bloom, usually dismissed as ironically bourgeois deflations of fairy-tale ideals (see Castle 1998, 138), make overt the connection between class and sex that the stories have depicted for centuries. Bloom also uses fairy tales to script his own fantasies in the scene, be they from storybooks or from pantomime stages. His utilization of the tales is rarely addressed but highly significant, since it undercuts the gendered hierarchy of male subject and female object that often informs interpretations of the chapter. Both figures' sexual fantasies are enabled by their knowledge of and interaction with fairy tales, then: they are modern subjects who capitalize upon the potential of mass culture and consumerism.

Central to most analyses of 'Nausicaa' is Gerty's apparent inability to read fairy tales and women's literature critically. She is seen to reflect the texts and messages she receives, as her attitudes are either produced (Burns 2000; Law 1990; Parkes 1997; Richards 1990) or constrained (Callow 1992; Devlin 1985; T. Jackson 1991; McGee 1987; Norris 1988; Senn 1971; C. Smith 1991) by fairy-tale fictions and the fantasies they promulgate. The underlying assumption here is that Gerty's real experiences as a woman in 1904 Dublin are ironically antithetical to the romantic and escapist plots of the fairy tales themselves (see Black 1997,

75). However, the stories of Snow White and Cinderella refer consistently to the very issues that Gerty faces in *Ulysses:* parental abuse, social and economic marginalization, and gender competition. As Gerty demonstrates, the language and imagery of fairy tales are effective in expressing her own position. She openly contrasts her situation as a lower-middle-class woman who has 'appallingly few alternatives' (Leonard 1991, 37), to the privileged roles of storybook and pantomime heroines: 'Had kind fate but willed her to be born a gentlewoman of high degree in her own right and had she only received the benefit of a good education Gerty MacDowell might easily have held her own beside any lady in the land and have seen herself exquisitely gowned with jewels on her brow and patrician suitors at her feet vying with one another to pay their devoirs to her' (13.99–104). The dream is the image of Cinderella-at-the-ball; the reality is the image of Cinderella-in-the-ashes: 'Had her father only avoided the clutches of the demon drink, by taking the pledge or those powders the drink habit cured in Pearson's Weekly, she might now be rolling in her carriage, second to none. Over and over had she told herself that as she mused by the dying embers in a brown study' (13.290–4). Her limp may be the thing that has left her 'on the shelf' (13.773), but her class, gender, and father have left her in the cinders and ashes of the hearth. Though she is not as young or beautiful as Cinderella – as she admits, she will 'never see seventeen again' (13.172–3) – she knows that she must transcend these limitations in order to improve her domestic situation.

Not surprisingly, Gerty attempts to alter her position by approximating her society's ideals of womanhood. Peggy Ochoa suggests that the looking-glass scenes in 'Nausicaa' can be interpreted according to Louis Althusser's concept of interpellation, where 'individuals see, in an ideological mirror, an idealized image with which they identify, and they become bound to the higher authority of the ideological absolute subject' (1993, 785–6). Certainly, the mirror in her bedroom allows Gerty to judge and compare herself to other women who approximate contemporary femininity: 'You are lovely, Gerty, it [the mirror] said' (13.192–3). Like the mirror that always speaks 'the truth' in 'Snow White' (Grimms 1972, 250), the looking glass and the women's magazines and advice columns represent the standards of beauty to which Gerty aspires. But 'Madame Vera Verity, dictress of the Woman Beautiful page of the Princess Novelette' (13.109–10) is not just the male gaze in a female guise; she is a Fairy Godmother whose advice Gerty uses to gain what footing she can in this society. Thus, while Ochoa may suggest the limitations of such narratives for Gerty, given this Snow White's age, limp, and family history, the only way that Gerty can change her situation is by approximating the ideals of womanhood she finds in magazines and fashioning a culturally determined identity that might cover over the cracks in her own body. Through this creative consumption, enabled by the system itself, she is able to 'react against, or possibly subvert' the norms of her culture and to use the narratives at her disposal in an enabling way (Leonard 1998, 13).

Money is a major factor in Gerty's presentation of a sexual identity, for money is what allows her to create the image that entices Bloom. Since she cannot afford to buy a hat or have one made, Gerty sews her own from the egg blue chenille she buys 'at Clery's summer sales [...] slightly shopsoiled but you would never notice, seven fingers two and a penny' (13:159–61). Later in the section, she notes that 'her face was suffused with a divine, an entrancing blush from straining back and he could see her other things too, nainsook knickers, the fabric that caresses the skin, better than those other pettiwidth, the green, four and eleven on account of being white and she let him and she saw that he saw' (13:723–6). Gerty displays here her knowledge of the advertising lingo of the Lady's Pictorial and her recognition that she is on display; but as importantly, she is thinking about the tools that she has used to create her look. Her fashioned image is in fact an investment, which may – though not in this scene – provide her with an alternative to spinsterhood, convent life, or prostitution, for if Stephen is haunted by the shabby image of his sister, Gerty is haunted by her vision of 'the fallen women off the accommodation walk' (13.660–2).

What is striking about Gerty's uses of fairy tales and narratives from women's magazines is that, at the same time that she produces an image that is fully in keeping with dominant visions of how women should look and act, she produces a sexual experience for herself that exceeds the social decorum of her gendered role. In a culture in which women's desire is unspoken by mainstream narratives, the fairy tale and the romantic stories in ladies' journals – those examples of a supposedly pernicious popular culture – represent a form of sexual fulfilment: 'It is Gerty's reading, after all, which provides the language of erotic exchange that makes Bloom a compelling object for her attention' (Leckie 1996–7, 74). If, as Luce Irigaray suggests, women's desires are traditionally located 'in the little-structured margins of a dominant ideology, as waste, or excess, what is left of a mirror invested by the (masculine) "subject" to reflect himself' (1977, 30), Gerty uses those fringe narratives to produce her own orgasm in a most creative way. Gerty is a consumer who 'derives pleasure' not just 'from being looked at,' as Sara Danius suggests (2002, 176), but from creating a sexual experience through her manipulation of culture.

Gerty's redeployment of literary fairy tales and pantomime scenarios does not change her circumstances – in fact, her limp indicates that she is a Cinderella perpetually without the slipper that guarantees the ideal happy ending – but it does signal her ability to rework both the stories and the social expectations of her society for her own pleasure. Over the course of her interior monologue, for example, she shifts from the impossible dream of Reggy Wylie to the more satisfying daydream of the mystery man at the beach:

> Strength of character had never been Reggy Wylie's strong point and he who would woo and win Gerty MacDowell must be a man among men. But waiting, always waiting to be asked and it was leap year too and would soon be over. No prince charming her beau ideal to lay a rare and wondrous love at her feet but rather a manly man with a strong quiet face who had not found his ideal. (13.206–11)

Here, Gerty represents herself first as a Cinderella figure who is waiting for Prince Charming. Upon noticing Bloom on the beach, however, she changes the focus of the narrative and turns the hero into 'a manly man with a strong quiet face.' In other words, she takes advantage of the material in front of her to compensate for the inattention of the youthful Prince, replacing the dubious attractions of 'his swank and his bit of money' (13.594) with the figure of an older man who needs rescuing: 'She would make the great sacrifice. Her every effort would be to share his thoughts' (13.653–4). The movement of her narrative is linked explicitly to economics, where Gerty downsizes her expectations just as she downsizes her male counterpart in the fantasy: the young Reggy Wylie becomes the older Bloom; the monied man becomes a working man; the estate becomes 'a nice snug and cosy little homely house' (13.239).

The role of heroine changes too, as her frustration at Reggy Wylie – or rather, her frustration at not being able to escape her drunken father's house through marriage – is replaced by her sense of control and desirability in the new fantasy. She will be needed and treasured by the wounded hero: 'If he had suffered, more sinned against than sinning, or even, even if he had been himself a sinner, a wicked man, she cared not'

(13.431–3). Gerty is no longer the passive heroine waiting to be noticed at the ball, but instead the more active figure of the Beauty who must save her Beast. In fact, 'Beauty' is the role that Bloom accords Gerty in his reading of the scene:

> His dark eyes fixed themselves on her again, drinking in her every contour, literally worshipping at her shrine. If ever there was undisguised admiration in a man's passionate gaze it was there plain to be seen on that man's face. It is for you, Gertrude MacDowell, and you know it. (13.563–7)

His constant attention validates the efforts Gerty has made to perform a youthful and attractive role, as his desire confirms the mirror's approval and Gerty's reading of herself.

It is not merely Gerty's voice but her eye that becomes central in this chapter, as she watches Bloom watch her and uses his responses in her fantasy: 'Yes, it was her he was looking at, and there was meaning in his look' (13.411–12). Just as she turns shopworn cloth into a stylish hat, so she turns Bloom into an object of titillation for her personal consumption. He becomes part of Gerty's erotic scenario. She 'exploits' his presence (Castle 1998, 126) by capitalizing upon his facial expressions and his silence to reflect the intensity of the emotion that her beauty has produced:

> She looked at him a moment, meeting his glance, and a light broke in upon her. Whitehot passion was in that face, passion as silent as the grave, and it had made her his. At last they were left alone without the others to pry and pass remarks and she knew he could be trusted to the death, steadfast, a sterling man, a man of inflexible honour to his fingertips. (13.690–4)

Bloom's silence alternately signifies passion, secrecy, the unimportance of verbal language, trust, and honour. Just as importantly, his lack of voice allows Gerty to control the fantasy and her own bodily responses. The dipping and swerving point of view can be seen, then, not as 'Gerty's inability to confine herself to the speech she herself deems appropriate' (Shelton 1996–7, 100), but a method that allows her to delay the orgasmic outcome of her narration.[6]

At the same time that Gerty MacDowell mines fairy tales for a satisfying plot line, she increases the intensity of the stories by combining them with explicit images of lust: the hidden pictures of 'skirtdancers and highkickers' from Bertha Supple's lodger (13.704); 'the image of the photo she had of Martin Harvey, the matinée idol' (13.416–17); even thoughts of the goods advertised in Dublin shop windows. All of these sources point to the staged and theatrical nature of the encounter. Certainly, Bloom's observations after his climax emphasize her role as an actress: 'See her as she is spoil all. Must have the stage setting, the rouge, costume, position, music. The name too' (13.855–6). But it becomes evident in the number of times that Gerty is depicted looking at Bloom that the woman is not the only one on display here. As John Bishop acknowledges, Bloom does 'some acting and posing himself' (1999, 196). Further, Gerty is not the only character who has narrated a sexual experience using the language and motifs of popular texts, for Bloom has also participated in a scripted and staged fantasy. Interestingly, both Bloom and Gerty use the same fairy tale, 'Beauty and the Beast.' Where Gerty has turned Bloom's silence into a mark of the passionate and noble nature of a wounded sinner, in his erotic reverie, Bloom has idealized Gerty's innocence and vulnerability. She is 'pathetic,' 'shy,' and 'guileless'; 'A fair unsullied soul' (13.742–6). He identifies himself as the villain: a 'brute,' a 'wretch,' and a 'cad,' who has been 'At it again,' 'He of all men!' (13.745–8). Where Gerty plays the character of Beauty, Bloom accords himself the position of the 'beast' (13.837). It seems to be a favourite scenario for Bloom, especially in the context of marriage. In 'Circe,' for instance, he tells Josie Breen of his jealousy of her husband: 'When you made your present choice they said it was beauty and the beast I can never forgive you for that' (15.476–7). It is a tale that allows Bloom to place himself in the role of an imposing but flawed hero, and a social outsider who can nevertheless be redeemed.

Madame Marie Leprince de Beaumont's popularization of 'Beauty and the Beast' for English girls in the mid-eighteenth century, as well as pantomime stagings of the text at the turn of the century, emphasize the patience and kindness that young women should display when married to older or less desirable men. Where the story becomes for Gerty an enjoyable plot of devotion and loyalty in which the woman rescues the man inside the beast, for Bloom its significance relates to his personal insecurities. Like Gerty, he judges himself against his society's ideals: 'Ought to attend to my appearance my age. Didn't let her see me in profile. Still, you never know. Pretty girls and ugly men marrying. Beauty and the beast. Besides I can't be so if Molly' (13.835–7). Despite his obvious interest in Gerty's image, his invocation of Molly here places her as the real heroine in the fairy tale. She has rescued the Beast by seeing beyond his gruff exterior, or has married Bloom 'despite' his being Jewish in this anti-Semitic society. His need for such redemption suggests the pressures of cultural standards on men and women alike. For Bloom, Molly is not just Beauty but a version of Madame Vera Verity or the Stepmother's mirror: it is her gaze and its reflection of the culture's ideology that he uses to stabilize his sense of identity. Though critics tend to view Bloom as the consumer in this scene and Gerty as the object that is consumed, their shared knowledge of 'Beauty and the Beast' and the different uses to which they put the tale place both as creative participants in this culture.

The fantasies that Bloom and Gerty create revolve around sexual gratification, the staging of gender, the consumption of fashioned bodies, and the bourgeois institution of marriage. Joyce makes overt the connection between these concerns and the fairy tale the characters cite when he renames it 'booty with the bedst' in a pantomime section of *Finnegans Wake* (1939, 560.20). It is a phrase that is resonant with meaning in the context of turn-of-the-century capitalism, where the phrase's association with treasure and beds invokes the link between money, sex, and commodity culture. But Joyce's play with the language of piracy and looting also suggests an appropriation of fairy tales that, thanks to the dynamics of consumerism, can be carried out despite official policings of desire. What we are shown in 'Nausicaa,' and what Stephen experiences throughout *Ulysses,* is not just the interpellation of subjects, but their interaction with the narratives and normatives that influence their lives. Culture for Joyce represents a flexible system in which the individual can engage with different forms of knowledge, different class and gender roles, and different sexual positions with varying degrees of success. In fashioning these different paths, individuals may not escape the labyrinth that is Joyce's Dublin, but their uses of fairy tales nevertheless open up spaces for movement within the city and its discourses.

3 Virginia Woolf: A Slipper of One's Own

'This is his writing-table. He used this pen,' and she lifted a quill pen and laid it down again. The writing table was splashed with old ink, and the pen dishevelled in service. There lay the gigantic gold-rimmed spectacles, ready to his hand, and beneath the table was a pair of large, worn slippers, one of which Katharine picked up, remarking:

'I think my grandfather must have been at least twice as large as any one is nowadays.'

Virginia Woolf, *Night and Day*

In his allusions to Continental fairy tales in the context of the Celtic Revival and against the backdrop of commodity-oriented Dublin, James Joyce depicts the interactive potential of the stories. Whether they are viewed as 'authentic' stories of the folk or as consumerist fantasies on the pantomime stage, these received narratives are used by characters in Joyce's texts who work within and at times against dominant visions of nation, class, gender, and sexuality. Joyce's characters are participants in their societies: though Stephen Dedalus finally declines his role as Cinderella, where Gerty MacDowell and Leopold Bloom embrace and reinterpret fairy-tale scenarios in their personal fantasies, all three engage with the narratives of their culture creatively and imaginatively.

As literary 'hand-me-downs,' however, fairy tales bear the weight of the past and not just the possibilities of the present. Fairy tales in modernity retain strong traces of the Victorian ideologies that permeated the childhoods of Joyce, Woolf, and Barnes. While the stories are reinterpreted and recirculated in different forms through the early twentieth century, the versions and morals of the previous generation have a lasting impact. What the works of Virginia Woolf exemplify is the sense of variability that arises from a modernist negotiation of inherited traditions. In her novels, essays, and diaries, Woolf's allusions to fairy tales suggest the layers of history and the various tellings and interpretations that have become associated with the stories. But even as she depicts the influence of her precursors, Woolf demonstrates the potential of fairy tales as texts through which legacies – both social and literary – can be drawn upon and opened up to further uses by current and future writers.

Like Joyce, Woolf connects fairy tales to the experience of the metropolis, as the modernity of London's Christmas pantomimes is coupled with the Victorianism of inherited written variants. This combination allows Woolf to explore 'the history of the everyday' (Cuddy-Keane 1997, 65), and, in particular, the dynamics of commodity culture which many fairy tales suggest through their depictions of fashion. Just as Woolf remodels the Victorian-encoded stories that would seem to demand a certain performance of narrative voice, so her characters interact with the urban fashion system that would seem to hem them in. In most cases, the modern subject realizes the difference between passing and failing. For example, Woolf's short story 'The New Dress' is a version of 'Cinderella' in which the protagonist uses a modish frock in order to participate in what she perceives to be a higher socioeconomic sphere. Unlike the fairy-tale heroine, however, Mabel Waring's appearance at Clarissa Dalloway's party is found wanting by Mabel herself, who sees only failure in her attempts to fit into the role that she has decided to play. The integrity of this Cinderella's identity begins to dissolve: 'all the time she could see little bits of her yellow dress in the round looking-glass which made them all the size of boot-buttons or tadpoles' (Woolf 1927a, 174).[1] The mirrors reflect back to Mabel the cracks that she perceives in her image. Like Stephen Dedalus, she recognizes that social mobility becomes possible through careful uses of clothing, but that her resulting position is still not fixed.

The same dynamic is at play in *Mrs Dalloway*. Though Rezia Smith can, like Gerty MacDowell, create a fashionable hat, she notes that it looks 'queer' when she sees it on her own head in the glass (Woolf 1925c, 106). Its incongruity arises from the gap between the status of her client, which the hat is intended to mark, and Rezia's much less privileged position. In a similar move, Rose from *The Years* glimpses not just a reflection of her own clothes in the store window, but the fashions that are located behind the plate glass, and it is this comparison that makes her feel that her dress is shabby (1937, 124–5). Miss Kilman's position as an outsider becomes obvious to her also in the context of shopping, when she sees herself 'with her hat askew, very red in the face, full length in a looking glass' at the Army and Navy Stores (1925c, 99). These women critique themselves by comparing their own images to the fashionable ideals they cannot fully imitate.

The mirrors that end the pageant in *Between the Acts* emphasize the discomfort that arises when the individual sees his or her identity as a performance, and not necessarily as a successful one. But along with the audience members who feel anxious when they are shown to be actors and not just spectators, Woolf presents the figure of Mrs Manresa. Instead turning away from the pressure of the moment, she uses the mirrors to reapply her make-up (1941, 110). Where the other audience members are forced to recognize that they are 'at once the viewers and the material of art' (Mao 1998, 87) – not only at the pageant but on an everyday level – Manresa's actions suggest her acknowledgment that identity is already social rather than natural, or 'plated,' as Isabella notes, 'not deeply interfused' (Woolf 1941, 119–20). Her application of the lipstick pits surface against surface, or her body's reflection of the feminine ideal against the reflective surface of the mirror. But her deliberate *maquillage* suggests also her recognition that the performance itself has parodic and subversive potential.[2] She is not just imitating an ideal here, as Mabel does in the short story; she is performing a gendered role knowingly and playfully.

Mrs Manresa's almost incongruous citation of social behaviour – 'Vulgar she was in her gestures, in her whole person, over-sexed, over-dressed for a picnic' (Woolf 1941, 27) – can be seen as a metaphor for Woolf's uses of fairy tales. Woolf's approach to the stories, and especially those associated with her mother's and father's generation, involves a double movement, as the inherited texts are both cited and refitted to her modern moment. What results is not a rejection of literary legacies, but an interaction with tradition that both hints at and averts incongruity. In *Mrs Dalloway*, for instance, Clarissa reworks the story of 'Sleeping Beauty,' casting herself as both a passive heroine and an active prince. Her lesbian-inflected reading of the tale foregrounds the narrative's malleability and the reader's potential in fashioning local or personal meaning. Another model of participatory reading is presented in *To the Lighthouse*, where Cam's random movements through the room in which Mrs Ramsay sits with James cause a fragmentation of the fairy tale that is being read out loud. Cam disrupts not only the transmission of the story but also a singular version of the tale, for what she hears will differ from what James hears (Woolf 1927b, 48–9). The relationships between the tellers and recipients of fairy tales in these novels are more fluid than stable, and the tales themselves shift in significance depending on the contexts of their interpretation.

The presence of fairy tales in the lives of Woolf's characters reflects Woolf's own inheritance of a literary tradition, particularly as it is modelled in *Night and Day*. Richard Alardyce's legacy to his grand-daughter is symbolized in the 'Cinderella' image of the slippers with which I have begun this chapter. Tellingly, they are too large for Katharine, who strives to assert a different identity (see Marcus 1980, 115). Woolf's own Victorian predecessors also seem to have worn shoes that are too big or too cumbersome to fill. Like the influence of 'great men' (Woolf 1929a, 69) such as Alardyce or the actual William Makepeace Thackeray, the fairy godfather may not be a helpful figure for the female heir. A Fairy Godmother, however, or one of the 'daughters of educated men' (1939c, 118), may be more useful. In *Night and Day*, Mrs Hilbery is a fictional version of Anne Thackeray Ritchie, an aunt and an alternate influence who adapted a number of Perrault's stories in the 1860s and 1870s. Though Woolf may have taken Oxbridge and 'Arthur's Education Fund' from Ritchie's father (B. Silver 1983, 10), it is her Aunt Anny who seems to have inspired Woolf to use fairy tales in order to critique gender relations.

Ritchie may be the writer to whom Woolf is most indebted, at least in terms of fairy tales, but she is also a literary precursor from whom Woolf consciously distances herself. The resulting double vision of Ritchie testifies to the ambivalence with which Woolf regards the Victorian era (see Paul 1987, 5). But it also suggests the enabling potential of fairy tales as they pertain to modernist uses of cultural legacies. Drawing upon multiple source texts that supplement her precursor's variants allows Woolf to link modernist experimentation to a range of nineteenth-century fairy tales, and to capitalize upon the instability not just of the source texts but of the gender roles and sexual desires they present. In contrast to the canonical works that would seem to follow a clear patrimonial line, fairy tales, perhaps more than any other form of cultural production, cannot be attributed to any one author, nation, meaning, time, or tradition. While Woolf's allusions to fairy tales have much to do with the morals of the Golden Age of Children's Literature, they are also sites at which interactions between texts and readers, writers and generations, and subjects and societies enable Woolf to move across cultural and literary divides.

Mrs Dalloway and 'Sleeping Beauty'

She would mend it. Her maids had too much to do. She would wear it tonight. She would take her silks, her scissors, her – what was it? – her thimble, of course, down into the drawing-room, for she must also write, and see that things generally were more or less in order.

Virginia Woolf, *Mrs Dalloway*

Cultural participation in the works of Virginia Woolf is modelled on the dynamic of consumption and links literature to the other commercial products that can be acquired by the modern subject. The commodification of both the modernist text and the persona of its author is a central issue in Woolf's 'Reviewing.' In Alex Zwerdling's reading, the essay suggests that Woolf thought 'of the writer in the glare of publicity as "like a trouser mender in Oxford Street, with a horde of reviewers pressing their noses to the glass and commenting to a curious crowd upon each stitch"' (1986, 110). For Reginald Abbott, the image of the tailor or artist in the shop window indicates Woolf's 'ambivalence toward the modern marketplace,' where the writer's work 'is demoted' to the status of a commodity (1992, 195). But in terms of *Mrs Dalloway*, this approach to commodity culture seems rather limited. While Woolf does indeed question the utopian promise of capitalism, especially through the figure of Doris Kilman, who seems to be excluded from both fashion and its purchase, she also emphasizes the possibilities of the economy. As Jennifer Wicke has noted, Woolf presents the 'active, even productive or creative process' of consumption as it can take place in the modern city (1994b, 14). In this approach, the commodity, like the intertext, can be consumed critically and used creatively: the consumer, like the writer, is an active member of the society.

The act of sewing that Woolf invokes in 'Reviewing' to discuss the modern writer's situation echoes the act of shopping; in both arenas, the individual interacts with existing cultural material. Like the woman who recreates the fashions that she sees in store windows, or the tailor who mends a client's trousers, the writer who alludes to fairy tales can reaffirm traditional interpretations of the texts and the ideologies that they reflect. But sewing and mending also involve adaptation, where garments are fitted to specific bodies or remade to approximate a more contemporary look. Like pargeting or plastering, sewing and writing indicate both the repair and the alteration of existing material. Where the seamstress mends or alters clothing, the writer updates or changes the fairy tale, either to conform to social standards or to remake those standards according to a new vision.[3]

Clarissa Dalloway is both a sewer and a storyteller, and she uses the materials at her disposal in order to face the challenge of Peter Walsh's visit. As Clarissa sews, she is watched and evaluated by Peter Walsh, who mirrors the crowds watching the tailor in the Oxford Street shop window. In this scene, which reflects the character's sexual fluidity, Woolf presents a series of variations on 'Sleeping Beauty' while Mrs Dalloway mends a tear in her green dress. Beverly Ann Schlack has summarized the main ties between the scene and the fairy story:

> Clarissa is sewing when Walsh arrives; her needle and scissors recall the circumstances of the fairy tale, in which the Princess's hand is pierced by a spinning needle, and the wound causes her to fall into an enchanted, hundred-year slumber. The Princess was shut up in a castle enclosed by trees, thorns, and *brambles;* so Clarissa is secluded in her solitary attic room, 'where she lies with *brambles* curving over her' (65, italics mine). The Prince climbed the staircase and entered Sleeping Beauty's bedchamber; Walsh bounds up the stairs and bursts in on Clarissa (59). The Princess was awakened to love by the Prince's kiss; in *Mrs. Dalloway,* Peter kisses Clarissa's hands (60) and later, in a gesture of rather maternal pity, Clarissa kisses Peter (69). (1979, 60; emphases in the original)

In one possible reading of the allusion, Clarissa, like the fairy-tale heroine, becomes the commodity or the object of desire in the window (on the chesterfield, on the bed, on the shelf) that is consumed by Peter. Certainly, when she has walked along Bond Street earlier in the novel, she is connected metonymically to the goods on display. She even thinks of her brand name: 'this being Mrs Dalloway; not even Clarissa anymore; this being Mrs Richard Dalloway' (Woolf 1925c, 10). The system of exchange at the basis of marriage seems to have stabilized her discursive identity as the wife of Richard Dalloway. In a similar sense, the allusion to the fairy tale becomes a *point de capiton:* just as the story of 'Sleeping Beauty' has been pinned down or threaded into the signifying field of patriarchal relations by writers such as Perrault, its role in *Mrs Dalloway* is to symbolize the heterosexual relationship of Richard and Clarissa, or of Peter and Clarissa. Either way it is a narrative in which, as Jack Zipes suggests, the heroine is characterized by 'docility and self-abandonment' (1983, 24), and is thus a passive recipient of her fate: the prick of the spindle, the prick of the prince, the pedestal of marriage.

But Woolf's allusion to 'Sleeping Beauty' does not necessarily lead to such a univocal narrative of gender, nor does it indicate the kind of sexual and textual stability that Schlack suggests. Mending is, after all, based on the fact that something has been rended in the first place and must be repaired. Following this line, Clarissa's pointed repetition of her married name acts like a needle and thread, as she confirms an identity that does not, perhaps, fit her as well or as comfortably as it could. Further, the fairy tale does not fully correspond to the situation. As Schlack herself points out, Clarissa's reaction to Peter while she sews is hardly positive or passive: she sees him as an enemy rather than as a lover. Indeed, Susan Squier reads his 'rescue' as 'embod[ying] a perspective on women that sustains male dominance' (1985, 104), where he actively places Clarissa in the role of victim to consolidate his own position of hero. And yet Peter's reaction to himself in the role of Prince Charming proves problematic too. Though his authority leads him to define and place Clarissa according to several different interpretations of her responses, that mastery collapses as he dissolves into tears and flees the room. Instead of a stoic Prince, he is affected as much as Clarissa, not just by their meeting but by the overwhelming expectations of his masculine role.

How then do we read Woolf's use of fairy tales if allusions to 'Sleeping Beauty' in *Mrs Dalloway* do not stabilize the characters' identities? One approach might be to see her references as ironic, where 'Sleeping Beauty' and other stories told in the past by rural, working-class women are placed incongruously in the context of a debased twentieth-century urban, upper-middle-class culture. But such a reading would have to ignore the historical circulation of fairy tales and the ways in which they have been told, retold, transcribed, written, rewritten, staged, filmed, used in advertising – in short, bought and sold by both men and women – for centuries. Another view might posit the irony as part of Woolf's critique of the fairy tale itself, where the patriarchal stereotypes on which 'Sleeping Beauty' is based are dramatically out of step with the lesbian desires and masculine failures depicted in the novel. But this would involve a definition of fairy tales as prescriptive texts that interpellate the reader completely, and this is hardly the case, given the number and range of variants that were available during Woolf's lifetime.

Woolf may be influenced in her use of the story by, for example, pantomime adaptations of the tale, since the pantomime was a theatrical tradition she attended from the time she was a child (see Woolf 1976b, 144–5, 163). In these stage adaptations, sex is anything but stable. Dame parts, such as Mother Goose or the Widow Twankey, are still played in contemporary pantos by a man, who often exaggerates the Dame's 'deluded fantasies that "she" was sexually alluring to other men on stage' (Boxwell 2002, 13). The Principal Boy was also a sexually fraught figure, despite panto's 'claims to be a theatre form safely directed to an audience of children' (Holland 1997, 203). The hero's role was not just played by a woman, but by a woman who read her lines while wearing a highly suggestive feminine costume (Herr 1986, 141). The spectacle of a woman wearing revealing tights and displaying a healthy bosom must have given some men a thrill, but the sight of a woman wooing another woman on stage – however much the lesbian dimension of the act was disavowed – may have given some female audience members a few shivers too. For both groups of consumers, the combination of role and actress opens up the interpretative possibilities of the bodies on stage as well as the possibilities of the fairy tale itself.

As these stagings suggest, the stories were altered in Woolf's day in any number of ways, not just by the producers of pantomimes but by the audiences and readers who interpreted them. Indeed, influenced by the panto tradition of the Principal Boy or not, Woolf explores how other desires refigure the significance of 'Sleeping Beauty' for Clarissa Dalloway. The image of Clarissa's bedroom, for instance, which has become an example of Woolf's critique of compulsory heterosexuality, is very much connected with the bower in which the Sleeping Beauty lies awaiting her Prince. 'Like [...] a child exploring a tower' Clarissa ascends to her room. She 'pierce[s] the pincushion' with her hatpin, just as Sleeping Beauty pierces her finger with the spindle (Woolf 1925c, 25). Her bed is also like the heroine's, associated by several critics with 'a death-bed' (Tambling 1989, 149), where nuns and virgins – those women to whom Clarissa compares herself – lie in an apparent state of sexual dormancy (Lyon 1983, 117–18; K. Moon 1980, 155). But while her withdrawal from the rest of the house has obvious drawbacks – as Emily Jensen writes, 'So much for her personal, sexual self' (1983, 176) – the solitude of the tower room is also a space of imaginative and indeed erotic possibilities, limited though they may be. It is in Clarissa's seclusion, for example, that she can re-experience the orgasmic moment: 'a match burning in a crocus' (Woolf 1925c, 26). She might be a Sleeping Beauty, frozen in a kind of virginity, but as she says, she sleeps 'badly' (25). I suggest that this failure to sleep well, especially in light of her 'failures' with Richard, is in fact a symptom of her resistance to the scripted role of woman.

In Charles Perrault's version of 'Sleeping Beauty,' the narrator lets us know that 'the good fairy had beguiled her long slumber with pleasant dreams' (1969, 15). Perhaps coincidentally, just after the passage in which Woolf describes the room as the tower of the Sleeping Beauty, Clarissa engages in her erotic reverie about Sally Seton at Bourton. Here, Clarissa alters the scene of love's first kiss:

> She and Sally fell a little behind. Then came the most exquisite moment of her whole life passing a stone urn with flowers in it. Sally stopped; picked a flower; kissed her on the lips. The whole world might have turned upside down! The others disappeared; there she was alone with Sally. (Woolf 1925c, 28)

It is the kiss from Sally that awakens Clarissa Dalloway to a lesbian sexuality, even though it is an experience that Jensen suggests must be disavowed in this society and replaced by the sleep of marriage (1983, 176). But her apparent repudiation of lesbianism is undercut by Clarissa's skillful uses of the fairy tale, as she recasts the gender roles of 'Sleeping Beauty' when she reworks the scene and Peter's position within it. Instead of rescuing her, Peter becomes the force in her memory that returns her to the tower of sexual isolation:

> 'Star-gazing?' said Peter.
> It was like running one's face against a granite wall in the darkness! It was shocking; it was horrible!
> Not for herself. She felt only how Sally was being mauled already, maltreated; she felt his hostility, his jealousy; his determination to break into their companionship. (Woolf 1925c, 28–9)

Tellingly, Sally becomes the Prince of the tale not just by virtue of the kiss but also by what Clarissa characterizes as her knightly behaviour: 'never had she admired her so much!' (29). Peter Walsh is only the inadequate male substitute for the more potent female gallant: where Clarissa thinks that Peter acts 'as if he guarded her,' Sally remains 'unvanquished' (29; emphasis mine).

When she brings herself back to present day, Clarissa takes up her green dress to mend the tear in the fabric, as if to resituate or sew herself back into her wifely role. But we are still in the world of the fairy tale, where identity is rarely absolute or unchanging, and 'Sleeping Beauty' is refigured again in the living room. Peter's half-hearted attempts at control are expressed in the image of his penknife, a truncated sword that is inadequate for hacking through Clarissa's defences. Unfortunately for Peter, the 'brambles' shelter rather than entrap Clarissa here (34). Clarissa changes her own fairy-tale role as well, becoming a kind of Prince Charming, matching him blow for blow.[4] Where Peter opens up his pocket knife, Clarissa counters by opening her scissors (32). While they can be read as a tool of castration, they also enable Clarissa to cut and loosen the threads of the narratives that would constrain her own sense of self.

For it is not just the story but Clarissa who changes here. Where Peter thinks her 'too cold' (34) – perhaps still asleep to his advances – Woolf makes it obvious that Clarissa is in fact enraged by his presence and by his challenge to her situation. It is anger that prompts her to rewrite the heroine's role in yet another version of the fairy tale:

> What an extraordinary habit that was, Clarissa thought; always playing with a knife. Always making one feel, too, frivolous; empty-minded; a mere silly chatterbox, as he used. But I too, she thought, and taking up her needle, summoned, like a Queen whose guards have fallen asleep and left her unprotected (she had been quite taken aback by this visit – it had upset her) so that any one can stroll in and have a look at her where she lies with the brambles curving over her, summoned to her help the things she did; the things she liked; her husband; Elizabeth; her self, in short, which Peter hardly knew now, all to come about her and beat off the enemy. (34–5)

At the moment Clarissa feels that Peter is situating her as the passive consumer who merely imitates her husband's and her culture's views – 'I detest the smugness of the whole affair, he thought; Richard's doing, not Clarissa's; save that she married him' (34) – she pulls the stitches out of one variant of the tale and creates a different version that better serves her purpose. Instead of remaining the passive Princess, she becomes an active Queen, defending herself against the unsettling presence of the Prince with needle, thread, and scissors; defending herself by restitching and thus reasserting the narrative she has chosen.

Instead of an intertext that rests upon the stability of gender and sexuality, Clarissa's uses of 'Sleeping Beauty' undercut traditional figurations of the hero and the heroine in *Mrs Dalloway*. Her scissors, needle, and thread suggest that socially constructed identities can be altered, and indeed, in Clarissa's deconstructions and reconstructions of the fairy tale, she is able to move between restrictive roles. She is alternately the Princess who is asleep in her attic room, the Princess who awakens herself, the Princess who is awakened to her lesbian desire by another Prince-Princess, and the Queen who fights off the Prince. At the end of the scene, when Peter breaks down, it is Clarissa who kisses him, taking the role of the triumphant Prince (36). Like the Principal Boy of pantomime, and like the Sally Seton of her memories, Clarissa is a heroine and a hero, and above all, an active reader. In her retellings of 'Sleeping Beauty,' Clarissa both remains in a position of emotional safety and financial security, and slides across the social and cultural narratives that would pin her in only one place.

To the Lighthouse and the Lessons of Childhood

[W]e went with Gerald to Peter Pan, Barries [sic] play – imaginative & witty like all of his, but just too sentimental – However it was a great treat.

Virginia Woolf, A Passionate Apprentice

Of course these books are not read, or are read without pleasure, by children: it is the adults who devour them, while the children satisfy their own romantic cravings with tit-bits of information purveyed by the popular press, opening wide their eyes and thrilling at the thought that if all the pins that are daily dropped in the streets within the four-mile radius were joined together lengthwise they would reach from London to Milan.

Max Beerbohm, '"Peter Pan" Revisited'

While the sewing scene that takes place in Clarissa Dalloway's living room reinterprets 'Sleeping Beauty' through a homoerotic lens, it also involves aspects of *Peter Pan*. Peter Walsh, like his namesake, is the freedom-loving boy who never grows up: 'Exactly the same, thought Clarissa' (Woolf 1925c, 32). Clarissa is a version of the Wendy-Mother who has continued to age: 'She's grown older, he thought' (32). Mrs Dalloway's mending of the green dress echoes Wendy's attempts to sew Peter to his shadow again and to bring him back to the realm of domesticity and responsibility. Unlike Wendy, though, who reasserts the status quo in most her actions (from exchanging a kiss for a thimble, to returning to home and hearth, to becoming a mother herself), Clarissa's uses of 'Sleeping Beauty' reflect her silent objections to patriarchal authority. In a world where the Law may originate with Mr Darling or Dr Bradshaw, and be enforced by the immediate influences of Mrs Darling or Mrs Bradshaw, Clarissa's similarity to the Principal Boy recalls instead the casting of the lead of J.M. Barrie's play.

Where Woolf acknowledges the provisionality of sexed identities, however, Barrie smoothes over or disavows this instability, particularly in relation to women. Significantly, the backdrop to *Peter Pan* is 'Cinderella,' the tale that Peter first comes to the nursery window to hear from the lips of Wendy's mother (Barrie 1999, 102). Interpreted as a tale of motherhood and domesticity, a tale of proper feminine behaviour, a tale of the social expectations brought to bear upon the protagonist by various mothers, the story is read by Mrs Darling to instruct (her daughter) as well as to delight (her sons and the Lost Boys). Indeed, it is for her storytelling abilities, or perhaps just for her knowledge of the fairy tale, that Wendy is chosen by Peter to come with him. Based on her mother's example, she becomes another Angel in the House, the value of which is thrown into relief by the mainly ineffectual maternal substitutes that plague Cinderella and Peter alike, be it in the form of the Dead Mother and the Wicked Stepmother, or the Incompetent Nurse in Kensington Gardens, the Ineffectual Nana, and most traumatically, the Mother-who-Forgets.

As Virginia Woolf and Max Beerbohm suggest in the epigraphs to this section, stories ostensibly for children are not only written *by* adults, they are often written *for* adults, just as *Peter Pan* is a play that features children but entertains their parents with its nostalgic constructions of childhood: 'The children are always on the stage, talking and talking, to reveal the sweetness and quaintness of their souls for the gratification of an audience of elders' (Beerbohm 1905, 118). Julia Briggs points out that 'the production of children's books is governed by what adults want children to be and to do,' even though the 'crude didacticism' of some of the earlier children's literature may have been replaced by 'subtler methods of persuasion' (1996, 21). Jacqueline Rose suggests that, despite the fact that 'the adult intention has more and more been absorbed into the story and, apparently, rendered invisible,' its effects are not diminished (1984, 60). Much of the didacticism of *Peter Pan*, for example, stems from its fetishism of the mother and of the values she represents, as the story presents the outcomes of both good and bad mothering. While the play is carnivalesque in its depiction of childish freedom, the idea of escape from the adult world is countered both onstage and offstage by the social and familial pressures that children face. Despite its continuing appeal for kids and grown-ups alike, *Peter Pan,* and indeed many texts for children, present 'a world in which the adult comes first (author, maker, giver) and the child comes after (reader, product, receiver)' (Rose 1984, 1–2). While these hierarchies are not necessarily stable or final, especially when the child-turned-adult revisits the tale in other contexts, the authority of the teacher-parent is often reinforced by the stories themselves as well as by the act of storytelling.

Mrs Ramsay in *To the Lighthouse* tells us that 'Children never forget' (Woolf 1927b, 54). An issue that arises from this statement, however, relates to *what* children remember: the lessons that are encoded in the text, or a version/subversion of those lessons that may lead to a critique of the power structures that the text would seem to affirm? Through Clarissa Dalloway, Woolf indicates that the morality encoded in a fairy tale can be broken down by the creative or resistant reader. While fairy tales and other literatures marketed towards children at the end of the nineteenth century and beyond are deeply involved in larger political and socioeconomic systems, then, local practices of reading have the potential to undermine the intended or implied messages of the texts. Woolf depicts these different levels of interaction at the beginning of *To the Lighthouse,* when James is looking through 'the illustrated catalogue of the Army and Navy Stores' (1927b, 7). The material that James reads situates him in the context of an adult, capitalist, Imperialist, and patriarchal society. But Woolf also emphasizes James's active response to the text in front of him, as he is shown cutting pictures from the catalogue and 'endow[ing]' them 'with heavenly bliss' (7). James's use of the catalogue – he takes the commodities out of their commercial context and places them according to his own desire – parallels Clarissa Dalloway's uses of 'Sleeping Beauty.' Consumerism is characterized by participation rather than interpellation in these scenes, as the reader becomes a creator in his or her own right.

Telling stories is another active engagement with the text as well as with the environment in which it is read. Mrs Ramsay knows that reading the story aloud will pacify her son, that the image of 'his wife reading stories to his little boy' will soothe her husband (40), and perhaps even that the 'sight of her reading a fairy tale to her boy' will make Mr Bankes feel 'that barbarity was tamed, the reign of chaos subdued' (43). But where the active reader/passive listener binary may result in a general pacification of the men of the house, the tensions that lurk underneath this relationship have the potential to upset the family's equilibrium. James knows, for instance, that he is at the centre of his mother's attention, and takes great satisfaction in cutting his father out of the action.[5] He also uses his position to keep his mother's focus: 'by pointing his finger at a word, he hoped to recall his mother's attention, which, he knew angrily, wavered instantly his father stopped' (34). James's anger at the various interruptions of his mother's reading of the fairy tale suggests that the actual story is less important to him than the attention of its reader. It's a feeling that Lily Briscoe shares. Operating from her own desire for Mrs Ramsay, she later takes the place of James at his mother's knee, 'close as she could get, smiling to think that Mrs Ramsay would never know the reason of that pressure' (45). The vision of the family here, symbolized in a sense by James and Mrs Ramsay, is thus unsettled on several levels, not only by Mr Ramsay's demanding presence or by Lily's sexually fraught restaging of the scene, but also by the erratically mobile figure of Cam.

Cam provides an interesting counterpoint to her brother's stationary position between his mother's knees. In contrast to James, Cam refuses to play the role of an obedient daughter, at least in the first section of *To the Lighthouse:* 'She would not "give a flower to the gentleman" as the nursemaid told her. No! no! no! she would not!' (22). When she does acknowledge her mother's authority, it is reluctantly: 'when Mrs Ramsay called "Cam!" a second time, the projectile dropped in mid career, and Cam came lagging back, pulling a leaf by the way, to her mother' (62). Cam is involved in her own fantasy world – what Mrs Ramsay thinks of as 'a fairy kingdom on the far side of the hedge' (48) – and it represents a story for which she is her own audience. Though she hears part of Mrs Ramsay's reading of the Grimms' 'The Fisherman and His Wife,' she remains in a liminal space, neither part of the scene nor apart from it: '"Come in or go out, Cam," she said, knowing that Cam was attracted only by the word "Flounder" and that in a moment she would fidget and fight with James as usual. Cam shot off. Mrs Ramsay went on reading, relieved, for she and James shared the same tastes and were comfortable together' (49). Cam's disorderly presence foregrounds the range of potential interpretations that arise not just from the story but from the act of telling.

These multiple responses to the storytelling scene undercut the more sentimental interpretations of mother and child that fortify and satisfy Mr Ramsay and Mr Bankes. Woolf emphasizes this further through Lily's painting, which appears at first to be an attempt to capture the primal relationship, but in fact participates in a larger cultural challenge to the political conservatism associated with the bourgeois family unit. The style of the painting places interpretative responsibility on the audience, where the work of art (like the commodity or the intertext) may take on a range of potential meanings. This is a lesson that Lily attempts to teach Mr Bankes:

> Mother and child then – objects of universal veneration, and in this case the mother was famous for her beauty – might be reduced, he pondered, to a purple shadow without irreverence.
> But the picture was not of them, she said. Or, not in his sense. There were other senses, too, in which one might reverence them. (47)

Interpretation is no longer anchored to a Victorian vision of beauty and women and children, and Lily indicates the possibilities of the reading rather than providing a specific explanation of intent. The painting and Lily's commentary are narratives that emphasize the viewer's gaze as much as the painter's eye, particularly in terms of the roles that the child and the mother play in the world of the Ramsays.

The same diversity of perspective characterizes the theme of marriage as it is presented in *To the Lighthouse,* and this is where the Grimms' 'The Fisherman and His Wife' that Mrs Ramsay is reading aloud has particular thematic relevance. Traditionally, 'the conflict of wills' figured in the fairy tale has been seen to echo the conflicted relationship of Mr and Mrs Ramsay (Dick 1992, xxv). In this interpretation, the allusion represents 'both an ironic and an appropriate commentary on the Ramsays' marriage' (Gillespie 1987, 3). Indeed, the variant that Woolf uses – an 1894 translation of the Grimms' tales (Dick 1992, 182) – points to a late-nineteenth-century vision of marriage that Woolf must certainly question. When a Fisherman catches a Flounder, which is in fact an enchanted prince, he releases the fish. The Flounder offers to grant him a wish as a reward for this kindness, but the Fisherman declines the fish's generosity. When he returns home, however, the Fisherman's wife sends her husband back for the reward, and back again with increasingly ambitious demands. It is when she wishes to become God that the Flounder turns all they have back to what it once was, and in doing so, reasserts the authority of the husband and the 'natural' order in which the woman knows her place.

Sharon Kaehele and Howard German, following a rather conservative reading of the tale, see Woolf's allusion as a commentary on Mrs Ramsay's 'tendency to manage, a fault which occasionally contributes a discordant note to the marital song' (1962, 194). Gillian Beer also uses the story to focus on Mrs Ramsay, suggesting that 'The fisherman's wife [...] longs for possession and for dominance, for control: that last wish is shared with Mrs Ramsay, and perhaps the other wishes too' (1996, 158). Similarly, for Thomas Vogler the tale points to Mrs Ramsay's 'desire for more than life can offer' (1970, 26), since, as Juliet Dusinberre points out, 'she too loves power and exercises it with the same ruthlessness as the Fisherman's wife' (1987, 144). In such readings, Mrs Ramsay is aligned with the role of the 'greedy wife' (Richter 1970, 106) or the 'self-centered harridan' (Cashdan 1999, 190) that the Grimms condemn and punish for expressing desires that disrupt the status quo. The wife's greed leads the couple to move from a pigsty to a hut to a castle, and more importantly, leads to her own ascension to the positions of King, Emperor, Pope, and God. Her 'pursuit of exalted status' and her 'tendency to be dissatisfied with [her] station in life' are what Sheldon Cashdan sees as the two central sins of the story (188). In other words, the conflict is caused by the woman's insatiability, and more importantly, her desire to take up a masculine position of authority not just within the relationship but within the society at large. The result of this ambition is that 'the desirous heroine of that tale (like Mrs. Ramsay, defined only by her sex role) cannot finally bend the world to her will and ends up defeated both by the male cultural realm her husband inhabits and by the natural world that the fish rules' (Gilbert and Gubar 1994, 35).

These interpretations have their limits. In contrast to the kind of worldly ambition shown by the Fisherman's wife, Mrs Ramsay remains fully within her conservative, feminine position despite the will that others perceive in her. Further, the demands of the Fisherman's wife cause immense turmoil: 'houses and trees toppled over, the mountains trembled, rocks rolled into the sea, the sky was pitch black, and it thundered and lightened' (Woolf 1927b, 53). However, Mrs Ramsay's control of others is not only subtle – 'Nor was she domineering, nor was she tyrannical' (51) – but fully in keeping with Victorian views of wives and of marriage. She matchmakes, she soothes her husband, she tells a fairy story to Cam in order to pacify James's desire for the skull, she knits the family together. Mrs Ramsay is an Angel in the House who effects action indirectly and in accordance with social expectations. Her choice of tale thus seems to demonstrate the 'belief that wives must be subordinate to their husbands,' which the Grimms would surely condone (Zwerdling 1986, 191). Though she manipulates her family and friends, and is indeed a 'powerful and magical figure' (Dusinberre 1987, 145), in a clear divergence from the Fisherman's wife, she uses her influence in order to fulfil her socially determined and thus socially acceptable role.

Perhaps the more significant issue here, however, is the unspoken assumption that Mrs Ramsay is the only character who manipulates or places demands on her family and guests. As we can see in the dynamics of the storytelling scene and in the power struggles that go on around Mrs Ramsay while she is reading aloud to James, she is responsible for fulfilling the conflicting desires of any number of characters. A version of the tale from Peter Cashorali's collection of 1995, *Fairy Tales: Traditional Stories Retold for Gay Men,* provides a useful foil for exploring in particular the role of Mr Ramsay. In 'The Fisherman and His Lover,' Cashorali emphasizes the Fisherman's desire to please his partner rather than his desire for personal gain or wealth. Above all, it is the Fisherman's concern with his partner's 'dissatisfaction *with him*' that leads him to speak the wishes to the fish (Cashorali 1997, 103; emphasis mine). As he explains to the fish while attempting to satisfy his partner by requesting a bigger penis, 'it's not for myself that I'm asking but *for Kevin*' (103; emphasis mine). The Fisherman's failings, which are pointed out to him when Kevin makes his requests, are, in this sense, really Kevin's.

In the context of *To the Lighthouse*, Mrs Ramsay's wish for control can be seen as a response to Mr Ramsay's anxiety and frustration. His search for 'R' moves along a trajectory of desire that is an uncanny echo of the Fisherman's wife's (Woolf 1927b, 32). Of course, the intellectual step that will complete Mr Ramsay's theory is always one term away, and however much Mrs Ramsay desires to be the term that satisfies her husband, is it an impossible task. She attempts to pacify him through her son, through her management of the family, through her work as a hostess, through her role as his Angel. But, like the Fisherman, she can never be that 'R(amsay)' that is the solution to his (apparently philosophical) problem. Inevitably, her efforts only soothe him for a moment, though ironically, her 'failure' allows Mr Ramsay to keep focusing on her drawbacks rather than on his own.

By acting almost as a screen onto which Mr Ramsay can displace his anxiety, Mrs Ramsay enables her husband to display his knowledge and authority:

The extraordinary irrationality of her remark, the folly of women's minds enraged him. He had ridden through the valley of death, been shattered and shivered; and now she flew in the face of facts, made his children hope what was utterly out of the question, in effect, told lies. He stamped his foot on the stone step. 'Damn you,' he said. But what had she said? Simply that it might be fine tomorrow. So it might. (Woolf 1927b, 30)

Indeed, she often enacts a role that creates a space for his performance of masculinity: 'And again he would have passed her without a word had she not, at that very moment, given him of her own free will what she knew he would never ask, and called to him and taken the green shawl off the picture frame and gone to him. For he wished, she knew, to protect her' (57). In taking up the shawl, Mrs Ramsay might as well be putting on a costume and drawing back the curtain for her staging of their marriage. She does this rather well, something that is attested to by the number of critics who note her tendency to manipulate the action, but who do not identify it as a symptom of her husband's lack. Lily, however, points out the theatricality of their relationship, noting that the Ramsays are 'symbols of marriage, husband and wife' (63). It is Mrs Ramsay's attempt to fulfil the role of Angel in the House that Mr Ramsay seems to need.

While its Victorian overtones place the tale as an object of critique, Woolf also uses 'The Fisherman and His Wife' to suggest the labour that is involved in performing the gendered, familial parts that the Ramsays play. Storytelling is just one aspect of Mrs Ramsay's role, but it effects are long lasting. The tale she tells has a significance that, like the relationship of Woolf's mother and father, can only be partially put into words. There is something about 'The Fisherman and His Wife' that resists the closure that we might expect from a fairy tale that ends happily ever after:

> But she did not let her voice change in the least as she finished the story, and added, shutting the book, and speaking the last words as if she had made them up herself, looking into James's eyes: 'And there they are living still at this very time.'
>
> 'And that's the end,' she said, and she saw in his eyes, as the interest of the story died away in them, something else take its place; something wondering, pale, like the reflection of a light, which at once made him gaze and marvel. (54)

Significantly, when James thinks about the scene later in his life, he remembers the experience of sitting with his mother rather than the story (158). It is the moment that he recalls, and the temporary sense of connection he has with his mother that matters, where their different uses of the fairy tale suggest that the act of reading, like the story itself, is open to interpretation.

Woolf's Fairy-Tale Inheritance

I want you to figure to yourselves a girl sitting with a pen in her hand, which for minutes, and indeed for hours, she never dips into the inkpot. The image that comes to my mind when I think of this girl is the image of a fisherman lying sunk in dreams on the verge of a deep lake with a rod held out over the water. She was letting her imagination sweep unchecked round every rock and cranny of the world that lies submerged in the depths of our unconscious being.

Virginia Woolf, 'Professions for Women'

Woolf's use of 'The Fisherman and His Wife' in *To the Lighthouse* is, in part, a revisitation of Victorian values by a high modernist, which relates to her critique of the nineteenth-century patriarchal order that governs the family unit, structures the nation, and limits the woman author in her attempts to write as she desires. But fairy tales and other forms of children's literature were for Woolf situated in a complex web of personal as well as cultural associations, particularly in relation to her own family's links to writers of fairy tales. Her allusions are not just sites at which she censures the previous era, then, but moments at which she makes obvious her connection to the past. What emerges is a view of fairy tales in which their relevance to modernity is paired with their Victorian past through her own experiences with the stories.

According to a number of biographical accounts, reading in the Stephen household was often a communal event, and the children were exposed to a range of texts in the nursery: 'not merely *Tom Brown's Schooldays* and *Treasure Island* but all Jane Austen, Hawthorne, Carlyle's *The French Revolution,* and the thirty-two volumes of the Waverley novels' (Annan 1984, 109). Julia Duckworth Stephen wrote stories, illustrated by Leslie Stephen, that were intended specifically for children (King 1994, 36). As Elizabeth Steele points out, these were influenced by a number of published children's authors, including Harriet Martineau, Frederick Marryat, Lewis Carroll, the Brothers Grimm, and Hans Christian Andersen (1987, 29). In Julia Stephen's 'Cat's Meat,' for instance, the children walk through London and note that one row house looks 'just like a house in Hans Christian Andersen's tales' (179). Woolf's mother's stories are didactic texts, outlining upper-middle-class visions of right and wrong in tales that are set in both the domestic and the metropolitan spaces of London, and which touch upon larger British social concerns. The texts focus primarily on misdemeanours and punishments, and though they address the behaviour of disobedient or cruel children, wayward parents are also critiqued.[6] The lessons in the stories and the strict and rigorous discipline they encourage are often undercut, however, by Julia Stephen's presentation of the mysteries and excitement of the city,[7] and of characters that enable a vicarious enjoyment of rebellion.[8]

Julia Stephen had personal connections with a number of writers of children's literature. Through her mother, Maria Jackson, and her aunt, Sara Prinsep, she knew William Makepeace Thackeray, whose *The Rose and the Ring* Leslie Stephen read to their children (Spalding 1983, 7). She also knew John Ruskin, who adapts the 'Cinderella' plot in his *The King of the Golden River* and is a major factor in the production of socially and politically oriented children's literature at the end of the nineteenth century (Knoepflmacher 1998, 39). Clearly, the absurdity of Thackeray's 'Fire-side Pantomime for Great and Small Children' (W. Thackeray 1855, 197) had as much of an influence on her writing as did the political intent of Ruskin. But for Woolf, Julia Stephen is associated with a more romantic vision. Describing her mother at Little Holland House, Woolf echoes the diction of a Victorian fairy tale: 'she had passed like a princess in a pageant from her supremely beautiful youth to marriage and motherhood, without awakenment. If I read truly, indeed the atmosphere of her home flattered such dreams and cast over the figure of her bridegroom [Herbert Duckworth] all the golden enchantments of Tennysonian sentiment' (1976b, 32).

Perhaps following her mother's lead, Woolf wrote tales that circulated in the nursery (see V. Bell 1974), in the *Hyde Park Gate News* (H. Lee 1996, 108–9), and among friends like Violet Dickinson, for whom she wrote *Friendship's Gallery*, 'a silly, tender fairy tale of two giant princesses with benign powers' (169). Later in life she wrote *Nurse Lugton's Curtain*[9] for her niece, Ann Stephen, and *The Widow and the Parrot: A True Story* for Julian and Quentin Bell's *Charleston Bulletin*. According to Quentin Bell, his aunt's story was 'a tease. We had hoped vaguely for something as funny, as subversive, and as frivolous as Virginia's conversation. Knowing this, she sent us an "improving story" with a moral, based on the very worst Victorian examples' (1988). The story takes its ironic impetus from the Victorian sentimentality and pedantry that offended Woolf's modernist sensibilities: 'if you are going to tell stories about orphan girls, blind boys, and deserted children the way to do it is with the perfect sincerity and good faith of Dr [Thomas Gordon] Hake. It is an art known to the Victorians [...] and this is what we cannot do' (Woolf 1917, 150). Like Joyce, she acknowledges the disjunction between these literary presentations of nostalgia, fantasy, or fine feeling, and the modern world.

Woolf had been immersed in the language and culture of such children's literature and fairy tales from an early age. As she writes in a 1925 letter to the *Nation* regarding the influence of Dickens, '[*David Copperfield*] is a book of such astonishing vividness that parents will read it aloud to their children before they can quite distinguish fact from fiction, and they will never in later life be able to recall the first time they read it. *Grimm's Fairy Tales* and *Robinson Crusoe* are for many people in the same case' (1925a, 69). These internalized stories, especially from the Brothers Grimm, are an important part of Woolf's essays on literature. Her criticism often involves the language of fairy tales, and she uses the stories and their motifs as metaphors in a system of reference that connects the author with her readers. In one essay she compares Ruskin to a Sleeping Beauty who has been given 'gifts' by fairies but who still succumbs to his position as an 'outsider' to literature (1950, 50). In a piece on Jane Austen, she suggests that 'One of those fairies who perch upon cradles must have taken her on a flight through the world directly she was born' (1925b, 136). Woolf's non-fiction also involves references to Lewis Carroll, whose books inspired a theme birthday party for Angelica Bell (Q. Bell 1972, 2:150) and to Jean Ingelow in 'I am Christina Rossetti' (1932, 241). She reviewed Washington Irving's *Tales* and wrote on Edmund Gosse, whose friendship with Robert Louis Stevenson was renewed at Leslie Stephen's dinner table (Thwaite 1984, 177). In the Gosse essay, Woolf also touches upon Andrew Lang, and thus addresses the two major collectors of fairy tales of her time and their obvious influence not just on her own work but on the society as a whole (1947a, 74).

As the careers of Gosse and Lang demonstrate, fairy tales are the stuff of both 'high-brow' scholarly inquiry and 'low-brow' children's literature. But even more than these academics, Woolf bridges the gap between art forms and audiences, placing herself into different interpretative frames by drawing upon fairy tales in a range of contexts. In her diary, for instance, she compares the generic opening of one entry to the stereotypical beginning of fairy tales: 'We were woken this morning (I see this is going to become a stock phrase like "Once upon a Time" in a Faery story)' (1977, 17). She also draws upon their imagery, referring to Lady Cunard as a 'stringy old hop o' my thumb' (1980, 202), and calling Phil Burne Jones a 'fairy God father to [...] fashionable young ladies' (248). Many of the comparisons seem to relate to pantomime stagings of fairy tales. She suggests that London's 'great shops are like fairies' palaces now' (1977, 35), writes that *The Voyage Out* seems like 'a harlequinade [...] an assortment of patches' (1978, 17), and decides that her next novel will 'be very Arabian nights' (1980, 236).

The pantomime was a tradition of which she was well aware. As she notes in her early diary, she went to a production of *Aladdin* in January of 1897 and to the first run of *Peter Pan* in January of 1905 (1990, 6, 228). George Duckworth, it seems, 'took children to the pantomime' regularly (1976b, 144–5). In 1918 she seems to have done the same for Julian and Quentin Bell when they visited her in London (H. Lee 1996, 381), and in 1930 she went with Angelica to the Lyceum for the pantomime *Puss in Boots* (Woolf 1980, 284–5). Indeed, she calls herself 'the good fairy Aunt,' albeit with a touch of irony (1982a, 239). But the fairy tales that Woolf experienced went beyond these popular forms of children's entertainment to include those variants that were adapted into the realm of high art. Thus, in the early 1920s she may have seen Lydia Lopokova, later Mrs Maynard Keynes, in the ballet *Sleeping Beauty* (Q. Bell 1972, 2: 90). She surely hears of Ethyl Smyth's harlequinade of 1934, *Fête Galante,* for which Vanessa Bell was the designer (H. Lee 1996, 591). Operatic adaptations of fairy tales were on her agenda in 1937, when she attended *Ariane et Barbebleue* by Paul Dukas (Woolf 1984, 81).

She also uses fairy tales to express her experiences of an everyday and lived London. In her diary, for instance, Woolf applies stories from the nursery to the world of the metropolis: 'London is enchanting. I step out upon a tawny coloured magic carpet, it seems, & get carried into beauty without raising a finger. The nights are amazing, with all the white porticoes & broad silent avenues. And people pop in & out, lightly, divertingly like rabbits' (1978, 301). In this description, images from *Aladdin* and *Alice in Wonderland* capture the magic of the city; and in comparing the dizzying experiences depicted in the stories to her sense of the city, Woolf indicates the connections between these literary fairy tales and their adaptations in a modern context.[10] The relevance of such works to the cityscape is tied not just to the speed and variety of the urban environment, but to how that space was figured in the pantomime. The harlequinade, for instance, often featured a street in which fabulous commodities were put on stage to dazzle the audience. This motif is what would seem to inform Woolf's presentation of Bond Street in *Mrs Dalloway,* as well as the Army and Navy Stores, which Abbott, following Woolf, calls 'a fairy palace of commodities' (1992, 206). London, the commercial centre of the Empire, is the stuff of which dreams are made, and those dreams are constructed and reflected in the pantomime.

Nevertheless, the realities of British social, political and economic systems were often at odds with the promises presented onstage. As Woolf writes, 'if everybody had spent their time writing about Donne we should not have gone off the Gold Standard – thats [sic] my version of the greatest crisis &c &c &c – gabble gabble go the geese, who cant [sic] lay golden eggs' (1984, 45). In this application of 'Jack and the Beanstalk,' one of the more popular pantomimes of the day, Woolf plays with the tale's idealistic depiction of capitalist ventures, where the intrepid individual is able to find the ultimate mode of production – the goose that lays the golden egg – in order to improve his own social standing. She uses the fairy tale to emphasize the fantastic and naïve nature of such a quest, particularly in the context of a British pound that had been dissociated from any concrete value. The economy has become an ogre in the clouds, mastering the bureaucrats who are nothing more than squabbling, ineffectual geese. Her comparison undermines the seriousness of the situation, as she becomes the Jack who chops the problem down to size through flippancy. While her use of fairy tales is in part a resurfacing of culturally latent imagery, these examples from her diaries, essays, and fiction show that the tales are also consciously chosen intertexts through which she addresses gender, class, money, and the experience of urban modernity.

Though Woolf alludes to fairy tales in order to explore her social context, she does not often rewrite them, despite the well-established practice of turning the stories into allegorical narratives or of using literature for children as a deliberate form of social critique. By the end of the nineteenth century, for example, writers such as Ruskin, Lewis Carroll, George MacDonald, Jean Ingelow, and Oscar Wilde had all written fairy stories for children that presented lessons in socialism, feminism, and environmentalism, as well as more conservative political perspectives. Using traditional fairy tales to do the same – that is, fairy tales from Perrault and de Beaumont and the Grimms – also had antecedents. In terms of published texts, however, perhaps none were as significant for Woolf as those written by her aunt, Anne Thackeray Ritchie. Ritchie's reconsiderations and re-evaluations of fairy tales provide a platform for Woolf's own use of the tales and for her modernist critique of gender roles and contemporary social structures. However, Woolf distinguishes her own politics and interpretations of the texts from her aunt's, as Ritchie represents a source that Woolf uses and critiques as both a modernist writer and a female author.

The Influence of Lady Ritchie

It is useless to go to the great men writers for help, however much one may go to them for pleasure. Lamb, Browne, Thackeray, Newman, Sterne, Dickens, De Quincey – whoever it may be – never helped a woman yet, though she may have learnt a few tricks of them and adapted them to her use.

Virginia Woolf, *A Room of One's Own*

She will be the unacknowledged source of much that remains in men's minds about the Victorian age.

Virginia Woolf, 'Lady Ritchie'

My only triumph is that the Ritchies are furious with me for Mrs Hilbery; and Hester is writing a life of Aunt Anny to prove that she was a shrewd, and silent woman of business.

Virginia Woolf, letter to Vanessa Bell

Diane Gillespie notes that one of the texts owned by Woolf was 'the volume of *Five Old Friends and a Young Prince* (1876) that Anny inscribed and gave to Julia' (1987, 7). This volume was originally published in 1868 and features a number of Anne Thackeray Ritchie's reworkings of Perrault's tales, including 'The Sleeping Beauty in the Wood,' 'Cinderella,' and 'Little Red Riding Hood,' as well as 'Jack the Giant-Killer,' probably inspired by a Grimms' story, and Madame de Beaumont's 'Beauty and the Beast.' It was followed by another book, *Bluebeard's Keys and Other Stories*, published in 1874, which contains versions of 'Bluebeard,' 'Riquet à la Houppe,' 'Jack and the Bean-Stalk,' and 'The White Cat' ('Thackeray' 1986, 182).

The stories are set in Ritchie's present and are accompanied by introductions that signal her critical engagement with both the source texts and the readings that had accrued to the tales. In prefaces to her stories, whether in the form of poetry or discussions between the storyteller and her fictional audience, Ritchie summarizes or provides commentaries upon the original texts and their adaptations. For instance, at the end of 'Bluebeard's Keys,' the speaker emphasizes that she has changed the plot of the original story: 'the point of my story was, that they did *not* marry. Most stories end with a wedding, the climax of mine was, that the wedding was happily broken off' (Ritchie 1902, 71). The speaker also challenges Perrault's narrative logic: 'What did the *first* wife see when she peeped in with the key?' (73). These perspectives on literature reflect the playfulness of Ritchie's writing, but the critique of women's roles as wives, mothers, and daughters is an equally important aspect of her work, particularly in relation to Virginia Woolf's response.

Anne Isabella Thackeray Ritchie was the sister of Leslie Stephen's first wife, Minny, and the eldest child of William Makepeace Thackeray. She lived with her sister during Minny's marriage to Stephen, and remained in Leslie's house after Minny died in 1875. Two years later, she married Richmond Ritchie, later Lord Ritchie, but stayed in touch with Stephen (Fuller and Hammersley 1952, 156), and introduced him to her friend, the widowed Julia Duckworth, who became his second wife. After Julia's death in 1895, Ritchie became a frequent visitor to the Stephen household and an important support system for Leslie Stephen and his children (Gérin 1981, 241). Nonetheless, Stephen's feelings for her were conflicted, though his irritation with her perceived shortcomings was often undercut by his genuine affection. In his *Mausoleum Book*, for instance, he emphasizes that, though her thoughts and actions seemed 'absurd or contradictory,' Ritchie 'generally came to sound conclusions' (Stephen 1977, 14). Given this ambivalence, Hermione Lee suggests that Ritchie was 'treated by the Stephen children (under parental guidance) as a figure of fun' (1996, 76). The Aunt Anny that Quentin Bell presents, for instance, is associated with an 'extraordinary youthful, vigorous and resilient optimism,' but also with an 'ebullience [that] must have been overwhelming' and 'exasperating' (1972, 1: 11).

Woolf's portraits of her aunt tend to reflect her father's opinions.[11] Her reservations are not, however, prompted solely by her aunt's combination of scattered charm and common sense, but by Ritchie's affiliation with another era and another literary moment. Elizabeth Boyd suggests that to the Bloomsbury group, 'Aunt Anny, like Lady Strachey, though so different from her, was an epitome' of the Victorian world (1976, 77). Woolf presents a similar view in a diary entry from March of 1919, just after Ritchie's death: 'unlike most old Aunts she had the wits to feel how sharply we differed on current questions; & this, perhaps,

gave her a sense, hardly existing within her usual circle, of age, obso-
leteness, extinction. For myself, though, she need have had no anxieties
on this head, since I admired her sincerely; but still the generations
certainly look very different ways' (1977, 247). Woolf's recognition of
the generational divide is here coupled with a real sense of affection,
and this doubled vision of Ritchie becomes typical of Woolf's depictions of her aunt.

Despite her admiration for her aunt, Woolf points out their ideological differences as well as Ritchie's professional shortcomings, which
undercut her potential as a role model for the modernist author. Ritchie
is 'a writer of genius' and 'a true artist' (1919a, 13, 14), but also a
charming woman who seems more often than not to be 'scribbling
brilliant nonsense' (1924, 399). Her work possesses life and immediacy,
but her writing is a 'gift' that stems instinctively from her 'distinct and
delightful personality' (1919a, 14, 13). This talented but rather flighty
Victorian woman writer is clearly the model for Woolf's Mrs Hilbery,
particularly in light of her non-academic approach to the genre of
biography. Like Ritchie, who wrote introductions for Thackeray's collected works, as well as her own vivid sketches of famous nineteenth-
century public figures, Mrs Hilbery is engaged in *Night and Day* in a
rather unorganized project based entirely on her father's life and times.
Their shared emphasis on unofficial, personal details tempers the official, public version of the father in question, and this kind of approach
is something we find in Woolf's own irreverent works of biography:
Flush, Freshwater, and *Orlando.* However, Mrs Hilbery's project is limited by the very legacy that both the fictional woman and her model
inherit. She is described as 'a child who is surrounding itself with a
building of bricks' (Woolf 1919b, 88), as the Father continues to exert his
authority in *Night and Day:* 'All the books and pictures, even the chairs
and tables, had belonged to him, or had reference to him' (89). She
remains the daughter of an educated man, supported but also constrained by his reputation.

Woolf herself is faced with a similar situation, as she must deal with
the immediate influence of her Aunt Anny as well as the dubious legacy
of the Victorian woman writer. The correspondence between the two is
something Woolf addresses through the recurring image of the thrush.
In 1919's 'Lady Ritchie,' the bird is associated with the light and natural
tone of Ritchie's sketches of the past: 'Again and again it has happened
to us to trace down our conception of one of the great figures of the past
not to the stout official biography consecrated to him, but to some little

hint or fact or fancy dropped lightly by Lady Ritchie in passing, as a bird alights on a branch, picks off the fruit and leaves the husk for another' (18). In *Night and Day,* the same image is associated with Mrs Hilbery's almost capricious approach to writing, where she fills 'a page every morning as instinctively as a thrush sings' (1919b, 27).[12] In *Orlando,* such music is connected with female emotion rather than with intellectual rigour: 'At one moment we deplore our birth and state and aspire to an ascetic exaltation; the next we are overcome by the smell of some old garden path and weep to hear the thrushes sing' (1928b, 102). In 'Women and Fiction,' the image of the bird is tied directly to the liabilities of feminine writing: 'In the past, the virtue of women's writing often lay in its divine spontaneity, like that of the blackbird's song or the thrush's. It was untaught; it was from the heart. But it was also, and much more often, chattering and garrulous – mere talk spilt over paper and left to dry in pools and blots' (1929b, 51). As Ellen Rosenman suggests in her reading of *A Room of One's Own,* 'The female "temperament" expressed in Mrs. Hilbery's giddiness and lack of discipline either disfigures art with personal grievance or prevents it from taking shape altogether' (1986, 64).[13] By the late twenties, the cluster of images that connect Ritchie, women's writing, and birds has come to signify the limitations of the Victorian precursor.

The ambivalence that surrounds the image of the inspired but impulsive song of the thrush provides an interesting backdrop to Woolf's statement that 'we think back through our mothers if we are women' (1929a, 69). Because the woman writer fears that there is no strong female tradition to engage with, she faces an ' "anxiety of authorship" – a radical fear that she cannot create, that because she can never become a "precursor" the act of writing will isolate or destroy her' (Gilbert and Gubar 1979, 49). The solution is to find female role models who will 'legitimize her own rebellious endeavors' (50), since the precursor, by 'acting as mother and mirror, affirms the daughter's identity as an artist' (Rosenman 1986, 139). This female literary tradition involves not only a recognition that 'each generation of women writers influences each other,' but also an acknowledgment that 'style evolves historically and is determined by class and sex' (Marcus 1988, 80). Evolution is a process predicated upon natural, or in this case, literary selection; that is, it entails a rejection of some women writers and a dependence upon others. In this sense, it becomes necessary for the modernist to determine which woman is an 'empowering ancestress' and which is only a 'trivial' or 'silly lady writer' (Gilbert and Gubar 1987, 203).[14]

In Woolf's portraits of Ritchie, however, Aunt Anny occupies both of these roles: she is an important female influence, but also a feminine writer of limited abilities. Instead of choosing between a powerful precursor and a 'weaker talent,' then, it would seem that Woolf chooses both in a layered presentation of the same writer (Bloom 1997, 5). This 'double positionality,' to use Melba Cuddy-Keane's terminology, speaks not just to a sense of ambivalence towards Ritchie and her writing, but to a deliberate rhetorical strategy in which Woolf herself occupies two positions (1996, 148). The 'multilevel discourse' through which Woolf self-reflexively muddies the transparency or reliability of her own status has obvious significance in relation to *Orlando*, in which the various levels of authorial presence are echoed in the combination of literary styles, genres, and multiple allusions to 'Cinderella.' Fairy tales are not just a system of reference, then, through which Woolf's identification with Ritchie as a precursor and as a female writer can be established and subverted. They are texts with a multifaceted history that allow Woolf to remove herself from the binary of either writerly rebellion or stifling acquiescence. By combining different responses to Ritchie in her biographical sketches, and by combining in *Orlando* Ritchie's interpretations of fairy tales with other versions and forms of 'Cinderella,' Woolf distances herself from a model of artistic production that is based upon a single, evolving line of inheritance. Instead of either rejecting or consolidating the legitimacy of the father or mother figure, and thus of the heir, Woolf patches together a different vision of legacy, where the multiple cultural influences that are connected through fairy tales provide an alternative to patrilineal tradition.

Orlando: Dragging Cinderella into 1928

'At twelve my horses turn into rats and off I go. The illusion fades. But I accept my fate. I make hay while the sun shines.'

Virginia Woolf, *Night and Day*

And the twelfth stroke of midnight sounded; the twelfth stroke of midnight, Thursday, the eleventh of October, Nineteen hundred and Twenty-eight.

Virginia Woolf, *Orlando*

In *Orlando*, Woolf puts into play the more disruptive aspects of 'Cinderella' in order to undercut two main aspects of her inheritance: Victorian gender roles and Victorian variants of fairy tales. Both are associated with the works of Anny Thackeray Ritchie. Ritchie's stories were primarily didactic, and her aim was to reform her society by adapting the stories to Victorian principles. Though the morals are not always as clear or as conservative as they might be, her portrayals of women who contend with the possibilities and pitfalls of courtship, marriage, and childrearing suggest the centrality of a stable family unit. Moreover, the tales become associated with what she regards as essential truths: 'Fairy stories are everywhere and everyday. We are all princes and princesses in disguise, or ogres or wicked dwarfs. All these histories are the histories of human nature, which does not seem to change very much in a thousand years or so, and we don't get tired of the fairies because they are so true to it' (Ritchie 1905, 5). Despite the claim to universality, her rewritings of the source texts tend to emphasize British, bourgeois, heterosexual norms of behaviour, which she seldom critiques.

Ritchie was, of course, exposed to fairy tales in part through her father, William Makepeace Thackeray, whose Christmas book of 1855, *The Rose and the Ring,* is one of a series of stories he wrote for children.[15] Where Thackeray's absurdly playful fairy story is clearly intended to entertain, Ritchie's tales are intended not just to delight but also to instruct. Her adaptations of Perrault are directed more towards women than children, and are influenced in part by her journalism for the *Cornhill Magazine,* which 'encouraged' the women who wrote for it 'to identify with key social issues of their own times' (Harris 1986, 389). Her articles address topics such as marriage, women's careers, and women's education. 'Toilers and Spinsters' (1874), for instance, explores the status of women who are financially and emotionally dependent upon unreliable men. While women's employment is a subject that Woolf later addresses in *A Room of One's Own* and 'Professions for Women,' unlike Woolf, Ritchie does not encourage widescale social change. Instead, she indicates ways in which women can use and work within the existing system. It is a pragmatic approach, and one that is reflected in her fairy tales, but through it she would seem to accept the status quo despite recognizing its inherent flaws.

Another influence on Ritchie's adaptations of fairy tales is the literary tradition of 'domestic fiction' (Boyd 1976, 77), which is echoed in her depiction of the growth and often the love life of the heroine. Though she presents insightful commentaries on class and gender within this form, Ritchie's emphasis on the marriage plot tends to overshadow the more overtly political aspects of her texts. In 'Jack and the Bean-Stalk,' from *Bluebeard's Keys and Other Stories*, for instance, the updated title character leads a labour revolt against the local squire (1902). The portrayal of social reform is gradually supplanted, however, by Ritchie's focus on a romance that remains firmly grounded in conventional roles. Her version of 'Sleeping Beauty in the Wood' entails a similarly conservative vision of gender relations. The heroine is Cecilia Lulworth, who has been lulled into an intellectual and emotional slumber by her overprotective and ignorant mother: 'though Mrs Lulworth had grown up stupid, suspicious, narrow-minded, soured, and overbearing, and had married for an establishment, and Miss Bowley, her daughter's governess, had turned out nervous, undecided, melancholy, and anxious, and had never married at all, yet they determined to bring up Cecilia as they themselves had been brought up, and sincerely thought they could not do better' (1905, 8–9). The issue is education, but the focus of the critique is the individual rather than the larger social factors that have encouraged such ignorance. Indeed, the spell is broken not by a direct challenge to a society in which poorly educated women are expected to turn children into productive citizens, but by Cecilia's cousin, who visits, falls in love with, and eventually marries the heroine. Cecilia becomes a symbol of the proper wife and mother, whose rewards are 'her children and her husband' (28).

Ritchie's version of Perrault's 'Cinderella,' in *Five Old Friends and a Young Prince*, also features the happy marriage of a rescuing hero and a rescued heroine. At twelve years of age, Ella Ashford is a budding Angel in the House: 'She was a cheery, happy little creature, looking at everything from the sunny side, adoring her father, running wild out of doors, but with an odd turn for house-keeping, and order and method at home' (Ritchie 1905, 42). The Evil Stepmother, however, turns her into a servant. It is only when the 'hesitating, flushing, blushing' Ella is fostered by Lady Jane Peppercorne and provided with clothes that better reflect her class position when she makes her debut in society, that the situation changes (56). In an echo of the second moral to Perrault's version of the story, the wealth and social connections of Ella's Fairy Godmother are what make the girl's beauty meaningful.[16] Similarly, although Ella's Prince Charming is 'a short ugly man,' he is desirable in large part because he is 'the next heir to a baronetcy' (61). Ritchie makes a point, of course, of informing her readers that the girl falls in love with the man rather than with his money, and that the would-be baronet falls in love with Ella's fairy-like perfection. Even so, the hero's desire is most obvious when Ella is wearing a 'beautiful white net dress' and her 'pearl necklace with the diamond clasp' (70). In ending the tale with a benediction encouraging 'happiness, content and plenty,' the narrator proposes a vision of marital bliss that is very much linked to the socioeconomic issues that have informed the story throughout (78).

As in most variants of 'Cinderella,' Ella's upward social shift depends upon the Prince's recognition not just of her beauty but of the class position that her beautiful dress signifies. In Perrault's tale, for example, Cinderella's sexual status at the ball is made possible by her gown, according to which she is identified as a 'beautiful princess' (1969, 72). Similarly, Ella Ashford's allure confuses the prince of Ritchie's tale when he sees her wearing dusty working clothes; her looks and body make sense, however, when she is clothed in her white dress and diamonds. In both cases, Cinderella's appeal can be acknowledged only when she is appropriately – that is, wealthily – clothed, whether by the ball gown or the glass slipper.[17] As Arthur Rackham and Edmund Gosse's adaptation of Perrault's 'Cinderella' suggests, the Prince cannot recognize the appeal of the heroine if she is not in costume: 'Amazed, the prince followed, but could not catch her. Indeed, he missed his lovely princess altogether, and only saw running out of the palace doors a little dirty lass whom he had never beheld before, and of whom he certainly would never have taken the least notice' (1916, 230). The ending of the Grimms' version makes the same point: it is the slipper that prompts the Prince's realization that the figure before him is a desirable woman (1972, 127). Again, clothes make the man or woman, and money makes the clothes; thus money makes gender material, or makes it matter in a society where the body is almost secondary to its social markings.

The connection between fashion and social identity, and the performative nature of gender and class are prominent aspects of Woolf's *Orlando* and of her multifaceted use of 'Cinderella.' But where Cinderella's transformation and social ascension consolidate an aristocratic, heterosexual, and patriarchal order in Perrault's story, or a bourgeois version of the same in Ritchie's domestic romance, Orlando's transformations tend to challenge these systems and to parody assumptions of control and consistency. The instability is personified by the title character, which is evident even in Woolf's opening description of Orlando: 'When he put his hand on the window-sill to push the window open, it was instantly coloured red, blue, and yellow like a butterfly's wings. Thus, those who like symbols, and have a turn for the deciphering of them, might observe that though the shapely legs, the handsome body, and the well-set shoulders were all of them decorated with various tints of heraldic light, Orlando's face, as he threw the window open, was lit solely by the sun itself' (1928b, 12). Orlando's body mocks the estate of patriarchy, here, as the father's coat of arms is reduced to 'various tints of heraldic light': identity becomes a temporary projection rather than an embodiment of inherited, propertied, sexed position. Like Cinderella, whose status depends upon her clothing, Orlando's social role seems about as stable as the shifting colors on his body. In this image, the family line and the heterosexual gender roles upon which it rests become a patchwork of conflicting subject positions and cultural impulses that – as the colors of the stained glass windows imply – change according to time and context.

The motley array of tints and hues also marks Orlando as Harlequin, a figure who symbolizes a 'temporary liberation from the prevailing truth and from the established order' (Bakhtin 1965, 10).[18] Woolf's allusion to Harlequin arises, I would suggest, in large part from her familiarity with the British pantomime, that bastard form of theatre that was heavily influenced by fairy tales and by the *commedia dell'arte*. Characters associated with the latter form become important images, not just for Woolf but for many artists of the day. Martin Green and John Swan note a heightened presence of figures such as Pierrot and Harlequin between 1890 and 1930 in texts as diverse as Pablo Picasso's *The Two Saltimbanques*, Serge Diaghilev's ballet *Le Carnaval*, and Wyndham Lewis's *The Wild Body*. The *commedia*, with its roots in street theatre, represents an alternative to 'society's dominant respectable values' (Green and Swan 1993, xiii). Edith Sitwell's *Façade*, which Woolf reviewed in the 1920s (H. Lee 1996, 470), contains a number of references to the *commedia* as well (Hunter 1987, 15). Indeed, Sacheverell Sitwell would issue *The Hundred and One Harlequins* in 1922, and Edith and Osbert Sitwell published a collection of poetry entitled *Twentieth Century Harlequinade* (Green and Swan 1993, 43).

One of the most striking Harlequins in modernist literature appears in Joseph Conrad's *Heart of Darkness* from 1902. The 'motley appearance, clownish mannerisms, and conspicuous gullibility' of the Russian sailor that Marlow encounters in the Congo situate him as a 'harlequinesque character' (Canario 1967, 225), and the costume becomes emblematic of the 'confused lack of order' at the heart of the novel (Helder 1975, 364). Conrad's use of the figure is informed also by the traditional associations of Harlequin with 'death and the underworld'

(Yoder 1980, 90), a connection that resonates in Dorothy L. Sayers's *Murder Must Advertise* from 1933. In the novel, Lord Peter Wimsey masquerades as Death Bredon by day and as Harlequin by night, linking a murder that has taken place at an advertising agency to the local drug trade. Wimsey's masquerades recall Orlando's shifts in identity and suggest the flux of modern subjectivity, for which, in Sayers's novel at least, the opiates of capitalism and cocaine would seem to compensate. A trickster figure, with one foot in the space of the carnival and the other in the realm of death, the modernist Harlequin occupies the shifting border territories of human experience.[19]

The role of Harlequin in the British pantomime speaks to the same sense of liminality, inversion, and social critique, but in a more comic way. Harlequin is traditionally a servant, 'loyal, credulous, greedy, always amorous, always getting his master or himself into a scrape' (Nicoll 1963, 73–4). Following his forerunner from the *commedia dell'arte,* the Harlequin of nineteenth-century pantomime is 'always in love, always in trouble, easily despairing, easily consoled' ('Harlequin' 1989). He is at the centre of the harlequinade, or transformation scene of the panto, in which the lovers from the main narrative line, usually based upon a fairy tale, are transformed into Harlequin and Columbine. In this topsy-turvy world, where Harlequin's magical bat or 'slapstick' gives him control, the love affair that is otherwise prohibited by the elder blocking characters from the main plot can be expressed. The bat becomes a carnivalesque phallus that enables play and parody, where the servant becomes the master and overturns the existing social order (Holland 1997, 198). But the harlequinade marks only a temporary shift in position. The pantomime ends in a reassertion of order, as both Harlequin and Columbine re-enter the existing social structure in their proper guises when the Good Fairy re-establishes the status quo.

Less easily contained by the ending of the pantomime, however, is the gender confusion posed by the figure of the Principal Boy. Orlando's 'shapely legs,' which Woolf notes in her description of his body, suggest the cross-dressed figure of the actress who would play the role of the hero of the fairy tale and the harlequinade. While later influenced by male impersonators from the music hall, such as Vesta Tilley, the Principal Boy was, as I have discussed above, traditionally played by women who 'were ample of figure' and whose 'considerable embonpoint' contrasted with the gender of the character's costume (Garber 1992, 176, 177). The incongruous combination of female-gendered body and male-gendered clothing represents another form of staged cultural confusion, however much this play with sexed roles was limited to the theatre.

The British pantomime's repressed challenge of social normatives is extended in *Orlando* through Woolf's multiple allusions to 'Cinderella.' Indeed, like the harlequinade, the appeal of 'Cinderella' lies in its representation of social inversion. The servant becomes the mistress in this fairy tale, and paradoxically, the significance of the role reversal is not undercut by the reader's knowledge of Cinderella's original, privileged class position. The ball that Cinderella attends is itself a carnival, which enables disguise and transformation, a plot point that is echoed in the celebration that takes place in *Orlando* during the extraordinary weather of the Great Frost. The suspension of the normal social order is marked in Woolf's text by the setting of the sun:

> As the orange light of sunset vanished and was succeeded by an astonishing white glare from the torches, bonfires, flaming cressets, and other devices by which the river was lit up the strangest transformation took place. Various churches and noblemen's palaces, whose fronts of white stone showed in streaks and patches as if floating on the air. Of St Paul's, in particular, nothing was left but a gilt cross. The Abbey appeared like the grey skeleton of a leaf. Everything suffered emaciation and transformation. (1928b, 34)

The church and its laws become 'nothing' in this scene, subject to the same kind of arbitrary control that the weather exerts on the countryside and the city, or that Harlequin's bat exerts in the harlequinade. This temporary overthrow allows for the interruption of other laws on the frozen Thames, and echoes the Prince's ball, in which he can make his choice of bride.

The Elizabethan carnival setting where Orlando falls in love with the Russian Princess also allows for the logic of the fairy tale itself to be overturned. According to Ritchie's version of the story, for example, the Prince should recognize his Cinderella and place her in a stable and privileged social position through the act of marriage. In *Orlando*, however, Sasha's identity remains as unstable as the fair and its setting. Indeed, she is associated most directly with the actors who present *Othello* on the Thames, where the theatrical production spills commedically onto the street.[20] Though the intertext suggests a gender correspondence, as Orlando identifies with the male title character of Shakespeare's tragedy – 'The frenzy of the Moor seemed to him his own frenzy' – and Sasha becomes the female Desdemona – 'it was Sasha he killed with his own hands' – the parallels only emphasize the provisionality of gendered identity (35).[21] The Desdemona to whom Sasha is compared is a fictional character; the wife with whom Sasha is associated is charged with infidelity; the woman's role that she occupies here would have been played by a boy-actor. At every turn, Sasha's position is false. Like the Principal Boy, her social, sexual, and gender roles are in flux, lying somewhere between, rather than firmly within, the binaries that order the world outside the theatre. Though Orlando names her (28), she shifts beyond his reach, almost embodying the spirit of the carnival itself. Significantly, her final evasion comes when she flees the ball and the Prince, or rather, the city and Orlando. Though this Cinderella does not leave behind a shoe, she does leave on the heels of another transformation, and the ice that breaks up on the Thames seems to represent a shattering of the glass slipper that might secure Sasha's identity and Orlando's own place in the fairy tale. As the clock strikes midnight and the party ends, she continues to slip away, and Orlando sees her ship 'standing out to sea' (62).

There are correspondences in imagery here, but the fluidity of the women's identities and the carnivalesque settings of the texts complicate the fairy tale's role as an interpretative anchor for the novel. In presenting a second and rather different use of the fairy tale in the next section of Orlando, and a second and rather different leading lady, Woolf continues to play with readerly expectations. Another midnight transformation sees Orlando descending from his privileged, masculine ambassadorial role: 'He stood upright in complete nakedness before us, and while the trumpets pealed Truth! Truth! Truth! we have no choice left but confess – he was a woman' (81). In a reworking of Cinderella's loss of classed and sexed position after the ball, this time it is the Prince that becomes the servant girl. Thus, just as Orlando's layered references to the fairy tale disrupt our reliance on a stable intertext, so Orlando's layered identities disrupt 'all concept of a stable "self"' (H. Lee 1996, 523).

Such multiplicity and flexibility is expressed in the novel, as it is in 'Cinderella,' in relation to fashion. Orlando comes to realize that clothes 'change our view of the world and the world's view of us' (Woolf 1928b, 108). Orlando's freedom from inherited British class and gender roles in the gypsy community, for example, is enabled by the Russian and Turkish trousers that are 'worn indifferently by either sex' (82). In contrast, her/his re-entry into the inherited social order is symbolized by the dress s/he wears upon returning to England and to Knole. In Orlando's Britain, clothes signal gender, and gender stands for sex, and, as Rachel Bowlby points out, 'the assignment of a sex is a prerequisite for any socially recognizable identity' (1992, xxxix). This poses a significant problem, however, when Orlando's multiply classed and sexed body comes into conflict with a system of patrimony that demands singularity and stability. Because Orlando cannot be recognized as the male heir, s/he must 'reside in a state of incognito or incognita, as the case might turn out to be' (Woolf 1928b, 98) and remain in a state of limbo, unable to claim the property that supports her/his class position, if not his/her gender position. Even so, in her/his 'ambiguous' role, Orlando occupies not a marginalized but a doubled position in this society that is less a punishment and more a reprieve. Orlando's motley identity enables him/her to combine categories rather than to be defined as either 'alive or dead, man or woman, Duke or nonentity' (98). The result is that s/he defers the final decision of the law, or, to put it in the context of the harlequinade, the final wand-waving of the Good Fairy. Unable to be finally classified, but able to draw upon the family's financial legacy, Orlando continues his/her disordered performance of identity in Britain. In one notable scene, the family's money and the privacy of his/her own room in the family manor enable Orlando to change out of 'a morning gown of sprigged cotton' and into a 'dove grey taffeta,' then into 'one of peach bloom; thence to a wine-coloured brocade' before adopting 'the neat black silk knickerbockers of an ordinary nobleman' (107–8). Echoing Cinderella's use of fashion, as well as the conflicting social markings of Principal Boy's body and clothes, Orlando does not reflect the singularity of identity that this society's gendered language and laws demand.

What results is a challenge to the logic of patrimony in both its literary and familial senses. Just as Woolf's use of 'Cinderella' is not restricted to Ritchie's version of the inherited story, so Orlando is not constrained by the monogamous heterosexuality upon which a line of inheritance is based. Orlando's autoerotic fantasy upon viewing him/herself in a mirror offers, for example, a different figuration of sexuality: 'the glass was green water, and she a mermaid, slung with pearls, a siren in a cave [...]; so dark, so bright, so hard, so soft, was she, so astonishingly seductive' (107). Orlando's fascination with the prostitute whom s/he desires when, as a woman, s/he is dressed as a man adds another dimension to her/his sexual identity. The prostitute's appearance – the 'exquisite shapeliness' of her head and the 'lustre' of her

eyes – 'rouse[s]' Orlando, and evokes Orlando's previous sexual encounters in male form (124). Even the Victorian Prince Charming who
rescues Orlando from a broken ankle rather than a lost slipper does not
so much stabilize Orlando's sexuality as prompt its continuing slide:
'"You're a woman, Shel!" she cried. / "You're a man, Orlando!" he
cried' (143). Instead of the stability of the traditional marriage plot of
'Cinderella,' Woolf presents the inconsistency of the harlequinade, which
flows into the main fairy-tale narrative.

The Victorian-encoded version of Orlando's story that ends in marriage is succeeded at the end of *Orlando* with a modern-day variant of
'Cinderella.' In its twentieth-century incarnation, the pumpkin-coach
becomes a car, 'an absurd truncated carriage without any horses' (168),
and the search for the glass slipper becomes Orlando's search for 'boy's
boots' (170) at Marshall & Snelgrove's. Woolf's combination of fairy-
tale variants, like her movement through diverse times and genres,
extends the possibilities of the source text and complicates the idea of
literary influence. At the same time that the fairy tale is cited, it is
critiqued; at the same time that the tradition is used, it is altered; at the
same time that the material is mended, it is remade. Woolf's novel ends
on this note of simultaneous difference, when Big Ben, the clock that
signals to Clarissa Dalloway the organization of time and the control of
the hours by a patriarchal system, also marks the countdown to Orlando's
next metamorphosis and the next upheaval of the status quo. The
carriage turns into a pumpkin, the gown turns into rags, the man turns
into a woman, as the writer turns to past narratives. At 'the twelfth
stroke of midnight, Thursday, the eleventh of October, Nineteen hundred and Twenty-eight,' Woolf presents her own turn with tradition,
participating in a modernist transformation of the multiple legacies
that are implicit in Lady Ritchie's fairy tales (187).

4 Djuna Barnes: Wolves in Sheep's Clothing

Very well – what is this love we have for the invert, boy or girl? It was they who were spoken of in every romance that we ever read. The girl lost, what is she but the Prince found? The Prince on the white horse that we have always been seeking. And the pretty lad who is a girl, what but the prince-princess in point lace – neither one and half the other, the painting on the fan! We love them for that reason. We were impaled in our childhood upon them as they rode through our primers, the sweetest lie of all, now come to be in boy or girl, for in the girl it is the prince, and in the boy it is the girl that makes the prince a prince – and not a man. They go far back in our lost distance where what we never had stands waiting; it was inevitable that we should come upon them, for our miscalculated longing has created them. They are our answer to what our grandmothers were told love was, and what it never came to be; they, the living lie of our centuries.

Djuna Barnes, *Nightwood*

In one of his lengthy monologues from *Nightwood*, Matthew O'Connor discusses 'this love we have for the invert,' identifying the fairy tale as a narrative axis around which sexuality turns (D. Barnes 1937, 136). The stories that Matthew has read and been read are 'primers' introducing him to traditional gender roles (136). But the transformation of the child into the adult in accordance with inherited stories of heterosexuality has been undercut in Matthew's case. Though he has been 'impaled' upon the lessons contained in these childhood books, there is a gap between the text and the body for whom that story's version of love 'never came to be' (137). David Copeland suggests that Matthew's is the modernist's recognition of fairy tales as 'romantic delusions' (1997,

7); Judith Lee argues that Barnes depicts the 'inadequacy' of the 'fairy-tale romance' in the setting of the Left Bank (1991, 208). I suggest that it is the very disjunction between the lesson and the lived experience that leads to Matthew's enabling interpretation of the source texts. For Matthew, the heterosexual characters of the fairy tales have been transgendered all along: it is not the bride or the groom, but the 'invert' that has been 'spoken of in every romance that we ever read' (D. Barnes 1937, 136). As Leigh Gilmore writes, 'the doctor has read in fairy tales the permanently perverse codes of gender, sexuality, and desire' (1994, 617). The hero is thus 'the sweetest lie,' for though he appears to be the representative of heterosexuality in the texts, Matthew's penetrating eye places him as a 'prince-princess in point-lace' (D. Barnes 1937, 136). Matthew reads the tales twice, then: first by focusing on what his Victorian 'grandmothers were told love was,' and second, by acknowledging his own 'answer' or response to nineteenth-century visions of gender and marriage (137). The fairy tale is turned into a palimpsest in Matthew's doubled view of its depiction of sexuality, as his 'miscalculated longing' for the 'Prince on a white horse' whom he has 'always been seeking' changes but retains traces of the original narrative (137, 136).

Matthew's manipulation of fairy tales reflects Barnes's own manipulation of source texts and of language. Like Joyce and Woolf, her modernist experimentations with diction, with narrative structure, and with intertextuality produce interpretative possibilities rather than stable points of reference for the reader. In the epigraph to this chapter, for instance, Barnes's repetition of the word 'come' draws attention to its multiple meanings: to move towards and reach a destination; to become perceptible; to descend from; to occupy spatially; to achieve orgasm (OED). Matthew's discussion of 'what our grandmothers were told love was, and what it never *came* to be' plays with these shades of significance (D. Barnes 1937, 137; emphasis mine). The definition of love has not been achieved, has not come to pass, has not come into sight. As a result, Matthew's interpretation has not descended from it, but instead from another source. Ultimately, Matthew suggests that the Victorian figuration of love lacks for him, as for his grandmothers, meaning and potency, and that it leads to a disappointment that is both emotional and sexual: neither Matthew nor the grandmothers 'came' to orgasm through it. Matthew has, however, arrived at an alternative reading of the love portrayed in fairy tales. Though he has been 'impaled [...] upon' the narratives, or penetrated by the messages of the texts, he has also 'come upon them' (136, 137). He has discovered a different meaning of the tales according to his own sense of sexual identity and has experienced an orgasmic pleasure by asserting (and inserting) his own interpretations. The Prince is thus 'the sweetest lie' in several senses: he indicates the deceptive nature of the heterosexual narrative, he represents Matthew's sweet discovery of inversion within the text, and he becomes a more fulfilling alternative, or a good 'lay.' Interpretation becomes copulation in Matthew's reading of the fairy tales, a moment of intercourse in which the adult who has internalized or been ridden by the stories of childhood is also able to ride them to a climax that is at once narrative and sexual, painful and pleasurable.

Djuna Barnes, like Joyce and Woolf, presents characters who exercise their authority as readers by acknowledging the lessons they have been taught and using those inherited visions of class, gender, and sexuality for their own ends. Allusions to fairy tales are sites where such readings are made evident. But the relationship between the source text and the reader, or between the ideology encoded in the fairy tale and the reader's response to that ideology, is complicated by the various social structures that Barnes depicts in *Ladies Almanack, Ryder, Nightwood,* and *The Antiphon.* Like Woolf's uses of 'Cinderella' in *Orlando,* where Lady Ritchie's version of the fairy tale is combined with other variants, Barnes's characters are involved in networks of power where authority arises from many different locations: mainstream and marginal, sexual and intellectual, familial and political. The different communities and spaces that are the settings for Barnes's works affect cultural interactions differently. Thus, though Barnes addresses the effects of a patriarchal order, such as the one suggested in the primers that Matthew encounters as a child, she also explores the hierarchies of the margins, including those positions of strength that Matthew himself occupies. Though he may defy the lessons of his childhood and assert an alternative vision of sexuality or desire, Matthew teaches lessons of his own to Nora, who must in turn deal with the control that Matthew wields in his Left Bank apartment. While Barnes presents the productive relationships that can occur between readers and texts, authors and audiences, and speakers and listeners, power is not necessarily decentred or diluted; rather, it is exerted by all parties. Interpretative certainty is foiled in this dynamic, not by an absence of authority but by the presence of multiple positions from which different forms of control can be exercised and resisted.

In reading Barnes in relation to the various social networks that she presents instead of according to a stable structure of dominance and opposition, I take a slightly different tack from other trends in Barnes criticism. In part, this is a response to some feminist reconsiderations of modernism, in which Barnes and other women writers of the era, such as Virginia Woolf, are seen to participate in a reaction against 'the men of 1914' – T.S. Eliot, Ezra Pound, Wyndham Lewis, and James Joyce – and the 'confining paternal, avuncular, and male modernist relationships and literary patterns' connected with those men (B. Scott 1995, 1:xxxvii). For instance, Mary Lynn Broe critiques Eliot's editing or 'text-bashing' of Barnes's play *The Antiphon*, and reads his influence as a 'suppression' of Barnes's feminist modernist project (1990, 22). Shari Benstock suggests that Barnes's invocation of 'disjointed, grotesque, and abstract' female figures in her early poetry is 'part of a developing critique of women's place in modern society' that shows the negative effects of the patriarchal culture on the female body and mind (1986, 241). Along similar lines, Sandra Gilbert and Susan Gubar assert that Barnes counters the norms of her society by 'compos[ing] in an English that predates the emergence of women writers, as if to reclaim lost dictions for her sex' (1987, 246). Jane Marcus also examines Barnes's response to patriarchal authority and emphasizes the liberatory potential of the transgressions against the Law of the Father that are depicted in *Nightwood*. In 'Laughing at Leviticus: *Nightwood* as Woman's Circus Epic' – one of the more influential works contained in Broe's 1991 collection of essays on Barnes, *Silence and Power* – Marcus argues that Barnes's novel includes 'a brilliant and hilarious feminist critique of Freudian psychoanalysis,' which undermines the foundations of the medical and political discourses that marginalize the characters of the novel (1991, 221). She reads *Nightwood* as an indictment of the dominant forces in society that have 'defined deviance and set up a world view of us and them, the normal and abnormal' (249). Barnes draws upon the carnivalesque traditions of Rabelais and the circus in this view to rebel against the divisive prohibitions of Leviticus and Hitler, as the 'grotesqueries' or the bodies that Barnes presents indicate the author's celebration of difference and her rejection of hierarchical purity (222).

Such approaches have led to an invaluable re-evaluation of the political nature of Barnes's work, which, as Marcus points out, had been dismissed to a large extent by previous critics (1991, 229). At the same time, this strand of critical inquiry regarding the 'outsiders' of the patriarchal order has had the paradoxical effect of privileging the mainstream and downplaying the complicated politics of the margins, or of those communities associated with the carnival, the circus, and the

Parisian Left Bank (221). Power can be exerted in a range of contexts and according to a number of ideologies, and while Marcus and other critics emphasize the liberatory potential of violating traditional social laws, Barnes depicts also the negative aspects of boundary crossings. In texts such as *Ryder, Nightwood,* and *The Antiphon,* where authority is invoked in unpredictable and often disturbing ways, systems predicated on the rejection of mainstream values are often abusive themselves. What Barnes indicates in these texts is the fluidity of power and its presence in a range of different communities.

The pluralistic nature of Barnes's work, which features multiple interactions rather than binary oppositions, is reflected in the formal aspects of her writing. Her irony, wordplay, and literary allusions produce many possible interpretations through which she troubles notions of textual authority and prompts the reader to participate in the creation of meaning. Her references to the Bible, to Chaucer's poetry, to Elizabethan literature, and to the texts of her contemporaries are fascinating examples of her engagement with sources and traditions. In her references to fairy tales, the same kinds of combinations take place, often in the same allusion, as different versions and interpretations of the stories overlap and, at times, come into conflict. Her descriptions of characters involve the same sense of combination and contradiction where, like the 'prince-princess in point lace' (D. Barnes 1937, 136), clothes, bodies, and sexualities are layered to produce an amalgam that is more than the sum of its parts. The overdetermination of the body echoes the overdetermination of the text and the fairy-tale intertext, as the characters' incongruous uses of fashion and Barnes's multileveled use of language hint at a range of potential identities and meanings.[1]

For example, Matthew O'Connor's cross-dressing aligns him with the Wolf from 'Little Red Riding Hood,' who disguises himself as the Grandmother. The Wolf's position in the fairy tale, like Matthew's place in the novel, indicates the enabling aspects of drag, where both figures use clothing in a socially prohibited way for their own pleasure. Dame Musset in *Ladies Almanack,* Barnes's roman-à-clef based upon Natalie Barney's 1920s lesbian salon, is a similar figure. Like Matthew and the Wolf, her body is ostensibly at odds with the clothes she wears, but in the context of the Parisian Lesbos that is the setting of the text, she represents the promise of sexual and social freedom. Indeed, Dame Musset is presented as a kind of Fairy Godmother, who turns the speaker into a successful Cinderella. But her role in the piece, like

Natalie Barney's role in Barnes's life, points to other restrictions, especially financial, which complicate the sense of liberation depicted in *Ladies Almanack*. While the different meanings that are combined in her name and her appearance undermine the fiction of a singular identity, they also signal a nexus of authority that has very real effects on the speaker and the author of the text.

The communities that Barnes explores often exist at the margins of 'normal' society, and while they represent spaces that are liberating in many ways, they too involve some significant costs to the individual. Nora's epiphany regarding 'Red Riding Hood and the wolf in bed,' for instance, speaks to the desire but also the anxiety that the child experiences in his or her confrontation with the composite, gender-bending figure of the Wolf-as-Grandmother (D. Barnes 1937, 79). Nora's dreams connect this highly sexual image from 'Little Red Riding Hood' to other fairy-tale scenarios in Barnes's works that feature an older, wolfish female figure. The Grandmother's cross-dressed body is both fascinating and frightening for the granddaughters whom she haunts in Barnes's fiction. Like Dame Musset, the Grandmother comes to represent a web of control – sexual, professional, literary, and familial – and one that is very much involved with Djuna Barnes's own grandmother, Zadel Barnes Budington Gustafson. Given Barnes's probable experiences with incest or sexual abuse within her unconventional family unit, this association is deeply disturbing. If there is a freedom that comes from breaking the laws of a patriarchal society, the family politics that are presented in *Ryder* and in Barnes's play *The Antiphon* suggest that there are abuses that can arise as a result.

Barnes explores the limitations and possibilities not just of social transgression, however, but of narrative control. If, as Judith Butler suggests, an incongruous citation of a sexed position is 'at once an interpretation of the norm and an occasion to expose the norm itself as a privileged interpretation' (1993, 108), allusions to fairy tales expose the provisionality of the writer's authority. This is enabling for Barnes, who is able to react against previous encodings of fairy tales or other intertexts and use them to respond to her past and present situations. But her temporary authority is also double-edged, since any reformulation can also be critiqued. The figure of the Grandmother has added significance for this reason. Zadel Barnes's story of 1875, 'The Children's Night,' features a range of fairy tales, and in her own uses of the texts, Barnes confronts not just the familial but the narrative control that the older storyteller wields. Barnes echoes Woolf's approach here by combining variants and by using the tales and their dramatis personae in different ways throughout her texts, thus asserting the place and potential power of the reader and the child. Zadel Barnes, the Mother Goose figure, is transformed into a character in Barnes's novels, and where the Grandmother is a loving maternal figure, she is also depicted as the Evil Stepmother or the disguised Wolf. Even so, she remains a traumatic as well as a chaotic figure who continues to haunt Barnes's protagonists. The issue that Barnes raises in her references to fairy tales, then, is not just what they mean, but whether authorial control is possible, desirable, and feasible in relation to the history of the tales and the settings in which they are and have been used.

'Little Red Riding Hood' and the Uses of Consumer Culture

Wolfed in fire even to galoshes:
All in scarlet, like a Cardinal,
A cherry ribbon 'round her neck, as murdered.
　Djuna Barnes, *The Antiphon*

Little girls, this seems to say,
Never stop upon your way.
Never trust a stranger-friend;
No one knows how it will end.
As you're pretty, so be wise;
Wolves may lurk in every guise.
Handsome they may be, and kind,
Gay or charming – never mind!
Now, as then, 'tis simple truth –
Sweetest tongue has sharpest tooth!
　　　　Charles Perrault, 'Little Red Riding Hood'

In *Nightwood*, the primary fairy-tale source text with which Matthew is associated is 'Little Red Riding Hood,' a story that depicts 'passing' at its most sinister level. 'Little Red Riding Hood' features two of the best-known consumers of fashion in the modern era. But where Red's reading of style assumes that there is a correlation between body and clothes – Red *is* what she wears – the Wolf plays with the assumption that the body wearing Granny's clothes must be Granny and uses the fashion system to his own advantage.

In their version of the tale, which cautions against the wayward impulses of the young protagonist, the Grimms depict Red as a spoiled child and posit greed as a major factor in her downfall (an aspect of the story that Sondheim and Lepine play with in their musical *Into the Woods*). According to the Grimms, Little Red-Cap consumes first the Grandmother's gift of the hood, refusing to wear anything except the 'little cap of red velvet' (Grimms 1972, 139). She then consumes the flowers at the side of the path: 'whenever she had picked one, she fancied that she saw a still prettier one farther on, and ran after it' (140). Indeed, Red gathers so many flowers that she can 'carry no more' (141–2). Her gluttony, which is of course encouraged by the Wolf, is matched by his own appetite, as the Wolf eats not just the little girl but the Grandmother too. This sequence is halted by the Huntsman, who cuts open the Wolf's belly with scissors to free the women and who sews it back up after filling the Wolf's stomach with rocks. Like the furrier who creates a luxury good out of a greedy varmint, the Huntsman refashions the Wolf, who returns in a different form into the economy.[2]

But Red is also a kind of commodity thanks to her own acts of consumption. The red cap that Red obtains from the Grandmother is more than a hat; it is her trademark, marking her identity and her place in the society. And just as Red partakes of the fashion that her grandmother produces, the Wolf partakes of the girl's fashionable body. It is a cycle that is echoed in a range of modernist texts, in which the citizens who shop and consume are in turn shopped and consumed. 'Little Red Riding Hood' is a narrative that can be read, then, in relation to the power dynamics of modern consumer culture, in which the goods advertised in the store windows are metonymically linked to the people who shop for them. The voyeurism that typifies the experience of the metropolis echoes the voyeurism that characterizes the forest, the setting for the Wolf's visual and literal consumption of Red. In the 'Calypso' section of Joyce's *Ulysses*, for instance, Bloom sights the Woods' servant in Dlugacz's butcher shop and connects her to the product that she has just bought: 'Sound meat there: like a stallfed heifer' (4.153). His subsequent fantasy extends the meaty metaphor: 'To catch up and walk behind her if she went slowly, behind her moving hams' (4.171–2). Bloom, the wolfish spectator, literally devours the image of the woman as she moves along the street, itemizing her body parts and their value, fantasizing about her sexual positions in other regions of the city: 'a constable off duty cuddling her in Eccles lane. They like them sizable. Prime sausage. O please, Mr Policeman, I'm lost in the wood' (4.179).

The music-hall song that Zack Bowen identifies as a source for Joyce here becomes the soundtrack to Bloom's erotic reverie (1974, 85), echoing 'Little Red Riding Hood' according to a highly sexual script. The little girl, lost on her way home, depends on the Law (Policeman, Hunter) to please (help) her. Little Red Riding Hood is the sexed body consumed visually by the man by virtue of her position in the (sexual) market.

Another version of the Wolf is Miss Kilman in Virginia Woolf's *Mrs Dalloway*, whose consumption of a pastry in the Army and Navy Stores also points to the contiguous relationship between the store-bought good and the object of sexual desire. The éclair that she wolfs down would seem to stand in for the body and heart of Elizabeth Dalloway: 'If she could grasp her, if she could clasp her, if she could make her hers absolutely and forever and then die; that was all she wanted' (Woolf 1925c, 98). But Elizabeth Dalloway, unlike the wayward figure of Little Red Riding Hood, is able to keep to the path and to take herself out of the woods. Instead of being willingly waylaid by the Wolf, and instead of enjoying a pleasure that exceeds the boundaries of appropriate behaviour, she chooses not to be tempted by Miss Kilman's entreaties: 'no, she did not want anything more' (141). In deciding not to consume, Elizabeth Dalloway declines to be herself consumed visually or sexually by Doris Kilman. Like Stephen Dedalus, who refuses to become a commodity in Dublin, Elizabeth Dalloway removes herself from a system of exchange for which greed is the foundation and in which reciprocity seems inevitable.[3]

What is evident in Charles Perrault's version of the story, as in these associated images, is that the Wolf's consumption of Red's body has sexual as well as gastronomic overtones. Marina Warner points out that the Wolf is a 'wellspoken seducer, urbane, not rustic'; indeed, he 'no longer stands for the savage wilderness, but for the deceptions of the city and the men who wield authority in it' (1994a, 183). The murderer in Fritz Lang's film *M* echoes much of this description of the threatening flâneur. Hans Beckert is characterized from the outset as a keen consumer of food and this, coupled with his charm and his circulation in the anonymous German city, mark him as a version of Perrault's Wolf. Significantly, the predator first sees a reflection of his youthful prey in a store window, and it is the child's own desire for candy, her own sweet tooth, that the Wolf uses to entrap her. Similarly, in Katherine Mansfield's 'The Little Governess,' the treats that the 'grandfather' buys the naïve protagonist – strawberries, beer, ice cream – represent the desire of the prey that is manipulated by the predator in order to satisfy his own desires (1945, 183). In this sense, the Wolf only masquerades as a regular consumer, for he uses the props and systems of the society in an unnatural – that is to say, non-normative – way. The Huntsman's role, then, is to reassert the 'true' status of the predator in order to bring him or her back into line. In *M*, Lang's murderer has the 'M' chalked upon the back of his coat, and it is this mark that allows him to be hunted down. In Mansfield's short story, however, though it is the governess who realizes that the 'grandfather' figure is the Wolf, and it is her own body that is marked by the waiter as having broken the social codes that regulate feminine behaviour: 'I told her [the employer] that you had arrived and gone out again immediately with a gentleman' (1945, 189).

Red's story begins in a space of definitional certainty, where she is identified by the clothing that her Grandmother gives her. But her trust in the correspondence between her body and the red hood causes problems when she later encounters the Wolf-as-Grandmother. Because she assumes that clothes represent – as they are 'supposed' to – stable gender roles, she cannot read the Wolf's male, animal body in its inappropriate context: 'she was astonished to see how her grandmother looked in her nightgown' (Perrault 1969, 28). The Wolf, however, has used fashion creatively, subverting ideologies and identities with great aplomb. He impersonates not only the Grandmother, but first the Granddaughter: '"It is your little daughter, Red Riding Hood," said the Wolf, disguising his voice, "and I bring you a cake and a little pot of butter as a present from my mother"' (26). Though Red eventually identifies the incongruity of the clothing and the body – the Wolf's arms, legs, ears, eyes, and teeth are too 'big'; the fashion does not fit – she is not capable of putting that identification into motion quickly enough.

A similar kind of definitional confusion awaits Nora Flood when she encounters 'Dr Matthew-Mighty-grain-of-salt-Dante-O'Connor' in *Nightwood* (D. Barnes 1937, 80). Her epiphany when she enters his Parisian flat and sees him in female clothing foregrounds the relevance of the fairy tale in modernity according to its presentation of sexuality: 'God, children know something they can't tell; they like Red Riding Hood and the wolf in bed!' (79). As a number of critics have pointed out, Matthew is the Wolf cross-dressed as the Grandmother here, or the trickster figure from the fairy tale who causes some confusion: 'The doctor's head, with its over-large black eyes, its full gun-metal cheeks and chin, was framed in the golden semi-circle of a wig with long pendent curls that touched his shoulders, and falling back against the pillows, turned up the shadowy interior of their cylinders. He was heavily rouged and his lashes painted' (79). The clothing and the make-up that Matthew affects are at odds with his male body, and indeed seem to mask it at least partially. But it is crucial to note here that Matthew does not try to 'transform [...] himself into a woman' (Benstock 1986, 258), or to appear 'as a woman' (J. Lee 1991, 216), or to 'pass as a woman' (Henstra 2000, 131). Rather, his unshaven 'gun-metal cheeks and chin' that are 'framed in the golden semi-circle' of a woman's wig indicate that he is combining what are usually viewed as incompatible signs of gender (D. Barnes 1937, 79). Though the doctor may have 'evacuated custom and gone back into his dress,' he does not evacuate the meaning of either his masculine body or the feminine clothes that he wears (80). In other words, he does not efface the 'already culturalized physical "givens" of the body,' but 'inhabit[s]' his male anatomy as well as a feminine gender role, juxtaposing and conflating various signifiers of sexuality (Moon and Sedgwick 1993, 220). Matthew's body, overtly at odds with the gender of the nightgown that he wears, is highly sexed as a result. Indeed, Marjorie Garber suggests that the 'confrontation with the wolf in bed, is pervasively and complicatedly erotic' precisely because of his cross-dressing (1992, 387).

Matthew is not a failed female impersonator; rather, he is exploiting the potential of fashion to produce a certain pleasure, though it remains uncertain whether his role is to be the Wolf who will consume an awaited object of desire, or, like Red Riding Hood and the Grand-mother, to be the character who will be consumed.[4] He may have been impaled on the heterosexual narratives of his childhood, but here, he uses those standards to assert not an alternative but rather a supple-mentary reading of their significance. His ability to do so arises from both his own creativity and the fashion system itself. Just as Joyce's Gerty MacDowell and Woolf's Mrs Manresa have been able to purchase and produce and perform their own identities, so has Matthew O'Connor. Unlike the women, he is not passing as wealthier or younger or ironi-cally acknowledging his socially constructed facade of masculinity; instead, he is moving beyond the oppositional logic according to which both Gerty and Mrs Manresa fashion themselves. In recalling the image of 'the prince-princess in point lace – neither one and half the other' (D. Barnes 1937, 136), he is taking advantage of capitalism, for even where commodity culture participates in a social scripting of gender and class, its gaps allow for unscripted interventions.

Robin Vote, Nora's lover, is another figure in *Nightwood* that Barnes characterizes through a combination of identities. Like the Wolf-as-Grandmother, Robin first appears in bed: 'half flung off the support of the cushions from which, in a moment of threatened consciousness she had turned her head, lay the young woman, heavy and dishevelled. Her legs, in white flannel trousers, were spread as in a dance, the thick-laquered pumps looking too lively for the arrested step. Her hands, long and beautiful, lay on either side of her face' (34). Robin's position identifies her most obviously as a Sleeping Beauty, which can and has been seen as an ironic use of the tale: 'a pantomime of Sleeping Beauty woken by the wrong prince' (Marcus 1991, 236). Certainly, neither of the men in the room fulfils the role of the heterosexual hero. Matthew does not steal her heart, but rather her perfume, her make-up, and a hundred-franc note from her bureau (D. Barnes 1937, 36). Felix may make her the 'Baronin' (43), but the title is fraudulent, and the marriage vows are undercut by her lesbian wanderings. Judith Lee claims that Robin is in fact a 'caricature of the "sleeping beauty"' (1991, 210), where, instead of reasserting its continuing relevance, Barnes 'parod[ies] the fairy-tale romance and the values mythologized in it' (211). But note that the fairy-tale symbol of male desire – the beautiful and passive young woman objectified on a bed – is here not replaced by but paired with an uncertainly sexed figure. The inherited fairy tale is not rejected, but rather joined by its current incarnation.

While it seems to be an incongruous juxtaposition, there are enough similarities to maintain the connection in a meaningful way. For instance, the fairy tale has particular bearing on the different states that Robin occupies here. She is a source of potential identity, not yet awakened to her role: 'lively' but static, almost conscious but still asleep, dancing but lying down. Her 'white flannel trousers' (D. Barnes 1937, 34), which are later identified as 'boy's trousers' (169), foreshadow Matthew's conflation of femininity and masculinity in the 'Watchman, What of the Night?' chapter, and in this bedroom scene, Felix observes Matthew 'dusting his darkly bristled chin with a puff, and drawing a line of rouge across his lips' with Robin's make-up (36). This is a hint that the Wolf is turning into the Grandmother, though in Nora's introduction to Robin, it is Robin who is described as the 'beast turning human' (37). Robin's relationship with Nora would, in fact, seem to fulfil the promise of 'Red Riding Hood and the wolf in bed' (79) when they meet at the Denckman circus and become lovers (53).[5] However, though she assumes the roles that correspond to her various partners – Felix's wife, Guido's mother, Nora's partner, Jenny's knick-knack – no single figure has final authority over Robin: she is always in the process of turning into something else. As Nora confesses, 'She was mine only when she was drunk, Matthew, and had passed out' (145). Nora's epiphany in Matthew's bedroom indicates the slipperiness of both characters, then, and of both bedroom scenes and both fairy tales as they are linked through the similarities of the episodes: the reader knows something about Robin and Matthew, but the specific significance remains hidden within the multiple meanings that accrue to their bodies.

Where Robin remains mostly silent, Matthew's voice and body dominate *Nightwood*. Perhaps it is his overwhelming presence in the text – and the sheer amount of signification that is represented by his monologues, his dialogues, his lectures, his non-sequiturs, his body, and his clothing – that leads to his centrality in readings of the novel. He is excessive also in the sense that, as with so many of Barnes's characters, he exists at the margins of a mainstream society and exceeds the boundaries of normalcy. T.S. Eliot's highly influential introduction to the 1937 American edition of *Nightwood* is among the first attempts to define the implications of Matthew and the world that he inhabits. Eliot warns the reader not to regard the book as a 'psychopathic study' since its 'deeper design is that of the human misery and bondage that is universal' (1937, xv). Eliot's aim is to incorporate or understand the 'horrid sideshow of freaks' according to a discourse of liberal humanism, and his attempt is prompted in part by the voice of Matthew, which produces a sympathetic identification (xvi). Indeed, for Eliot, Matthew is the central figure of the text, as his speeches testify to the apparent sterility of modern life: 'he is talking to drown the still small wailing and whining of humanity, to make more supportable its shame and less ignoble its misery' (xiv). Kenneth Burke suggests that Matthew is an embodiment of a sense of 'tragic dignification' and argues that the novel recommends a political stance through Matthew, where Barnes 'show[s] people who are willing to undergo sacrifices in behalf of the cause' in order to prompt her readers to do the same (1966, 345). In other words, Barnes is politically motivated to demonstrate the inequities of the social system that castrates or marginalizes Matthew and the rest of the bodies in the Left Bank. In his lamentations, he prompts the reader's pity, performing 'regret both for a safety he cannot find in symbolic categories and for what is barred from desire in order to exist as a legitimate social subject' (Henstra 2000, 132). Matthew and Barnes's other marginalized figures must thus be reintegrated or 'recuperat[ed]' (V. Smith 1999, 195) into a new formulation of social identity, one erected in accordance with Barnes's apparent reminder that 'the human condition is a sister- and brotherhood of difference' (Marcus 1991, 250).

In such readings of *Nightwood*, the novel is seen to reverse or invert the patriarchal gaze, as Barnes 'turns the entire social order upside down, privileging the resistance of all outsiders' (Broe 1989, 52). 'Carnivalesque' is the term most often used for this world that features the temporary and transitory subjectivities that are situated outside the Law, and that signifies the 'communal resistances of underworld outsiders to domination' (Marcus 1991, 221). But as Peter Stallybrass and Allon White observe, it is the mainstream bourgeoisie that '*made* carnival into the festival of the Other. It encoded all that which the proper bourgeois must strive *not to be* in order to preserve a stable and "correct" sense of self' (1986, 178). While Marcus shows how the denizens of *Nightwood* engage in an enabling and parodic destabilization of traditional identities, in its very status as an 'escape from the usual official way of life' (Bakhtin 1965, 8), carnival is dependent upon its opposite term for meaning. In its promise of a 'temporary suspension, both ideal and real, of hierarchical rank' (10), it indicates the limits of its own efficacy and remains tied to the authority itself. Bound within the calendar time of the mainstream, for which it acts as a steam valve, carnival represents a revolving system of inversion that maintains the given hierarchical relationships that produce the centre/margin system in the first place. Marcus's figurations of carnival speak to inclusion, then, but not necessarily to systemic change: the 'enthronement of the fool' only '*implies* dethronement of hierarchy' while using the same symbols of power (1991, 247).

Dianne Chisholm suggests that Barnes 'flaunts a queer scepticism concerning sexual liberation and its bohemian milieux' (1997, 176), and does not fully embrace the idea of inversion as a carnivalesque tactic that leads to political freedom. Indeed, reading Barnes's presentation of sexual politics according to an opposition between a monolithic mainstream and a community of like-minded outsiders seems antithetical to the varied performances of identities that Barnes depicts. Matthew's personal experiences of pleasure and pain stem, for example, from his role as both the consumer and the consumed, rather than from his alignment with one term of a binary. If nothing else, his doubled position as the Wolf-as-Grandmother indicates that he is not just a victim who needs to be rescued from the abuses of patriarchal Law. A more promising strand of interpretation regarding Barnes's politics examines the boundaries that the individual confronts and views these barriers as being 'relational, unstable, and vulnerable' in Barnes's work (Henstra 2000, 144). Instead of reversing the oppositional structure of outside and inside, or of patriarchy as Power and the marginal communities as the Lack Thereof, such an approach emphasizes dialogue. The 'permanent instability' that results from local negotiations of borders has the potential to result in a different kind of community, one not necessarily dominated by a single authority or group (Cuddy-Keane 1990, 280). This model is something that Butler suggests in *Bodies That Matter*, pointing to the necessity of 'establish[ing] a kind of political contestation that is not a "pure" opposition, a "transcendence" of contemporary relations of power, but a difficult labor of forging a future from resources inevitably impure' (1993, 241). Such an approach recognizes the provisionality of identity and of the social codes that affect individuals on an everyday basis.

The practical ramifications of these rewritten boundaries and of the kind of 'resistance and change' to which they lead (Henstra 2000, 144), however, seem rather vague. While this is perhaps inevitable, a view of relational and conditional identities as leading to productive engagements with authority becomes problematic in terms of Barnes's specific depictions of social relations. In *Nightwood* as well as in her other works, Barnes shows that occupying a marginalized position can be unnerving, for though it may enable sexual boundary-crossings, it also leaves the subject open to threat. For example, Matthew's cross-dressing sets the stage for his (unrealized) experience of sexuality the night that Nora comes to visit, but the incest, bestiality, and paedophilia intimated by the composite fairy-tale figure of the Wolf-as-Grandmother may not represent an equally enjoyable set of experiences. Further, while critics sympathize with and at times celebrate the transgendered bodies of Robin and Matthew, we are less willing to embrace the potential of Nazi sadism as a site of marginalized sexuality in *Nightwood*. The issue here is that power does not vanish in a liberal humanist approach, through which difference is kindly brought into the critical fold, nor does authority cease to exist when individuals engage in dialogic 'troublings' of boundaries.

We need to address the limitations of the alternative communities that appear in Barnes's work if we are to acknowledge the complexities of the spaces and subject positions that she depicts. Power is not immanent in the figure of the Wolf, nor is it exercised only by the Huntsman, and as commodity culture tells us, the difference between consumer and consumed is not always easy to pin down. Barnes shows us the politics of these overlapping positions, and of the margins within margins, which complicate a reading of resistance as opposition only. Marcus has outlined persuasively the larger political situation in which Barnes is writing, where the characters of *Nightwood* – 'Jews, homosexuals, lesbians, transvestites, gypsies, blacks, and circus performers – were all to perish in the Holocaust' (1991, 229). In *Nightwood*, however, fascism is only one of many ideologies, and the time is ripe for looking at how Barnes figures other forms of control.

Ladies Almanack and the Sexual Economics of Lesbos

The Vixen in the Coat of red,
The Hussy with the Honey Head,
Her frontal Bone soft lappéd up
With hempen Ringlets like the Tup,
The Doxy in the Vest of Kid
Rustling like the Katie-did,
With Panther's Eyen dark and wan,
And dovës Feet to walk upon.   Djuna Barnes, *Ladies Almanack*

Joseph Allen Boone proposes that, in '*Nightwood*, we *only* see a queer world, from which the status quo is entirely banished' (1998, 217). In his reading of Barnes's Left Bank, the traditional, heterosexual centre has been pushed to the margin: 'Barnes creates a *conceptual space* in which the normative becomes, for once in history, the excluded, the taboo, and the unmentionable [...] There is no 'mainstream' in this novel – or, rather, its social misfits and undesirables have *become* the mainstream' (235). Boone reads the novel, in which Barnes 'transposes those who generally exist on the margins (of society, of texts) to center stage' (235), as representing the 'world of carnival and circus' with its 'suspension of the rules of order and class' (235). The drawback to the reading is that carnival time is by definition a temporary state, and what we see in *Nightwood* is that the Law is not suspended indefinitely, but reasserted both overtly and covertly throughout the text. Felix's willingness to bow down to masculine authority figures – whether Nazi party members or members of the European aristocracy – indicates his investment in the rules of the mainstream. Similarly, though Matthew O'Connor occupies an eccentric position, his 'eternal fear of meeting with the law (he was not a licensed practitioner)' signals a very real anxiety about the regulations that officially govern medical practioners (D. Barnes 1937, 35). Robin is actually detained by the police in one of her movements through Paris, and the authority they possess is evident in the ways the officer gains sexual and legal control of her body: 'She put her head down on one of the officers' shoulders. She was drunk. He had her by her wrist, one hand on her behind' (144).

These moments in *Nightwood* demonstrate not the separation of two worlds, but their interpenetration, as they remain in a dynamic relationship of mutual influence. This means that both are implicated in the kinds of hierarchies that speak to the abuse or manipulation of authority. For example, while Matthew may fear the Law, he still draws upon its clout, calling himself 'Doctor' within the Left Bank community while practising his dubious medicine. Though Robin seems to be exploited by the police officers, she herself exploits Nora by alternately insulting and caressing her in 'Bow Down, Matthew,' and she is alternately caressed and physically assaulted by Nora in turn. In this sense, Boone's identification of *Nightwood* as 'queer' refers not only to the characters and their sexual preferences, but to the many different frames of reference by which they can be read. As Eve Kosofsky Sedgwick argues, the term 'queer' can encompass 'the open mesh of possibilities, gaps, overlaps, dissonances and resonances, lapses and excesses of meaning when the constituent elements of anyone's gender, of anyone's sexuality aren't made (or *can't* be made) to signify monolithically' (1993, 8). These 'gaps' and 'overlaps' signal the body's position in a complicated web of different kinds of societies. The 'excess' that results undercuts attempts to make sense of the characters and politics of *Nightwood*, or of any of the worlds that Barnes depicts.

Barnes's language is itself 'queer.' Words have multiple meanings that also overlap in incongruous ways. Her diction becomes a form of allusion, through which Barnes cites multiple definitions and contexts. Such levels of linguistic significance reflect the ideological encodings that accumulate to the gendered and sexed bodies in her texts. In *Ladies Almanack*, for instance, Barnes presents the flaps and folds of lesbian bodies, and draws from the discourses of fashion and literature to describe their anatomies: 'What they have in their Heads, Hearts, Stomachs, Pockets, Flaps, Tabs and Plackets, have one and all been some and severally commented on, by way of hint or harsh Harangue, praised, blamed, epicked, poemed and pastoraled, pamphleted, prodded and pushed, made a Spring-board for every sort of Conjecture whatsoever, good, bad and indifferent' (1928, 47–8). The clothes are the women and the women have become their clothes in this interpenetration of language and body. Stomachers, or the front panels of dresses, become the 'stomachs' that they cover; mouths become 'pockets'; vulvae become 'flaps and tabs'; 'plackets' or slits in women's garments seem to stand in for vaginas. Like Clarissa Dalloway, these female figures appear to have been sewn into linguistic identities, where fashion and literature are the textual systems that ostensibly constrain them. They are verbed to definition: 'praised, blamed, epicked, poemed and pastoraled, pamphleted, prodded and pushed.' But where the bodies are designated by their apparel and by their textual status, there is a disjunction between the women and the discursive garments that is foregrounded by the number of terms that Barnes uses here. Both the fashions and the terms that are intended to control the women are overpowered, as the epic list of words draws attention to its own artificiality, and consequently to the gap between the body and its social markings. The diction thus signals contradiction, as the language collapses under its own weight.

In *Ladies Almanack,* such lesbian bodies are subject not just to the culturally dominant figurations of women in fashion or fiction, but also to the authoritative discourses of their own communities. To apply Boone's reading of the world of *Nightwood* to *Ladies Almanack,* the politics of the margins becomes the politics of a different kind of mainstream, as the lesbian community is itself predicated upon a division between insiders and outsiders. Not surprisingly, the text is a roman-à-clef, written and illustrated by 'A Lady of Fashion,' published in a limited print run in 1928, and intended for a coterie audience consisting primarily of its real–life subjects (Herring 1995, 151). Its satire thus depends on the reader's insider knowledge as much as upon the author's ironic eye. The community in the novel is the lesbian salon of Dame Evangeline Musset, which echoes that of Natalie Barney, Barnes's friend and patron. The character's name symbolizes several strands of reference that Barnes explores in the text. A prodigious lover of women, Dame Musset seems to be associated with Alfred de Musset, a French Romantic who died of an unusual heart condition. Musset signifies the amorous nature of Barney herself, whose Sapphic community in the garden at 20 rue Jacob was both an artistic and a sexual retreat (Benstock 1986, 304). Alfred de Musset's famous affair with George Sand in the 1830s also seems significant, since her name plays into the kind of linguistic cross-dressing that Barnes revels in (Liukkonen 2000, par.1–

2). There are less complimentary associations with the word 'musset,' too. A musette is, for instance, a 'small bagpipe with bellows' (OED), which seems to suggest Barney's long-windedness. In the context of Barney's reputation as a sexual predator, the name recalls the character Musetta from Giacomo Puccini's opera *La Bohème*. The heterosexual bohemia that is the setting of the opera is replaced by Lesbos in the novel, and the coquette with a heart of gold becomes the femme with a large bank account. 'Evangeline' signals the evangelical zeal with which Dame Musset encourages the dissemination of lesbian passion (Kent 1993, 90), and it situates her as the new Eve, or the mother of a new sexual order. The possible reference to Henry Wadsworth Longfellow's poem may signal that lesbianism is a viable alternative to the frustrations of heterosexual love; it could also suggest that Evangeline Musset's mission may itself be ultimately frustrated. 'Dame' also invokes different cultural contexts, as the American slang term for a common woman is coupled with the British formal term for the female equivalent of the title 'Sir.' In the latter sense, Dame indicates Barney's social status and 'underscor[es] her generational claims, if not to a title, at least to wealth' (Jay 1990, 206). The word's derivation from the Latin *domina* or mistress is also significant, not only in terms of Barney's dominating personality but in terms of her promiscuity. Dame refers, of course, to the dame from the pantomime, which connects the excesses of Barnes's wordplay to fairy-tale transformations of identity. But references to the male actor in female drag and to the feminine Musetta who becomes (linguistically) the more masculine Musset signal that Barney is also a highly sexed figure herself.

Linguistic cross-dressing is linked to actual cross-dressing in Barnes's sustained description of Dame Musset: 'Evangeline Musset [...] had been developed in the Womb of her most gentle Mother to be a Boy, when therefore, she came forth an Inch or so less than this, she paid no Heed to the Error, but donning a Vest of a superb Blister and Tooling, a Belcher for tippet and a pair of hip-boots with a scarlet channel (for it was a most wet wading) she took her Whip in hand, calling her Pups about her, and so set out upon the Road of Destiny' (1928, 7). The 'gentle' maternal female figure is contrasted to the active and aggressive figure of the daughter, whose sexual status is stabilized by neither her clothes nor her body. Karla Jay suggests that Barnes deliberately and 'insulting[ly]' misrepresents the ultra-feminine Barney as a 'pseudo-man' in this passage according to stereotypes of lesbians as women who had 'unnaturally elongated clitorises' (1990, 207). Kathryn Kent, on the

other hand, argues that instead of a 'reinscription of sexology's stereotypes of lesbian penis envy,' Barney represents in this portrait 'Barnes's
appropriation of the phallic and a representation of possibilities for the
(re)productive power of lesbian desire' (1993, 92). The more general
point is that the lesbian or female body is here oversignified to the point
of irreducibility; or to borrow from Marina Warner's reading of multiple rewritings of popular fairy tales, 'the palimpsest becomes so dense
that the text beneath is obscured' (1994b, 15). Musset is another figuration of the hero/heroine of the fairy tale from *Nightwood*, 'the pretty lad
who is a girl' and 'the prince-princess in point lace – neither one and
half the other' (D. Barnes 1937, 136).

For Barnes, the cross-dressed body is not an easily interpreted text for
it invites the reader to consider its many possible and often incompatible meanings. Dame Musset (or rather, her genital area) is actually
described as a book: 'My Love she is an Old Girl, out of Fashion, Bugles
at the Bosom, and theredown a much Thumbed Mystery and a Maze'
(D. Barnes 1928, 15). The well-sexed and oft-bedded woman is, like the
fairy tale, a well- and oft-read text. Instead of being 'impaled,' the
woman has been 'Thumbed,' as Barnes links the experience of the lover
to the experience of the reader and the act of interpretation to the act of
sexual intercourse. But Barnes also explores the anxiety that reading
and loving involve, where the interpreter or sexual partner must figure
out not just the text or the body, but the past readings and beddings that
affect its reception: 'Shall one stumble on a Nuance that twenty Centuries have not pounced upon, yea worried and made a Kill of?' (15). Like
the stories 'our grandmothers were told' (D. Barnes 1937, 137), Dame
Musset's body seems to have been already permeated with meaning by
previous lovers, and the possibilities for new readings or sexual encounters are, in consequence, restricted. The book or body has already
been tamed, and as the narrator asks, 'Who can make a New Path
where there be no Wilderness?' (D. Barnes 1928, 15). However, just as
Matthew's doubled view of the fairy tale speaks to the reader's ability
to assert a supplementary meaning, it also shows the malleability of the
source text. So the body of Dame Musset confounds singular sexual
ownership or interpretation through her library-like circulation and
thus remains available for new readings.

Of course, such an accessible and open-ended position is easier to
enjoy when the body occupies a privileged class role. It is socioeconomic status that allows the subject to buy clothes; it is also socioeco-

nomic status that limits the subject's expression of his or her sexuality. Where Matthew's 'custom' (D. Barnes 1937, 80) is to dress like a man and to pass as a member of the heterosexual community, Dame Musset is able, like Natalie Barney, to pay 'no Heed to the Error' of her position by virtue of her fortune (D. Barnes 1928, 7). Natalie Barney's wealth in the 1920s has been estimated at between two and four million dollars (Jay 1990, 215). This gave her much personal latitude, especially since her financial freedom also entailed freedom from her family. When she was twenty-six her father died, leaving her in a financially stable and liberated position in Paris (Benstock 1986, 271). In contrast, as a writer without a wealthy family to draw upon for support, 'Barnes had to consider the financial repercussions of adopting a fully alternative lifestyle' (Elliott and Wallace 1994, 137). Janet Flanner, who was in a position similar to Barnes's, avoided potential problems by keeping her 'private life separated from her public career during her own lifetime,' a split in identity that her journalistic tag, Genêt, demonstrates (Benstock 1986, 115). In *Ladies Almanack,* Flanner appears with Solita Solano under another pseudonym as the pair 'Nip and Tuck,' and was one of many expatriates who took advantage of what the lesbian communities in Paris had to offer (Herring 1995, 154). Barnes, Barney, and others were lured to Paris not only because of its rich cultural history but also because homosexuality was not illegal in France. As William Wiser points out, 'Homosexual exile in Paris was a tradition that might extend from Oscar Wilde at the turn of the century to his granddaughter [*sic*] Dolly Wilde in the 1920s' (1983, 21).[6] The financial appeal of Paris was perhaps equally tempting for Barnes. The American dollar was much stronger than the French franc at this time: in 1920, one American dollar was worth 27 francs (the equivalent of a month's supply of bread), and by 1924, 50 francs (Wiser 1983, 29). For a woman who made her money by working as a journalist through the 1920s, and who depended upon book sales and patrons to support her from the 1930s and after, buying power must have been a factor in Barnes's decision to become part of the Left Bank society.

Barnes's financial situation informs not only the production of *Ladies Almanack,* the profits of which went to pay for her partner Thelma Wood's medical bills (Herring 1995, 151), but also the satirical tone of the book. Her relationship with Barney and with Barney's *Académie des Femmes* was, like most of Barnes's relationships, characterized by a certain ambivalence.[7] Jay suggests that, amidst the wealth of Barney's

Lesbos, Barnes 'was perpetually placed in the role of the beggar at the feast, the celebrant in the borrowed gown, the one to partake of others' hospitality without being able to return it in kind' (1990, 205). And while Shari Benstock argues that 'Woman's body – which has been made the vehicle by which man satiates his lust – is returned to woman's control' in *Ladies Almanack* (1986, 250), Barnes suggests that other forms of control still exist in relationships between women. Financial need leads to a sense of economic subservience, and Barnes depended upon the inherited money of Peggy Guggenheim and Natalie Barney for most of her life. The fortunes with which these women supported Barnes came, however, from their fathers. Where the daughters live upon the profits of the patriarchs, the artists in turn live upon the inheritances of the daughters.[8] The history of the money shows how an inheritance can be manipulated to move well beyond the original value of the estate. *Ladies Almanack* represents not the heir's negotiation of a legacy, however, but Barnes's negotiations with Barney's sexual prowess, social persona, and most of all, her financial power. Barney is the muse who inspires the project and the main subject of the text, but she is also the patron who funds the artist and the mistress of a community that operates according to her rules.

The 'February' section of *Ladies Almanack* indicates most overtly the tensions that arise from Barnes's position in Barney's Lesbos. The narrator of the chapter is the new lover of the older woman, and realizes that she 'has nothing original except her words to give the legendary lover Dame Musset' (Lanser 1991, 165). The anxiety here is both sexual and artistic, where the subordinate figure of the speaker must find a different way of celebrating her 'sainted' lover (D. Barnes 1928, 14). The anxiety is also financial: 'Will she unpack her Panels for such a Stale Receipt, pour out her Treasures for a coin worn thin?' (15–17). The dynamics of the relationship are explored by Barnes through an allusion to 'Cinderella,' a fairy tale in which sexuality and gender are deeply tied to class and money. Barnes places Dame Musset, or Natalie Barney, in the role of the Fairy Godmother to whom she, as Cinderella, cannot give a gift in recompense, in gratitude, or in an assertion of equality. Her alternative is, at first, abjection: 'As it is, shall I not pour ashes upon my Head, gird me in Sackcloth, covering my Nothing and Despair under a Mountain of Cinders, and thus become a Monument to No-Ability for her sake?' (17). The speaker denigrates herself by becoming the Cinderella in the ashes, against whom the greatness of Dame Musset is contrasted. The fairy tale intertext suggests, however, that

Musset's authority rests on her economic clout, and that while the debasement of the narrator/Cinder-slut is a symptom of that control, the artist herself can draw upon alternative-sites of power.

Indeed, in the next paragraph the speaker redefines their relationship by manipulating the language in which she describes her patron: 'Verily, I shall place me before her Door, and when she cometh forth I shall think she has left her Feet inward upon the Sill and when she enters in, I shall dream her Hands be yet outward upon the Door – for therein is no way for me, and Fancy is my only Craft' (17). When Dame Musset leaves her house, the speaker will think of her as still being inside; when Musset enters in again, the speaker will see her as being without. This semantic transformation of Barney's physical position is made more significant by the speaker's emphasis on Musset's feet. Where in the first paragraph the speaker occupies the position of Cinderella to Musset's Godmother, here Musset is a kind of Cinderella who relies upon the speaker's linguistic magic to be transformed into art. The assertion that 'Fancy is my only Craft' is not just a testament to the imaginative fruits enabled by Dame Musset's patronage, then, but also a statement of the speaker's control of the text. She places the relationship in the context of a different and literary economy.[9] In essence, the author bites 'the very hands that brought *Ladies Almanack* into existence' (Jay 1990, 205), signalling both her reliance upon and resistance to Barney's financial and sexual authority.

'Cinderella' is thus refigured according to its new Parisian context. Where Perrault's heroine desires to enter into the heterosexual, aristocratic economy of the Prince's ball through her use of ideal fashion and class behaviours, Barnes's heroine is reluctant to pay the price that the Fairy Godmother asks for accessing the lesbian, aristocratic economy of Barney's salon. The political dynamics here have less to do with patriarchy and the subject's desire for male approval and more to do with the economic and social politics of Barnes's Left Bank society. Relationships within this community are created not just in accordance with or in opposition to the mainstream, then, but arise also from interactions between variously gendered, sexed, and financed bodies. Though Barnes is the scribe who depends upon the aristocratic Dame Musset to survive in Paris, out of her dependence she is able to create an independent text that critiques the lesbian society at the same time that it celebrates it. The overlapping identities and roles that such art reflects indicate the complexity of power as well as the opportunities for resistance that attend the circulation of the subject in any community.

Families, Fairy Tales, and Zadel Barnes

There in my sleep was my grandmother, whom I loved more than anyone, tangled in the grave grass, and flowers blowing about and between her; lying there in the grave, in the forest, in a coffin of glass, and flying low, my father who is still living; low going and into the grave beside her, his head thrown back and his curls lying out, struggling with her death terribly, and me, stepping about its edges, walking and wailing without a sound.

Djuna Barnes, *Nightwood*

In texts such as *Nightwood* and *Ladies Almanack*, Barnes depicts the shifting nature and local exercise of power, but certainly not its absence. Just as Dame Musset's name and clothed body produce a range of possible meanings, she also represents a range of authoritative positions in *Ladies Almanack*, which, though too complicated to be overturned, may be critiqued. Like Matthew and his interpretations of fairy tales, the reader has the ability to rework ideologically encoded texts and bodies, but it is a daunting task. As he says in *Nightwood*, 'Man has no foothold that is not also a bargain. So be it!' (D. Barnes 1937, 32). There is no one perspective or reading to be rejected or accepted in Barnes's work; instead, communities are depicted as having the potential to be both useful and hostile for the subjects involved. This is what Nora realizes in her sudden rereading of 'Little Red Riding Hood.' As she finds upon encountering Matthew, his largely enabling form of drag combines sexual pleasure and sexual threat. Perrault warns his readers that the Wolf is seductive but also rapacious; Bettelheim's Freudian reading suggests that the Wolf represents the 'dangers of overwhelming oedipal feelings' (1975, 178). Frightening as well as compelling, the Wolf exceeds the boundaries of the villain category, and it is his ambiguity that Barnes depicts through Nora's epiphanic statement, itself an ambivalent insight.

The danger and the allure that the Wolf represents stem in large part from his imitation of the Grandmother's role. In an echo of the power and appeal of Dame Musset, the Wolf combines his own charisma with the elder figure's authority, and Red Riding Hood is lured into bed through this trickster's voice:

'Put the cake and the little pot of butter on the bin,' he said, 'and come up on the bed with me.'
    Little Red Riding Hood took off her clothes, but when she climbed up

on the bed she was astonished to see how her grandmother looked in her nightgown. (Perrault 1969, 28)

That the seduction is carried out by a version of the Grandmother indicates the disturbing implications of border-crossings, where Matthew's sexuality is coupled with the Grandmother's control. Indeed, the boundary between the Wolf and the Grandmother is virtually imperceptible in *Nightwood*, especially in the context of Nora's dreams of her grandmother. In the first dream, Nora attempts to enter her grandmother's bedchamber 'knowing that it was impossible because the room was taboo' (D. Barnes 1937, 62). When Nora does find the older woman, whether in the dream or in an associated memory, the grandmother is playing the cross-dressed role of the Wolf: 'the grandmother who, for some unknown reason, was dressed as a man [...] her arms spread saying with a leer of love, "My little sweetheart!"' (63). In Nora's second dream, she sees her grandmother 'lying there in the grave, in the forest, in a coffin of glass' (149). Here, 'Snow White' is the source text, but again identities become conflated. In the first scene, as in the image of the Wolf-as-Grandmother, the figure's simultaneous citation of masculinity and femininity both fascinates and frightens the granddaughter. In the second scene, the figure's bridging of death and life prompts Nora's interpretative confusion. In both, a taboo frustrates a connection between the two women – whether the taboo of incest or death – and prevents the child from acting upon what she 'like[s]': though the girl wants her grandmother, or rather, a version of the grandmother, she cannot 'tell' it – enunciate, distinguish, determine, or understand it – because that desire has been foreclosed.

The incestuous implications of Red Riding Hood and the Wolf-as-Grandmother in bed, and the incestuous connotations of Nora's second dream in which the granddaughter seems to be a Prince waiting at the edge of the grave to kiss her Snow White-Grandmother back to life (Marcus 1991, 244), become increasingly fraught in the context of Djuna Barnes's relationship with her paternal grandmother, Zadel Barnes Budington Gustafson. The organization of Barnes's highly unconventional family, and the sexual dynamics that characterize the bond between Zadel and Djuna in particular, have been explored in recent biographies of Barnes and biographical interpretations of her works. It is difficult to ascertain, however, the limits and ramifications of their relationship. Anne Dalton, for instance, reads Zadel's correspondence with Djuna as evidence of abuse and sexual exploitation, especially the letters that express Zadel's 'erotic desire for her granddaughter' and make detailed references 'to past sexual encounters between them' (1993, 121). These letters include drawings of the women's breasts and genitals, and depictions of the women hugging, kissing, and tumbling each other. Bonnie Kime Scott interprets this material to suggest that Barnes's 'first experience of physical love may have been with her grandmother' (1995, 1:16–17). But in light of Djuna's troubled relationship with her apparently abusive father, Mary Lynn Broe argues that the correspondence asserts 'a law and a vocabulary of female desire' that was enabling rather than damaging (1989, 54). Alternatively, Philip Herring sees the often absurd images and playful language of the missives as forms of 'bawdy entertainment by two women who happened to share a bed, as everybody in the family seemed to do in their small farmhouse on Long Island' (1993, 112). The grandmother occupies a number of different roles here, and while the letters can be read through a family language of earthy humour and openness about the body, the family is still headed by the matriarch. Her role in the household indicates the unequal ground upon which such exchanges may have taken place. In this context, the Grandmother becomes a Wolf, and the girl who is Red Riding Hood must find ways to cope with her seductive authority.

Zadel Barnes's sexual and familial position is further complicated by the influence she exerts as an author and as 'the primary literary model for Djuna' (B. Scott 1995, 1:16). Interestingly, among other narratives, Zadel wrote and published fairy-tale fantasies, including a story called 'The Children's Night,' which appeared in *Harper's New Monthly Magazine* in 1875. For Broe, Zadel's stories indicate the grandmother's embodiment of both mothering and writing, and the fairy tales with which Zadel is associated – 'those old wives' tales that celebrated matriarchal societies before the DWEMS (Dead White European Male Scholars) got hold of them' – signal a women's oral cultural tradition in which Djuna participates (1989, 54). Shari Benstock celebrates Zadel's power as a storyteller too, and reads Matthew as Barnes's ironic figuration of the misappropriation of woman's voice: 'Playing the grandmother, bewigged and rouged, Matthew O'Connor parodies woman's language, steals her stories and her images in order to teach her about herself' (1986, 266). But the grandmother is also cross-dressed in *Nightwood*, and if Zadel's fairy tales or fantasies are drawn upon and renegotiated in Barnes's modernist works, so too is the voice of the Mother Goose figure. Indeed, in her contiguity with the Wolf, the storytelling Grandmother is a dangerous if compelling figure who has the ability to manipulate the child. In this sense, Barnes's writing and refiguring of the Grandmother through fairy tales has, perhaps, less to do with her desire to assert a woman's voice in a patriarchal world and more to do with her desire to assert her narrative control over her family's past. By placing her grandmother in the context of fairy tales, Barnes rewrites or re-presents not just the texts but the voice and body of the precursor who also drew upon them. Barnes's use of fairy tales is thus a response to Zadel's authority as a grandmother and as a storyteller.

In *Ryder* and in *The Antiphon,* the Grandmother figure signals both the positive and the highly disturbing aspects of Barnes's upbringing in rural New York. The Barnes family's unconventional views of sexuality stemmed largely from Zadel, who was the matriarch and main source of income for the family (Dalton 1993, 119). The Barneses lived initially in Cornwall-on-Hudson at Storm King, a farm owned by Zadel's second son, Justin Budington. She and Justin supported her first son, Djuna's father Wald Barnes (one of several names he used through his life). He met Djuna's mother, Elizabeth Chappell, in London through Zadel, and married her in New York in 1889. By 1897, Elizabeth Frances Faulkner Clark, or Fanny, had joined the family as Wald's mistress, also by Zadel's invitation (Herring 1995, 29). Djuna Barnes grew up, then, in a family that was funded by Zadel, run by Wald and his wife and mistress, and peopled by the eight children that resulted from the marital and extramarital relationships. When the log cabin was no longer big enough for them all, the family moved to New York, and by 1902, to a farm in Huntington, Long Island, where Barnes spent her teenage years (36). By 1912, however, the household was under financial and familial stresses that could no longer be contained, and it appears that with the urging of Zadel, Wald chose to retain his mistress rather than his wife. Elizabeth filed for divorce in July of 1912, and moved to New York with her daughter Djuna and three of her sons – Zendon, Saxon, and Shangar (Thurn was living on his own at the time; 40–1). Djuna thus began her writing career in earnest at the age of twenty in order to support her mother and siblings through her journalism. Barnes was not just 'empowered by her grandmother's words' to become a reporter (Broe 1989, 55), then, but also by the aging woman's inability to support her financially.

Zadel actively encouraged Barnes's literary pursuits, however, by establishing a household centred upon the arts. She was a journalist, an interviewer, a novelist, a poet, a short-story writer, a spiritualist, a teacher, and a political critic. She had connections to many prominent

Americans, including Henry Wadsworth Longfellow, John D. Rockefeller, Abraham Lincoln, and John Greenleaf Whittier (Herring 1995, 8). In 1880 she was sent to London by *McCall's*, a magazine that Barnes would write for in the Paris of the 1920s, and she met many well-known British figures too, including Lady Speranza Wilde (Herring 1995, 12). It was this atmosphere of culture and literature that she brought back to New York and that influenced Barnes's early reading and writing. In a list that was vetted by Djuna, James Scott indicates the range of texts and authors to which she was exposed. Zadel's fireside readings included the works of Charles Dickens, George Eliot, Edgar Allan Poe, Shakespeare, and Barnes's personal favourite, Geoffrey Chaucer. Fairy tales that were read included works by Lewis Carroll, the Grimms, Mother Goose, and Hans Christian Andersen (38). Andrew Field indicates that William Makepeace Thackeray's *The Rose and the Ring* was read to her as well, and that Wald was interested in Rudyard Kipling's children's stories (1983, 175). Since none of the children went to school, these texts and the lessons provided by Zadel, Wald, and Elizabeth represented all the formal education that Barnes would receive, aside from her later attendance at the 'Pratt Institute and at the Art Students League' (J. Scott 1976, 16).

Zadel also had a formative influence on Barnes's sense of sexuality. Having divorced her first husband Henry Budington in 1877, she married Axel Carl Johan Gustafson soon after. She separated from Gustafson in 1890, apparently having carried on a number of extramarital affairs for many years. Zadel shared with her son a 'free-love philosophy' (Herring 1995, 19): if Wald 'made what amounted to a religious cult out of sex' (Hanscombe and Smyers 1987, 87), he was encouraged in it by his mother, who had been exposed in London to the theory that 'love was sufficient grounds for sexual involvement, and [...] that both prostitution and the oppression of women would end if polygamy became widespread' (Herring 1993, 110). Djuna's own experiences were as extensive as her father's and grandmother's, and her disregard for social or sexual categories characterized her personal relationships as well as her writing (see Wittig 1992, 61). Barnes lived with several men, including Courtney Lemon in the late 1910s and Charles Henri Ford in the early 1930s. She also lived with women, most famously with Thelma Wood in the 1920s. By her own reckoning, Barnes had literally dozens of lovers including Marsden Hartley, Jane Heap, Laurence Vail, and Horace Liveright (Hanscombe and Smyers 1987, 93–4). Her open attitude towards sex, at least earlier in her life, was determined in great part by the openness with which the body was treated in her extended family.

The effects of Barnes's upbringing are complicated, since the family was itself implicated in a range of power struggles – financial, generational, social, political, and sexual – that are difficult to unweave. Control was exerted by the grandmother, the father, the wife, the live-in mistress, the eight children, the father's numerous sexual partners, and the larger community from which the Barneses separated themselves. In *Ryder,* which was first published in 1928, the characters are constantly dealing with these varied forms of authority. Wendell Ryder's patriarchy is thus one of many kinds of power in the text that are exerted not only within the family but without, and different masculine and feminine systems challenge its primacy. In this sense, *Ryder* is less a parody of the Father's position, or a 'mockery of the patriarch (and his discourse)' (Stevenson 1991, 82), and more an exploration of the complicated dynamics that inform any exercise of control. For instance, Father Lucas, representing the patriarchy of the church, does not enforce the tenets of Catholicism in the confessional with Matthew but instead (and perhaps innocently) invokes a personal relationship that challenges gender boundaries: 'Go, my daughter, he says, and love thy fellowmen' (D. Barnes 1995, 137). Dr Matthew O'Connor, representing the authority of the male-dominated medical profession, exceeds, as we know from *Nightwood,* the masculine social position that Amelia Ryder would knit for him: '"Matthew, it's time that you were assisting at the birth of your own, for never saw I such a man for loving-kindness, and such a way with little things. So if some good, strong woman ..." But she got no further, for Dr. Matthew O'Connor had burst into tears' (124). Even when Ryder, the Fathering Phallus himself, invokes laws based on patriarchal constructs, such as the authority that paternity grants, they are rendered uninterpretable by other characters' references to additional forms of authority. When Ryder asserts his claim to the child of a pregnant dog breeder, Molly Dance counters his declaration of fatherhood with a suggestion of uncertainty: 'how shall she, or I, or you, or another know but that Dan, the corner policeman, be he?' (199). Her sexual experiences with a number of other men complicate Wendell's patriarchal claims. In another scenario, when Ryder beds Lady Terrence and asks what name the resulting child will assume, he is again struck silent by the woman's answer: 'Nothing and Never [...] He shall accomplish all the others leave undone. You need No Child also, my good man, all fathers have one. On him you shall hang that part of your ambition too heavy for mortal' (211). In this way too does the woman's knowledge – not of men here but of mortality – undermine the assertion of the father's name.

Barnes also shows that patriarchy is itself a heterogeneous and complicated system. Though Wendell Ryder is a father, he refuses to follow a variety of patriarchal rules: he rejects monogamy, he rejects the church, he rejects formal education, and he rejects expectations that he will hold down a job outside the house. Instead, he includes his mistress and her children openly in his life, forms his own religion, teaches his own children, and relies on his mother, wife, and mistress for economic support. Ryder, like the Circean Bloom, is a highly uncertain figure. He spreads joy and semen throughout the countryside, as a good picaro would, but as a child he has 'a body like a girl's' (17), as an adult he cries with his 'tears streaming like a woman's' (122), and on his deathbed he says that he will 'die like a child, most terribly frightened' (204). Though Wendell's role as a father is attested to by his wife, mistress, and children, his masculinity is undercut by his emotions, by the women who assert a different kind of authority, and by a mainstream patriarchy that sees his unruly sexuality as offending the letter and spirit of the law. The result is that his body is forcibly marked, restricted, and punished by the larger authority: 'the mayor said, gallantly enough, that Wendell should go to jail, felt boots and all; the school authorities said, still more gallantly, that unless the various children now living on what was known as 'Bulls'-Ease' farm did not attend school, it would be not only much worse for them, but for their parents, *whoever* they were!' (213). Ultimately, he is forced by these authorities to choose between his wife and mistress. But again, he rejects mainstream morality and chooses his mistress over his wife. *Ryder* is a critique of patriarchal systems, then, but Barnes indicates patriarchy's own complexities and possibilities, and its demands not just on women, children, lesbians, and homosexuals, but on fathers too.

Like the household of Wendell Ryder, the Barnes family was dominated by a father and his mother who challenged social expectations. Nevertheless, the unconventionality of the family dynamic was not just empowering in its distance from the mainstream, it was also at times highly disturbing. Anne Dalton suggests that the Barnes family operated according to a philosophy of free love and polygamy, which resulted in the systemic abuse of the children: 'the father isolated them from outside influences, intensifying the effect of his self-aggrandizement as prophet, his physical and sexual abuse, and both parents' inability to provide material security. The mother's acquiescence in face of these dynamics, and the grandmother's sanctioning of the father's practices through her economic and emotional support of him, left the children remarkably vulnerable to the father's power' (1993, 120). To contextualize this statement, we can look at biographies of Barnes, which point consistently to her traumatic relationship with her father. Here, Barnes fiction seems to connect to Barnes fact, though there are complexities introduced by the range of narratives that biographers can draw upon, which have been at times censored or altered or destroyed by Barnes herself. Nonetheless, incest haunts most representations of Barnes's childhood, whether it is expressed in her comments to friends, in letters, in interviews, or in her works of fiction.

The most dramatic version of a crucial scene of abuse from Barnes's life occurs in a draft of her play of 1958, *The Antiphon*, in which Titus Hobbs, the father figure, attempts to rape his daughter, Miranda. When she beats him off, 'Titus binds her up like a side of beef and hoists her up to hang from a rafter in the barn while he goes off to barter her virginity for a goat among the local men' (Field 1983, 193). Broe characterizes this scene as a realistic portrayal of Barnes's 'father's attempted rape, his "virginal sacrifice" of the daughter, then his brutal barter of his daughter-bride' (1989, 56). Field suggests that Djuna was 'not exactly seduced or raped but rather "given" sexually by her father like an Old Testament slave or daughter' to another man (1983, 43). Philip Herring summarizes with some skill the various strands of these narratives of sexual abuse:

> Convinced that sex was beautiful, Djuna allowed herself to be manipulated into a humiliating sexual encounter when Wald arranged for a man down the road to take her virginity [...].
>
> One might easily conclude that in Barnes's own life the man was Percy Faulkner, Fanny's brother, but Faulkner apparently claimed that there was no blood on their 'wedding night,' which supports the theory that another man (either Wald or his surrogate) earlier took her virginity. Despite the confusion, Barnes seems to be saying that whether her father enjoyed incest directly or vicariously, he bears equal moral blame. It would be hard to disagree. (1995, 268–9)[10]

It is redundant here to state that Barnes was involved in a deeply disturbing situation based on family sexual politics and subversive border-crossings. As Broe states, in cases of incest, 'Boundaries are transgressed; the duty to protect and the right to use get irrevocably confused' (1989, 48). Such abuses indicate the threat that any community, marginal or mainstream, poses to the subject, and especially to the child, whose agency is the most limited.

This central episode from Barnes's life and fiction represents a rather different interpretation of the carnivalesque, then, especially as the Rabelaisian world is depicted in *The Antiphon*. As the title suggests, Barnes's play is based upon a range of voices and thus perspectives, when a fragmented family gathers on the eve of World War II to revisit various traumas. The father has died, and his Law is becoming the Law of the Lords of Misrule. The play is rife with figurations of the carnival, the stage, the circus, the masquerade ball, the fairy tale, and, as Andrew Field suggests, 'the modern pantomime' (1983, 224). When the main character, Miranda, is 'playfully' attacked by her two brothers, for instance, they are wearing costumes: 'DUDLEY *donning a pig's mask,* ELISHA *an ass's, as if the playthings would make them anonymous*' (D. Barnes 1962, 175). The brothers here participate in an enabling adoption of disguise through which they can express their childish selves and in turn repress their worldly roles as businessmen. In this carnival, the sister represents the norm that is abjected, since she is the successful writer who has marginalized her brothers, or has refused to be judged by them or 'clapped between the palms of their approval' (177). But it becomes unclear whether Dudley is the pig in revolt against Miranda's Wolf-like power in the family – 'Who's afraid?' – or if he is the Wolf dressed as the pig who will destroy Miranda – 'I'll huff, and I'll puff, and I'll blow your house down!' (176, 175). Like the trickster figure Jack, who turns out to be their brother Jeremy in disguise, all the family members are transformed in the play, both to escape the control of others and to assert the authority of their own liberated voices.

In the masking of identities and in the transformation of bodies and roles according to the fairy tales, however, the threatening aspects of both the stories and the brothers' manipulations of the Law come to light. Dudley is both the prey and the predator from 'The Three Little Pigs,' and his shifting position allows him to mock and exploit his sister in a temporary exercise of power that is masked as play. Similarly, Elisha is the Ogre from 'Jack in the Beanstalk' who both kills and is killed: 'Fe-fo-fi-fum – I smell the blood of an Englishman!' (D. Barnes 1962, 152). The intertexts' depictions of wealth, property, and unlawful greed seem to connect to the careers of the two brothers, merchants who dismiss Miranda's socioeconomic position – 'Aristocrat, pauper, artist, beggar!' (178) – and attempt to swindle their mother (220–1). Their consumption of money and their misuse of wealth become gradually associated with their father Titus's sexual consumption and misuse of women. 'Little Red Riding Hood' is invoked as a composite metaphor for one of Titus's many mistresses, Juliette of Camberwell: 'Wolfed in fire even to galoshes: / All in scarlet, like a Cardinal, / A cherry ribbon 'round her neck, as murdered' (157). This dense description plays with the sexual subtext, didacticism, and violence of the fairy-tale source. In a disturbing combination of fragmented roles, the woman is characterized as both a prostitute and a religious symbol. Though she is a sexual predator or Wolf, the red choker suggests that she is also a sacrificial lamb, punished by strangulation or by having her throat slit. 'Wolfed in fire,' her body is burned at the stake; perhaps she has been impaled upon Titus, destroyed or 'Wolfed' by him, or by the larger society, which has punished her for her sexuality. Regardless, she has been left for this family or pack of wolves, who literally tear her identity apart in a retrospective assertion of control.

Barnes uses fairy tales in *The Antiphon* to point out the limits of 'what our grandmothers were told love was' (1937, 137), and to expose the truth of Titus's rather brutal husbandhood. However, the mother of the adult children and the widow of Titus is still stuck on the lessons of the fairy-tale primers and refuses to acknowledge that such romance stories 'never came to be' in the context of her marriage (137). In Act III, Augusta looks to fairy tales as escapist fantasies and refuses Miranda's attempts to help her confront a realistic vision of the family's traumatic past and of the mother's own complicity:

> [*Thinking herself into fairy-tales and legends*]
> Was I ever a princess in a legend?
>   [*Whispers*]
> *Did I sleep a hundred years?*
> [...]
>   [*In a frantic whisper*]
> *Was I stolen?* (D. Barnes 1962, 199–200)

Augusta's memories of the past are covered over or repressed by idealistic interpretations of 'Cinderella' and 'Sleeping Beauty,' in which female figures – changelings or captives – are returned from exile and restored to favour by the actions of a noble Prince. The mother thus replaces the truth of her marriage with the ideals of the stories, invoking a view of Titus and of herself that the rest of the family exposes as a fantasy. Though she assumes the innocent and passive role, she has been an active agent in her husband's abuse of their daughter; indeed, Miranda seems to associate her mother and not Titus with Bluebeard: 'Dearest, worst and sorriest, had been a man / You'd been the bloodiest villain of us all' (201). Again, fairy tales become palimpsests in Barnes's work, testifying to the agency of the different readers but also to the entangling of different interpretations. Where the children expose the brutal and disturbing realities of the family's past through the tales, Augusta embraces them as utopian figurations of love. For the mother, these living lies are the alternatives to guilt.

The Antiphon revolves around struggles over the story of the family, where different interpretations represent conflicting exercises of narrative control. The figure of Victoria, Miranda's grandmother, is at the centre of such expressions of authority and symbolizes the family's most powerful speaker. Although it is never directly represented, the grandmother's voice resonates in *The Antiphon*. For Augusta, the daughter-in-law, Victoria's appeal is sexual as well as oral; indeed, Victoria, perhaps even more than her son Titus, has been the seducer of the young Augusta: 'She had my purse, my person, and my trust / In one scant hour' (D. Barnes 1962, 154). While Victoria corresponds to the comforting figure of Mother Goose, her 'ready and [...] milking tongue' also recalls the seductive tale-telling of the Wolf (154). Victoria is another alluring and controlling presence who echoes Zadel Barnes's own force as both a grandmother and a writer.

Barnes works through Zadel's influence in the fictional characters of Victoria, Sophia Ryder, and Nora's grandmother, but also in allusions to texts that her precursor drew upon in her own fiction, and these include fairy tales. Zadel's story 'The Children's Night' is based upon a number of traditional stories from Perrault and the Grimms. By incorporating the tales into her own texts, Barnes draws upon her grandmother's example but asserts a subsequent authority over both the tales and their teller. In this sense, Barnes is continuing the tradition of 'The Children's Night,' though in a rather different form and to different ends. The central relationship in Zadel's story features a maternal figure who is the speaker and a daughter who is the subject of the tale. The hierarchy of adult and child is echoed in the binary relationships between writer and reader, and author and audience, that Zadel reinforces by taking the role of Mother Goose. It is her assertion of authorial control that Djuna Barnes plays with in her own engagement with fairy tales, where the writer's presence becomes less stable and reliable.

'The Children's Night' takes place on Christmas Eve. In the tradition of the Christmas pantomime, the story features a range of characters drawn from fairy tales as well as from nursery rhymes, the *Arabian Nights*, 'Babes in the Woods,' and 'Undine.' The child's exploration of Fairyland is witnessed and written down by the maternal figure, who is the story's narrator. The text becomes 'the mother's gift to her young daughter,' as the girl is given the book on Christmas Day (B. Scott 1995, 2:75). But such a gift entails an assertion of parental authority as well as of love, and the relationship is characterized by the kind of power dynamics that surround Dame Musset in *Ladies Almanack*. The opening lines of the text, for instance, indicate the narrator's concern for the girl, but also reassert the differences in their positions that stem from age and experience. By emphasizing the purity and innocence of the unknowing and ignorant child, she establishes her own more knowledgeable position: 'My Liebling's trustful prayers were said, / She lay at peace in her guileless bed' (Z. Barnes 1875, 153). Downstairs, as the speaker sits by the fire and sews, a figure enters the house and calls to the sleeping girl to prepare for Cinderella's ball (153). The 'Children's Night' is a carnival in which the laws of Fairyland take precedence, and where characters from bedtime stories come to life for the child's enjoyment. But in a sense, the experience of the ball is a metaphor for the experience of the story itself, where the magic is really the parent's imaginative abilities. This is a world created by the adult and controlled by her, though the subject and active participant of the story is the child.

Thus the child takes centre stage, representing the focus of the text and dominating the action to which the narrator is only the witness. For instance, the speaker depicts herself as the passive audience while her Liebling, or dear one, dresses for the Fairyland party:

Soft bosom and arm and pearl-white side
Shone where her night-dress parted wide.
Cinderella kissed the rose-leaf cheek,
And the parted lips that they might speak,

And the lidded eyes that they might see;
Then Liebling laughed, and the laugh was glee;
And 'Tell me, Cinderella,' she cried,
'Shall I wear glass shoes, and be Prince's bride?' (Z. Barnes 1875, 154)

This loving description nevertheless indicates the larger impulses – adult, narrative, gendered, classed – in which the child is enmeshed. While Cinderella's kisses may be chaste and playful, they still partake of a Victorian fetishization of the young girl. The nightgown, the lips, and the eyes are 'parted' in a rather erotic figuration of a body that is ready to be penetrated. Indeed, the girl is pierced with the ideology of fashion in this scene, which is associated with wealth as well as with sexuality. By the end of the costuming, the girl is 'brightly dressed, / In dainty robes as were ever planned / By the head modiste of Fairy-land' (154). The girl has become a debutante, judged approvingly by the speaker's eyes and words, and ready to enter into the aristocratic marriage market represented by the ball.

Zadel Barnes draws upon the plots of traditional fairy-tale narratives here that her audience would already be familiar with. Moreover, she demonstrates how children imaginatively participate in the stories they read: the young girl identifies so strongly with depictions of Cinderella's transformation that she actually transforms herself in this scene and becomes Cinderella. The power of the child and of the process of reading is obvious, but it does not replace or overshadow the power of the adult narrator. While there is an emphasis in the story on children acting like children, playing with dolls and giving squirrels nuts to eat (1875, 155), there is an equally sustained emphasis on the heterosexual politics found in Perrault and the Grimms. Marriage and sexual marketing crop up consistently in the story, especially when the Prince makes an appearance and tells all that '"Cinderella is our bride; / But" – and he smiled like a prince upon her – / "Liebling is chosen first Maid of Honor"' (158). The authority of the Prince over this girl, the girl's authority over other girls, the authority of the writer over the reader, and the authority of the adult over the child are reasserted in a hierarchical arrangement of gendered, classed, and generational roles. Even the Liebling's reception of her present is scripted according to the adult narrative of Christmas, here spoken by Kris Kringle:

'For little Liebling, in cloth of gold,
A wonderful book, in which is told –
But locked, my dears, till the morrow's light –
The history of the Children's Night.' (164)

The story represents a performative speech act, a 'practice that enacts or produces that which it names,' and that signifies the authority of the speaker (Butler 1993, 13). The Christmas present, and the ritual of Christmas in which it is presented, is controlled by the adult, who has put into action the words she has spoken.

To paraphrase Matthew, this 'wonderful book' represents the stories through which Barnes's grandmother was told what love was. However, the combination of sources and layers of control in 'The Children's Night' emphasize the dominance of Zadel Barnes, who retells the tales in her own way. Djuna Barnes thus becomes the writer who inherits this power, re-presenting not only the fairy tales but the image of the storyteller. In one sense, Barnes's allusions to and reworkings of fairy tales seem to indicate the command that the granddaughter finally has over the traditional stories and the grandmother who has told them. But on another level, the source texts themselves invoke multiple interpretations and tellings, and make overt the fiction that is narrative authority.

Nora's dreams in *Nightwood* seem to play with the ramifications of the fairy tale's palimpsestic nature, where no single version of the tale or of the Grandmother exerts a final authority. In Nora's first dream, for instance, the older woman appears leering and in drag, 'wearing a billycock and a corked moustache, ridiculous and plump in tight trousers and a red waistcoat' (D. Barnes 1937, 63). The disturbing sexual subtext of the image recalls the Grandmother-as-Wolf and the physical and emotional intimacy of Zadel and Djuna, who called her grandmother her 'first love' (Herring 1995, 22). The cross-dressed figure is also a symbol of mastery, as she is dressed as a kind of military commander or circus ringmaster. But at the same time that the image indicates Zadel's very real status in the family, the home is depicted as a kind of chaotic circus, and the ringmaster becomes a figure of fun, both outrageous and laughable, engaging and enjoyable for the granddaughter who 'loved' her grandmother 'more than anyone' (D. Barnes 1937, 148). In this sense, Barnes is parodying the Grandmother's power, playing with it just as she plays with the Grandmother's voice and image in her texts. The older woman is a 'master' but also a mistress; she is clothed in the garments of authority, but 'plump[ly]' tests their boundaries. Her cross-dressing is disturbing but also 'ridiculous' and, most importantly, prevents a final interpretation of her significance by virtue of the different identities that she portrays. Though the fairy tales and the Grandmother figure may be reconstituted in the night world of Nora's dreams and in Barnes's fiction, she is not ultimately contained in either form. Like the fairy tale, she accrues significance but is not reducible to one meaning.

If Matthew has been impaled upon the lessons of his grandmothers' stories, Nora and the other granddaughters of Barnes's fiction have been impaled upon the Grandmother herself, and must engage with the axes of their desire in similar ways. Matthew conflates interpretations and retellings of fairy-tale heroes and heroines, viewing the Prince as both the heterosexual norm and the homosexual love interest. Nora also participates, albeit less consciously, in a series of interpretations and recuperations, as the grandmother appears in different guises in her granddaughter's dreams and memories. Matthew suggests that a primal lack or want prompts the refigurations of the central text; for him, the reinterpreted fairy-tale heroes and heroines 'go far back in our lost distance where what we never had stands waiting; it was inevitable that we should come upon them, for our miscalculated longing has created them' (D. Barnes 1937, 137). But where Matthew longs for something he has never had, Nora longs for something she cannot fully restore: 'There in my sleep was my grandmother [...]; I was weeping and unable to do anything' (148–9). If Matthew is the Wolf who can mimic the Grandmother, who can use her narratives creatively and transgressively, Nora is the Red Riding Hood who is caught by the Grandmother, and by the seductive but slippery authority of her voice and body.

Though Barnes celebrates, parodies, and troubles the Grandmother's sexual, familial, and authorial power, the figure of the older woman signals the limits of Barnes's writerly control, and comes to represent an excess that cannot ultimately be redressed through narrative. Barnes seems to acknowledge as much in *Ryder*, where Julie's grandmother, Sophia, attempts to control her own status after death by leaving explicit instructions regarding her burial. She is to be placed with the body of her husband in a coffin that has a 'slightly convex lid, inset with a heavy chamfered plate glass' (D. Barnes 1995, 78). The passage is fragmented, having been censored by the U.S. Post Office in 1928 and not restored by the author in later editions, but it appears that their hands are to be placed on each other's genitals, and thus both are to be 'in death as in life, but a little parted' (78). Sexual desire and its textual rendering are here asserted as ways to overcome the finality of death. Nevertheless, the authority implied in the detailed description and language of the legal document is finally undercut: 'In after-life, Sophia looked upon this document with amazement' (80). The grandmother who attempts to control death pre-emptively through the narrative of the will is an ironic echo of the granddaughter who attempts to recover her in works of fiction that range over decades of modernism.

Nora's second dream is perhaps Barnes's most poignant depiction of the response of a granddaughter to the loss of a Zadel figure. Nora stands 'wailing' at the edge of the older woman's grave, seemingly within reach of the figure and yet unable to connect (D. Barnes 1937, 149). Revived in the dream, the grandmother can be seen through the glass of the coffin, but unlike Snow White, she cannot be touched or kissed back to life. The glass of the grandmother's coffin that appears in both *Ryder* and *Nightwood* is thus a barrier, as the 'grandmother who was not entirely her recalled grandmother' in both dreams is the simulacrum that only reminds Nora of what has been lost in the process of narrative reconstitution (63). The image of the Grandmother-as-Wolf testifies to this unrecoverability. Consumed by the Wolf in 'Little Red Riding Hood,' the Grandmother is represented through his impersonation of her role, but the incongruous presence of the nightgown also signals the absence of the Grandmother's body. For Barnes, the Grandmother, like the fairy tales with which she is associated, is a palimpsest that can be reread and reinterpreted, but cannot be reduced to a tidy reading.

In its interpretative potential, the figure of the Grandmother-as-Wolf remains the stuff of further writings and reinterpretations. As a reflection of the story from which the reference is derived, the allusion is predicated upon instability, multiplicity, excess, and possibility. Like fairy tales and their multifaceted status in modernity and modernism, the excessively signified body is a site of flux that opens up the text for participation in the process of making meaning, and for interaction in the process of asserting desire. Here, the reader, like Nora, brings personal connections to the cultural associations of the fairy tale, and meets the writer on the rich and common ground that fairy tales represent in this early-twentieth-century moment.

Conclusion: Slipping Out from Between the Sheets

And must I, perchance, like careful writers, guard myself against the conclusions of my readers?

Djuna Barnes, *Nightwood*

Though the role that fairy tales play in modern culture derives from earlier eras, from previous encodings, and from prior interpretations of the tales, it sets the stage for further revisions of and experiments with the inherited tradition. Particularly in the aftermath of the Second World War, fairy tales become the grounds for feminist responses to the increasingly insistent forces of commercialism, perhaps best demonstrated in the example of the Walt Disney Studios, and to the continuing sway of a patriarchal order. Simone de Beauvoir identifies the gender dynamics of this post-war society according to the language of fairy tales, where the texts are metaphors and models of the disenfranchisement of women: 'It is clear that in dreaming of himself as donor, liberator, redeemer, man still desires the subjection of woman; for in order to awaken the Sleeping Beauty, she must have been put to sleep' (1952, 184). After the changes arising from suffrage, from the city, and from a new economy, women are still assigned a domestic and codedly submissive role that does not fit with their actual needs, as Betty Friedan argues in *The Feminine Mystique* (1963, 27). In what Colette Dowling terms 'The Cinderella Complex,' women are trained to be passive and encouraged to be dependent on others: 'Only hang on long enough, the childhood story goes, and someday someone will come along to rescue you from the anxiety of authentic living. (The only saviour the *boy* knows about is himself)' (1981, 4). In some visions of this cultural dynamic, the girl's 'adoption of femininity is at best shaky and partial' (Walkerdine 1984, 163), which indicates the constructed and contradictory nature of gender. But the options for women seem limited, and many appear to have internalized such norms to the point of abnegation: 'we (the girls) aspired to become that object of every necrophiliac's lust – the innocent, *victimized* Sleeping Beauty, beauteous lump of ultimate, sleeping good. Despite ourselves, sometimes unknowing, sometimes knowing, unwilling, unable to do otherwise, we act out the roles we were taught' (Dworkin 1974, 33). It is the feminist's job, then, to awaken these Sleeping Beauties and Snow Whites, and to rouse women from their cultural complicity. In this scenario, in which 'fairy tales are unique parables of feminine socialization,' subjects can be prompted into action and readers into interaction with texts that are not just the conduits of their subjugation but the bases for their rebirth (Kolbenschlag 1979, 4).

Contemporary writers and rewriters of fairy tales thus engage with the inherited body of stories to raise questions not only about the previous encodings of the literature, but about contemporary gender relations. Barbara Walker's *Feminist Fairy Tales*, for example, is written with the express intent to counter the 'misogynous messages' of stories that 'have filtered through centuries of patriarchal culture' (1996, ix). Cheryl Moch's play *Cinderella, the Real True Story* participates in a similar project of rewriting inherited sexed and gendered roles, as the author reinterprets the fairy tale according to the heroine's desire for a Princess rather than a Prince. The text ends with a utopian vision of inclusivity, as the King issues a proclamation in which he declares: 'Let women love women! Let men love men! Or any combination thereof! Let love decide!' (1989, 145). Peter Cashorali's collection *Fairy Tales: Traditional Stories Retold for Gay Men* delves into a more complicated vision of social interactions, addressing not just a range of sexual identities but also the threat of AIDS and homophobia in tales that are placed in both contemporary and traditionally timeless settings (1997). Anne Sexton's collection of poetry, *Transformations* (1971), and Neil Gaiman's stories, such as 'Snow, Glass, Apples' (1994), involve other kinds of formal and ideological responses to inherited stories. Where Sexton's speakers have contemporary and rather sardonic voices, Gaiman's narrator tells a chillingly Gothic tale, in which the Stepmother represents herself as a victim of a vampirish Snow White. However, while they shift the perspective of the narratives and present previously marginalized voices, both authors still address the texts according to a traditional emphasis on the stories' links to psychoanalysis. These are works that delve into the 'dark' regions of sexual and family dynamics, and explore the gendered politics of societies in which women strive against men and against each other.

Linda Hutcheon suggests that postmodern versions of folklore and fairy tales are often based upon the doubled vision of irony, in which the citation forces the reader to critique the hegemonic norms that are being re-presented as well as subverted (1994, 32). As a form of resistance to social and literary normatives, irony is something that Margaret Atwood uses in a number of her texts. In *Surfacing*, for instance, the narrator feels constricted by the images of Princesses she reproduces as an illustrator of fairy tales: 'I outline a princess, an ordinary one, emaciated fashion-model torso and infantile face' (Atwood 1972, 53). Her repressed resentment of such images and recognition of their effects on real bodies, including Anna's, results, however, in an almost unconsciously narrow vision of gender politics that must be reworked if she is to survive. In this sense, Joe is the Beast, 'only half-formed,' who does not save the narrator as much as offer her the opportunity to collaborate with him and work through the baggage of the gendered roles of the stories and of the society itself (192). In a similar case of ironic misrecognition, Sally, the protagonist of 'Bluebeard's Egg,' realizes that she has been constructing a fairy tale rather than viewing her marriage accurately. 'Her version of Ed' has shifted by the end of the short story, as has her vision of 'Bluebeard' thanks to the writing course she has taken (1983, 145). But just as the fairy tale depicts a discovery that is both threatening and ultimately enabling for the heroine, so Sally's discovery of her husband's infidelity may lead to a kind of rebirth. The readings and uses of fairy tales by characters in Atwood's works speak, then, to a form of labour that has both social and literary ramifications. By engaging with inherited narratives, characters engage with the cultural ideals the texts convey, and come to recognize their own internalization of such norms. The generational politics of such feminist enterprises are, however, rather fraught, and speak to the divide between older and younger women in terms of their cultural knowledges and experiences. Where Paula and Erin, the young twins of *The Robber Bride*, are able to change the gender of the protagonists in the stories they are read with ease, the adults have much more trouble in reworking the narratives they have constructed of their own lives (1993, 331). Indeed, if Zenia is the witch or screen onto which Tony, Roz, and Charis have projected their gendered insecurities, she is a slippery figure indeed, representing at once the potential for closure and a kind of resolution, and the potential for the women's continued abdication of personal responsibility.

While reactionary adaptations and readings of the stories are the objects of critique for many writers, especially in relation to the pedagogical role that fairy tales play in childhood, others use the fairy tale's flexible cultural status, and perhaps most importantly, its characteristic depiction of transformations, to explore those sites of identity that slide out from between the sheets of traditional variants. Jeannette Winterson's version of 'The Twelve Dancing Princesses' in *Sexing the Cherry* is one example, where instead of complying with the 'happily ever after' ending and remaining married, all the Princesses have 'in one way or another, parted from the glorious princes and [are] living scattered, according to [their] tastes' (1989, 44). This is an attitude that, while coded feminist, offers the consistent instability that becomes possible in the realm of capitalism, rather than a specific social organization that is seen as an alternative to consumerism. Angela Carter participates in a similar disruption of narrative expectations. 'Little Red Riding Hood' is retold several times in *The Bloody Chamber,* where different versions of the tale assert women's desires and undercut the patriarchal imperatives of the stories, if not their heterosexual biases (1979). Emma Donoghue's collection of short stories, *Kissing the Witch,* involves stories that are changed not just by the sexualities of their protagonists, but by acts of storytelling that, as we see in Carter's and Winterson's texts, resist the finality of a single political or narrative position. The subtitle of the collection, 'Old Tales in New Skins,' signals the interactive nature of her project, as well as its ramifications for future writers. In her reference to Mark 2:22, Donoghue makes overt the intoxicating potential of fairy tales when they are adapted to new contexts. Like wine, the old tales ferment over time and must be accommodated by new containers or forms, through which the stories can expand and contract.

In this postmodern and post-feminist vision, the tales are self-reflexive texts that demonstrate an awareness on the part of Donoghue's narrators of their own involvement in a tradition. 'I didn't have to listen to the barking voices to know how the story went,' says the Cinderella-like protagonist of 'The Tale of the Shoe,' in her recognition of the power of social narratives larger than herself (1997, 5). As she later acknowledges, however, she gets 'the story all wrong' (6); she has misinterpreted the potential of the tale, and has risked confining herself to an inappropriate variant. In discovering her love for the Fairy Godmother, in rejecting the Prince, and in throwing the glass slipper away, this Cinderella opens herself up to a new set of narrative possibilities. As importantly, she learns from the older woman of another tale and of another experience. By creating a collection that is in fact a series of interlocking stories, where characters not only tell their own tales but listen to those of the women whom they meet, Donoghue challenges the linearity and stability of narrative as well as of sexed identity. The multiple perspectives and voices that she presents forestall a reduction of the meaning of text and undermine the sense of closure with which narratives traditionally end. The stories thus retain traces of previous encodings, while suggesting new opportunities for their exchange in different situations, just as the language that the characters use, while it is tied to a system of inherited uses, changes according to the contexts and situations to which it is applied. Thus Beauty states, upon realizing that the Beast she has fallen in love with in 'The Tale of the Rose' is a woman, 'This was a strange story, one I would have to learn a new language to read, a language I could not learn except by trying to read the story' (Donoghue 1997, 39). By drawing the reader through a series of uses, tellers, stories, and audiences, Donoghue suggests the continuing slide of language, narrative, and the fairy tale through this century and well into the next. Her final move is to leave the final story of her collection, 'The Tale of the Kiss,' unresolved:

> And what happened next, you ask? Never you mind. There are some tales not for telling, whether because they are too long, too precious, too laughable, too painful, too easy to need telling or too hard to explain. After all, after years and travels, my secrets are all I have left to chew on in the night.
> This is the story you asked for. I leave it in your mouth. (1997, 227–8)

Notes

Introduction: Modernism's Fairy Tales

1 Recent critics such as Garry Leonard (1998), Melba Cuddy-Keane (1987), and Laura Winkiel (1997) have, for example, addressed the roles of advertising, modern history, and circus spectacles in the works of James Joyce, Virginia Woolf, and Djuna Barnes respectively.

2 'Culture' is often used to refer to 'works and practices of intellectual and especially artistic activity' such as 'music, literature, painting and sculpture, theatre and film' (Williams 1983, 90). It has also come to be associated with a certain sense of prestige, particularly where the term designates works of 'high art.' As Marc Manganaro points out, when Gerty MacDowell in *Ulysses* notes that Leopold Bloom's voice has 'a cultured ring in it' (13.548), she means that Bloom is a cultivated individual, a well-bred modern subject who has been schooled and civilized (2002, 127). But culture can also be read as 'a particular way of life' that is associated with a society as a whole (Williams 1983, 90), what Manganaro might say is culture in its ethnographic sense (2002, 113). An example would be the panorama of 1904 Dublin culture that is represented in (and in a sense constructed by) *Ulysses* (see Herr 1986). Here, Dublin culture includes the discourses of the church and of the British-dominated state, the propaganda of nationalist movements, the advertisements that appear throughout the city, the theories of Shakespeare's plays discussed in the National Library, the titbit stories and ladies' magazines that Gerty MacDowell consumes, and the pornographic novels that Leopold Bloom buys for Molly. The diversity and complexity conveyed by this second sense of 'culture,' and its many connections with the first sense of the term, are what inform my readings of fairy tales in the works of James Joyce, Virginia Woolf, and Djuna Barnes, in which children's

stories and academic collections of variants and Christmas pantomime adaptations of the tales are all part of the cultures they depict.

3 As Jack Zipes points out in relation to fairy tales and Nazi Germany, the stories were used to reassert the purity of races as well as of nation states (1983, 134–69).

4 'Little Red Riding Hood' exemplifies the dynamic nature of the fairy tale and its changing role in various societies. In Charles Perrault's version, Red dies (1969, 28); in the Grimms' 'Little Red Cap,' Red lives (1972, 142). Andrew Lang's written translation of Perrault's 'Little Red Riding-Hood' (1889) does not include the scatological and cannibalistic elements of the oral variants collected by Wolfram Eberhard (1970). The Asian tales collected by Eberhard differ in turn from the French oral variants collected by Paul Delarue (1956), particularly in the kinds of cannibalism they portray. Where the Red character ingests a sibling or grandmother, and thus breaches a family taboo, in the first set, she ingests the bottled flesh and blood of the grandmother in the French versions, in a move that has sacrilegious overtones. In the Stephen Sondheim and James Lapine musical *Into the Woods* (1987), Little Red Riding Hood is a greedy little girl; in Neil Jordan's film *The Company of Wolves* (1984), based on a story by Angela Carter, Red is a sexually maturing teenager. In Matthew Bright's movie *Freeway* (1996), she is a symbol of disillusioned American youth (Orenstein 2002, 219–37). Versions by James Thurber – 'the little girl took an automatic out of her basket and shot the wolf dead' (1940, 26) – Roald Dahl – 'The small girl smiles. One eyelid flickers. / She whips a pistol from her knickers' (1995, 40) – and James Finn Garner – 'Red Riding Hood screamed, not out of alarm at the wolf's apparent tendency toward cross-dressing, but because of his willful invasion of her personal space' (1994, 3–4) – are contemporary rewritings that parody Perrault's warning to women about the wiles of predatory men, or the Grimms' demand for girls to obey their parents. The 'remarkable mercurial properties' of the tale (Orenstein 2002, 12), in which familiarity is coupled with flexibility, keep the story's significance open for comparison, debate, and most importantly, reinscription.

5 All references to James Joyce's *Ulysses* are followed by chapter and line numbers in parentheses. Citations are from *Ulysses: The Corrected Text*, edited by Hans Gabler, Wolfhard Steppe, and Claus Melchior (New York: Vintage, 1986).

Chapter 1: Turning Back the Covers

1 John Rowe Townsend suggests that '"folk" indicates the origin, "fairy" the nature of the story' (1974, 90). For Alan Dundes, 'a myth is a sacred narra-

tive explaining how the world and humanity came to be in their present form; a folktale is a fictional narrative set in no particular place and time (often signaled by an introductory opening formula: "Once upon a time"); and a legend is a story told as true, set in the post-creation real world' (1989, 64).

2 *The Young Misses Magazine: containing Dialogues between A Governess and several Young Ladies of Quality her Scholars* (Grey 1968, 65).

3 Regina Bendix points out that 'Once a cultural good has been declared authentic, the demand for it rises, and it acquires a market value' (1997, 8). In this sense, anxiety regarding the purity of fairy tales may have much to do with the forces of modernization that would flood the market.

4 In America, circuses also performed fairy tales: Laura Winkiel indicates that in 1916, Barnum and Bailey staged the spectacle of *Cinderella* at Madison Square Gardens with a cast of 1370 (1997, 12).

5 We see this link in the seasonal popularity of, for example, Tchaikovsky's ballet *The Nutcracker,* taken from E.T.A. Hoffmann's tale of *Nussknacker und Mausekonig* (Taylor 1963, 107).

6 Fairy tales in the Aarne-Thompson Index are categorized as tales of magic or wonder tales and are listed as the tale types 300 to 749 (Aarne and Thompson 1964, 88–254).

7 I am indebted to Richard Greene for his suggestion of Sitwell and Melba Cuddy-Keane for her suggestion of Mansfield.

8 As Peter Hunt points out, 'Almost every fear that lay beneath the surface of Kenneth Grahame's *The Wind in the Willows* was realized,' including suffrage, suburbia, paid holidays, and vacations in the country (1995, 193).

Chapter 2: James Joyce

1 These sources include *The Book of Invasions,* which would seem to influence the structure of *Ulysses* (Tymoczko 1989, 19), the figure of the banshee in 'Clay' (Cowan 1969, 214), the hero Cú Chulainn in *Portrait* (Radford 1987, 253), the consubstantial father image of Lir in *Ulysses* (Paterakis 1972, 35), and the supernatural midwife figure in the 'Proteus' (Herr 1999, 36–7).

2 Not surprisingly, the integrity of Irish folklore becomes a central concern for the Revival, since the purity and authenticity of the tales is directly linked to the purity and authenticity of the nation. In 1890, for instance, Douglas Hyde criticizes the haphazard collection and the rather free translation of folk tales by writers from Crofton Croker to Patrick Kennedy to Lady Speranza Wilde: 'folk-lore is presented in an uncertain and unsuitable medium, whenever the contents of the stories are divorced from their original expression in language' (1890, xvii). Yeats points to a similar

problem, where for many citizens, the organic interpenetration of folk and faery has been threatened with disruption: 'the hum of wheels and clatter of printing presses, to let alone the lecturers with their black coats and tumblers of water, have driven away the goblin kingdom and made silent the feet of the little dancers' (1892, 301). Both theorists of the Revival indicate the vulnerability of the source texts that guarantee national identity and emphasize the importance of authenticity. Like Dickens's 'Bluebeard,' the pure Celtic narrative seems to be receding into the distance, overwhelmed by counterfeits that threaten the stability of Irish nationalism's cultural gold standard.

3 It seems that in *Stephen Hero* there is room for only one romantic figure: the artist, for whom 'the serious business of life [...] loomed like some monstrous jinni out of the *Arabian Nights* before him' (Gorman 1940, 117).

4 Homi K. Bhabha's explanation of colonial mimicry has much to do with my sense of imitation or citation, where the Other is *'almost the same, but not quite'* (1983, 381).

5 To quote Luce Irigaray, 'just as a commodity has no mirror it can use to reflect itself, so woman serves as reflection, as image of and for man, but lacks specific qualities of her own. Her value-invested form amounts to what man inscribes in and on its matter' (1977, 187).

6 I read Gerty's orgasm as the 'little strangled cry' and the six 'O's that accompany the Roman candle's trajectory.

Chapter 3: Virginia Woolf

1 On the other hand, in 'Moments of Being: Slater's Pins Have No Points,' it is the very fragmentation of the social persona that allows Fanny Wilmot to intuit the love that dare not speak its name. When the pin holding Miss Craye's rose drops to the floor, lesbian desire slides into and among the possibilities of sexual subject positions (Woolf 1928a).

2 Manresa's theatrical flirtation also points to her deliberate staging of gender, as does her assumption of a male role through the assumption of the male gaze: '"All I need," said Mrs Manresa ogling Candish, as if he were a real man, not a stuffed man, "is a corkscrew." She had a bottle of champagne, but no corkscrew' (Woolf 1941, 27). Candish is placed as the straight man here, but her music-hall innuendo is anything but. Does she want a man to pull out her cork and allow her to explode emotionally, or to fill a need and allow her to implode sexually? Or does she want the corkscrew for herself as a substitute phallus with which she can penetrate Candish?

3 I am indebted to Heather Murray, who pointed out this connection between pargeters (cf. Woolf's Pargiter family) and tailors.

4 See Sandra Gilbert and Susan Gubar's *No Man's Land*, vol. 3, for another view of this battle in which the gender positions are seen as more stable: 'During her reunion with her old lover, Peter Walsh, in fact, Clarissa is drawn into a Popeian mock-heroic battle of (male) pocketknife against (female) needle' (1994, 21).

5 The Oedipal resonances of the scene have been noted by, for example, Madeline Moore (1984, 64–7), Sandra Kemp (1994, 20), and Sandra Gilbert and Susan Gubar (1994, 31).

6 For instance, in 'Cat's Meat,' two children ignored by their philanthropic mother and father decide to enact the roles of poor children in London in order to get their parents' attention.

7 In 'The Black Cat or the Grey Parrot,' for instance, children are taken on magical journeys by animals into different city worlds.

8 See 'Tommy and His Neighbours,' where upper-middle-class Londoners never do find out who has thrown stones down their chimneys. In 'The Mysterious Voice,' Jem is allowed to be as naughty as he likes (though he finds the experience of not being punished so odd and unnerving that he starts to behave).

9 An inspiration for this story may be *Gammer Gurton's Needle* (1575), which Woolf discusses at length in her essay 'Pure English' (1920).

10 Significantly, Woolf uses nursery rhymes primarily to depict personal issues, such as the childish antics of the schoolyard bully, Clive Bell, or 'George, Ring the Bell & Run Away' (1982a, 132). Her own response is taken from 'Jack Be Nimble': 'I played my tricks: jumped over the candlestick' (104).

11 Indeed, in an essay from 1924, 'The Enchanted Organ,' Woolf seems to echo her father's conflicted view of Anny's financial acumen, or lack thereof. According to Stephen: 'Unsystematic and confused as her statements might be about business and so forth, she yet had always a strong substratum of common sense' (1977, 14). According to Woolf: 'if [Ritchie's] random ways were charming, who, on the other hand, could be more practical, or see things, when she liked, precisely as they were?' (1924, 400–1).

12 The image is applied directly to Ritchie by Carol Hanbery MacKay (1987, 75) and by Winifred Gérin (1981, 241).

13 Similarly, Elizabeth Boyd suggests that, for Woolf, Ritchie writes 'as naturally as the bird sings' but does not 'rewrite, select, and perfect,' a distinction that represents the crucial difference between the two artists (1976, 89).

14 Ritchie's stories seem to echo the plots of the '*mind-and-millinery* species' of novel that George Eliot critiques, just as Ritchie's lack of 'patient diligence'

places her in proximity to the lady novelists from whom Woolf would seem to distance herself (G. Eliot 1856, 301, 323).

15 Though the delightfully silly adventures of Prince Giglio of Paflagonia are subtitled a 'Fire-side Pantomime for Great and Small Children' (Thackeray 1855, 197), Thackeray emphasizes less the theatrical conventions of the pantomime form and more its fairy-tale plot, which ends through magical interventions in marriage.

16 Godmothers are useful things
Even when without the wings.
Wisdom may be yours and wit,
Courage, industry, and grit –
What's the use of these at all,
If you lack a friend at call? (Perrault 1969, 78)

17 Contemporary films predicated upon the basic plot of 'Cinderella' demonstrate the same gendered move. In *Maid in Manhattan*, for example, the Jennifer Lopez character is acknowledged by the wealthy politician 'when he catches her trying on a Dolce & Gabbana suit worth several thousand dollars' (Gordon 2002, J3).

18 Martin Green and John Swan state, in fact, that *Orlando* is a 'commedic novel' in which Woolf adapts 'the archetypal figures to the subject matter of literature and history' in the text (1993, 9). Unfortunately, they do not present a reading beyond this very suggestive point.

19 We can think here particularly of Pablo Picasso's use of Harlequin: not just the playful designs he produced for *Parade* in 1917, the commedic performance piece on which he collaborated with Eric Satie and Jean Cocteau (Nichols 2002, 38), but also two specific Harlequin paintings he produced in 1901 and 1915 that are connected with the deaths of Casagemas and Eva Gouel (Green and Swan 1993, 164, 179).

20 The staging of the play is compared to a Punch and Judy show, another connection to the *commedia dell'arte*, Punch being derived from the character Pulcinella (Nicoll 1963, 84).

21 See Jane de Gay's work on theatrical allusions in *Orlando* and their connection to moments at which 'conventions of gender' are disrupted (2001, 31).

Chapter 4: Djuna Barnes

1 As David Copeland suggests, in *Nightwood* 'images are reappropriated from [...] fairy-tales and redeployed as intimations, rather than revelations' (1997, 2).

2 The (ex)change is suggested by Roald Dahl's version, in which Red kills the Wolf herself:

A few weeks later in the wood,
I came across Miss Riding Hood.
But what a change! No cloak of red,
No silly hood upon her head.
She said, 'Hello, and do please note
'My lovely furry WOLFSKIN COAT.' (1982, 40)

3 Stephen's fascination with *The Count of Monte Cristo* and with Edmund Dantes's 'sadly proud gesture of refusal' of 'muscatel grapes' is another version of this independence (Joyce 1916, 51–2). As R.B. Kershner suggests, 'the source of the Count's empowerment, paradoxically, is his exile' (1989, 196) – that is, his rejection of the community and the reciprocity that communities involve.

4 Of course, Nora is neither the Wolf nor the Red Riding Hood whose arrival Matthew has been awaiting: 'he was extremely put out, having expected someone else' (D. Barnes 1937, 80).

5 If Nora's grandmother corresponds to Zadel Barnes, Robin Vote stands in for Thelma Wood, Barnes's partner through the 1920s (see, for example, Hanscombe and Smyers 1987, 97–102). Barnes identified a connection between the two, according to Hank O'Neal, who came to know Barnes in the late 1970s: 'I had known her but a few weeks when she recounted the first stories about Wood resembling her grandmother' (1990, 137). In this association, fraught with meaning, the lover and the grandmother would appear to be combined in the image of the Wolf in bed with Red Riding Hood.

6 It cannot be a coincidence that Dolly Wilde appears in *Ladies Almanack* as 'Doll Furious,' the modernist embodiment of decadence.

7 Janet Flanner testifies to the distance that Barnes established in most of her friendships: 'I was devoted to Djuna and she was quite fond of me, too, in her superior way' (1972, xvii).

8 Barnes was also funded by the Ellerman fortune, since *Ladies Almanack* was published first by Robert McAlmon, whose Contact Editions was financed by an alimony settlement from Bryher (Winnifred Ellerman) (Benstock 1986, 246).

9 See also Cheryl Plumb, *Fancy's Craft* (1986, 94).

10 Percy Faulkner was the brother of Wald's live-in mistress. It was with Faulkner that Djuna Barnes appears to have entered into a 'failed common-law marriage' that was arranged by both Wald and Zadel when Djuna was 18 (Herring 1993, 107).

References

Aarne, Antti, and Stith Thompson. 1964. *The Types of the Folktale: Classification and Bibliography.* 2nd rev. ed. Helsinki: Suomalainen Tiedeakatemian.

Abbott, Reginald. 1992. 'What Miss Kilman's Petticoat Means: Virginia Woolf, Shopping, and Spectacle.' *Modern Fiction Studies* 38 (1): 193–216.

Andersen, Graham. 2000. *Fairytale in the Ancient World.* London: Routledge.

Andersen, Hans Christian. 1998. *Hans Andersen's Fairy Tales: A Selection.* Trans. L.W. Kingsland. Oxford: Oxford University Press.

Annan, Noel. 1984. *Leslie Stephen: The Godless Victorian.* New York: Random.

Apuleuis, Lucius. 1996. *The Golden Ass.* Trans. William Adlington and S. Gaselee. Ware, UK: Wordsworth.

Arabian Nights' Entertainments. 1998. Ed. Robert L. Mack. Oxford: Oxford University Press.

Archer, William. 1898. *The Theatrical 'World' of 1897.* London: Walter Scott.

Arnold, Matthew. 1866. 'On the Study of Celtic Literature.' In Vol. 5 of *The Works of Matthew Arnold in Fifteen Volumes,* 1–150. London: Macmillan, 1903.

Atwood, Margaret.1972. *Surfacing.* Toronto: New Canadian Library, 1994.

– 1983. 'Bluebeard's Egg.' In *Bluebeard's Egg,* 115–46. Toronto: Seal, 1984.

– 1993. *The Robber Bride.* Toronto: Seal, 1994.

Avery, Gillian. 1995. 'The Beginnings of Children's Reading to c. 1700.' In Hunt 1995, 1–25.

Avery, Gillian and Margaret Kinnell. 1995. 'Morality and Levity 1780–1820.' In Hunt 1995, 46–76.

Bailey, J.O. 1966. Introd. to *British Plays of the Nineteenth Century: An Anthology to Illustrate the Evolution of the Drama.* New York: Odyssey.

Bakhtin, Mikhail. 1965. *Rabelais and His World.* Trans. Hélène Iswolsky. Bloomington: Indiana University Press, 1984.

Barnes, Djuna. (A Lady of Fashion, pseud.) 1928. *Ladies Almanack*. Normal, IL: Dalkey, 1992.

– 1937. *Nightwood*. New York: New Directions, 1961.

– 1962. *The Antiphon*. In *The Selected Works of Djuna Barnes: Spillway / The Antiphon / Nightwood*, 77–224. London: Faber, 1998.

– 1995. *Ryder*. Normal, IL: Dalkey. (Orig. pub. 1928; rev. 1990.)

Barnes, Zadel. 1875. 'The Children's Night.' *Harper's New Monthly Magazine* 50 (296): 153–64.

Barrie, J.M. 1999. *Peter Pan*. In *Peter Pan and Other Plays*, 73–154. Oxford: Oxford University Press.

Barthes, Roland. 1967. *The Fashion System*. Trans. Matthew Ward and Richard Howard. Berkeley: University of California Press, 1990.

Baum, L. Frank. 1900. *The Wonderful Wizard of Oz*. New York: Dover, 1960.

Beer, Gillian. 1996. *Virginia Woolf: The Common Ground*. Ann Arbor: University of Michigan Press.

Beerbohm, Max. 1904. *The Poet's Corner*. London: Heinemann.

– 1905. 'Pantomime for Children.' In *Last Theatres: 1904–1910*, 116–20. London: Rupert Hart-Davis, 1970.

– 1907. 'Peter Pan Revisited.' In *Last Theatres: 1904–1910*, 334–7. London: Rupert Hart-Davis, 1970.

– 1915. *The Happy Hypocrite*. London: John Lande.

– 1997. 'Mr W.B. Yeats presenting Mr George Moore to the Queen of the Fairies.' In *Max Beerbohm Caricatures*, 49. Ed. N. John Hall. New Haven, CT: Yale University Press.

Bell, Quentin. 1988. Afterword to *The Widow and the Parrot*, by Virginia Woolf. New York: Harcourt.

– 1972. *Virginia Woolf: A Biography*. 2 vols. London: Pimlico, 1996.

Bell, Vanessa. 1974. *Notes on Virginia's Childhood*. Ed. Richard J. Schaubeck, Jr. New York: Hallman.

Bendix, Regina. 1997. *In Search of Authenticity: The Formation of Folklore Studies*. Madison: University of Wisconsin Press.

Benjamin, Walter. 1929. 'Children's Literature.' In vol. 2 of *Selected Writings, 1927–1934*, trans. Rodney Livingstone, ed. Michael W. Jennings, Howard Eiland, and Gary Smith, 250–6. Cambridge, MA: Harvard University Press, 1999.

– 1936a. 'The Storyteller.' In *Illuminations: Essays and Reflections*, trans. Harry Zohn, ed. Hannah Arendt, 83–109. New York: Schocken, 1968.

– 1936b. 'The Work of Art in the Age of Mechanical Reproduction.' In *Illuminations: Essays and Reflections*, trans. Harry Zohn, ed. Hannah Arendt, 217–51. New York: Schocken, 1968.

Ben-Merre, Diana A., and Maureen Murphy, eds. 1989. *James Joyce and His Contemporaries*. New York: Greenwood.

Benstock, Shari. 1986. *Women of the Left Bank: Paris, 1900–1940*. Austin: University of Texas Press, 1988.

Bett, Henry. 1924. *Nursery Rhymes and Tales: Their Origin and History*. London: Methuen.

Bettelheim, Bruno. 1975. *The Uses of Enchantment: The Meaning and Importance of Fairy Tales*. New York: Vintage, 1977.

Bhabha, Homi K. 1983. 'Of Mimicry and Man: The Ambivalence of Colonial Discourse.' In *Modern Literary Theory: A Reader*, 4th ed., ed. Philip Rice and Patricia Waugh, 380–7. New York: Oxford University Press, 2001.

– 1990. 'DissemiNation: time, narrative, and the margins of the modern nation.' In *Nation and Narration*, ed. Homi K. Bhabha, 291–322. London: Routledge.

Bishop, John. 1999. 'A Metaphysics of Coitus in "Nausicaa."' In Devlin and Reizbaum 1999, 183–209.

Black, Martha Fodaski. 1997. 'S/He-Male Voices in *Ulysses:* Counterpointing the "New Womanly Man."' In *Gender in Joyce*, ed. Jolanta Wawrzycka and Marlena G. Corcoran, 62–81. Gainesville: University Press of Florida.

Blake, William. 1789. 'The Ecchoing Green.' In *The Complete Poetry and Prose of William Blake*, rev. ed., ed. David V. Erdman, 8. New York: Doubleday, 1988.

Block, Francesca Lia. 2000. *The Rose and the Beast: Fairy Tales Retold*. New York: Harper.

Bloom, Harold. 1997. *The Anxiety of Influence: A Theory of Poetry*. 2nd ed. Oxford: Oxford University Press.

Boone, Joseph Allen. 1998. *Libidinal Currents: Sexuality and the Shaping of Modernism*. Chicago: University of Chicago Press.

Booth, Michael. 1976. Introd. to *Pantomimes, Extravaganzas and Burlesques*. Ed. Michael Booth. Oxford: Clarendon.

Bowen, Zack. 1974. *Musical Allusions in the Works of James Joyce: Early Poetry Through 'Ulysses.'* Albany: State University of New York Press.

– 1998. 'All in a Night's Entertainment: The Codology of Haroun al Raschid, the *Thousand and One Nights*, Bloomsusalem/Baghdad, the Uncreated Conscience of the Irish Race, and Joycean Self-Reflexivity.' *James Joyce Quarterly* 35 (2–3): 297–307.

Bowlby, Rachel. 1992. Introd. to *Orlando: A Biography*, by Virginia Woolf, ed. Rachel Bowlby. Oxford: Oxford University Press.

Boxwell, David. 2002. 'The Follies of War: Cross-Dressing and Popular Theatre on the British Front Lines, 1914–18.' *Modernism/Modernity* 9 (1): 1–20.

Boyd, Elizabeth French. 1976. *Bloomsbury Heritage: Their Mothers and Their Aunts*. London: Hamilton.

Briggs, Julia. 1995. 'Transitions, 1890–1914.' In Hunt 1995, 167–91.

– 1996. 'Critical Opinion: Reading Children's Books.' In *Only Connect: Readings on Children's Literature*, 3rd ed., ed. Sheila Egoff, Gordon Stubbs, Ralph Ashley, and Wendy Sutton, 18–31. Toronto: Oxford University Press.

Broe, Mary Lynn. 1989. 'My Art Belongs to Daddy: Incest as Exile, the Textual Economics of Hayford Hall.' In *Women's Writing in Exile*, ed. Mary Lynn Broe and Angela Ingram, 41–86. Chapel Hill: University of North Carolina Press.

– 1990. 'Djuna Barnes (1892–1982).' In *The Gender of Modernism: A Critical Anthology*, ed. Bonnie Kime Scott, 19–29. Bloomington: Indiana University Press.

– ed. 1991. *Silence and Power: A Reevaluation of Djuna Barnes*. Carbondale: Southern Illinois University Press.

Buchan, John. 1931. *The Novel and the Fairy Tale*. Oxford: Oxford University Press.

Budgen, Frank. 1934. *James Joyce and the Making of 'Ulysses.'* New York: Smith & Haas.

Burke, Kenneth. 1966. 'Version, Con-, Per-, and In- (Thoughts on Djuna Barnes's Novel, *Nightwood*).' *Southern Review* n.s. (2): 329–46.

Burnett, Frances Hodgson. 1911. *The Secret Garden*. Maidenhead, UK: Purnell, 1975.

Burns, Christy L. 2000. *Gestural Politics: Stereotype and Parody in Joyce*. Albany: State University of New York Press.

Butler, Judith. 1993. *Bodies That Matter: On the Discursive Limits of 'Sex.'* New York: Routledge.

Butts, Dennis. 1995. 'The Beginnings of Victorianism, c. 1820–1850.' In Hunt 1995, 77–101.

Callander, Marilyn Berg. 1989. *Willa Cather and the Fairy Tale*. Ann Arbor, MI: UMI Research Press.

Callow, Heather Cook. 1992. 'Joyce's Female Voices in *Ulysses*.' *Journal of Narrative Technique* 22 (3): 151–63.

Canario, John W. 1967. 'The Harlequin in *Heart of Darkness*.' *Studies in Short Fiction* 4: 225–33.

Carpenter, Humphrey. 1985. *Secret Gardens: A Study of the Golden Age of Children's Literature*. London: George Allen & Unwin.

Carpenter, Humphrey, and Mari Prichard. 1984. *The Oxford Companion to Children's Literature*. Oxford: Oxford University Press, 1999.

Carroll, Lewis. 1988. *The Complete Works of Lewis Carroll*. London: Penguin.

Carter, Angela. 1979. *The Bloody Chamber*. New York: Penguin, 1993.

Cashdan, Sheldon. 1999. *The Witch Must Die: How Fairy Tales Shape Our Lives.* New York: Basic.

Cashorali, Peter. 1997. 'The Fisherman and His Lover.' In *Fairy Tales: Traditional Stories Retold for Gay Men,* 100–7. New York: Harper.

Castle, Gregory. 1998. 'Colonial Discourse and the Subject of Empire in Joyce's "Nausicaa."' In *European Joyce Studies 8,* ed. Ellen Carol Jones, 115–44. Atlanta: Rodopi.

– 2001. *Modernism and the Celtic Revival.* Cambridge: Cambridge University Press.

Cheng, Vincent J. 2000. 'Authenticity and Identity: Catching the Irish Spirit.' In *Semicolonial Joyce,* ed. Derek Attridge and Marjorie Howes, 240–61. Cambridge: Cambridge University Press.

Chisholm, Dianne. 1997. 'Obscene Modernism: *Eros Noir* and the Profane Illumination of Djuna Barnes.' *American Literature* 69 (1): 167–206.

Cixous, Hélène. 1972. *The Exile of James Joyce.* Trans. Sally A.J. Purcell. New York: David Lewis.

Clarke, Desmond. 1977. London: Batsford.

Colum, Padraic. 1922. *Dramatic Legends and Other Poems.* New York: Macmillan.

Conrad, Joseph. 1902. *Heart of Darkness.* New York: Dover, 1990.

Copeland, David. 1997. 'A Fairy-Tale Undressed?: Little Red, Children, and Narrative Revelation in *Nightwood.*' Paper presented at the annual meeting of the Modern Languages Association, Toronto.

Cowan, S.A. 1969. 'Celtic Folklore in "Clay": Maria and the Irish Washerwoman.' *Studies in Short Fiction* 6: 213–15.

Cuddy-Keane, Melba. 1990. 'The Politics of Comic Modes in Virginia Woolf's *Between the Acts.*' *PMLA* 105 (2): 273–85.

– 1996. 'The Rhetoric of Feminist Conversation: Virginia Woolf and the Trope of the Twist.' In *Ambiguous Discourse: Feminist Narratology and British Women Writers,* ed. Kathy Mezei, 137–61. Chapel Hill: University of North Carolina Press.

– 1997. 'Virginia Woolf and the Varieties of Historicist Experience.' In *Virginia Woolf and the Essay,* ed. Ruth Carole Rosenberg and Jeanne Dubino, 59–77. New York: St Martin's.

Dahl, Roald. 1982. 'Little Red Riding Hood and the Wolf.' In *Revolting Rhymes,* 36–40. New York: Puffin, 1995.

Dalton, Anne B. 1993. '"*This* is Obscene": Female Voyeurism, Sexual Abuse, and Maternal Power in *The Dove.*' *Review of Contemporary Fiction* 13 (3): 117–39.

Danius, Sara. 2002. *The Senses of Modernism: Technology, Perception, and Aesthetics.* Ithaca, NY: Cornell University Press.

Darton, F.J. Harvey. 1932. Children's Books in England: Five Centuries of Social Life. Cambridge: Cambridge University Press.

de Beaumont, Madame Marie Leprince. 1804. 'Beauty and the Beast.' In *The Classic Fairy Tales,* ed. Iona Opie and Peter Opie, 182–95. New York: Oxford University Press, 1980.

de Beauvoir, Simone. 1952. The Second Sex. Trans. and ed. H.M. Pashley. New York: Vintage, 1989.

de Certeau, Michel. 1984. *The Practice of Everyday Life.* Trans. Steven Rendall. Berkeley: University of California Press, 1988.

de Gay, Jane. 2001. '"though the fashion of the time did something to disguise it": Staging Gender in Woolf's *Orlando.' Virginia Woolf Out of Bounds: Selected Papers from the Tenth Annual Conference on Virginia Woolf.* New York: Pace University Press. 31–9.

de la Mare, Walter. 1927. Told Again. Oxford: Basil Blackwell.

Delarue, Paul. 1956. 'The Story of the Grandmother.' In Dundes 1989, 13–20.

Demoor, M. 1989. Introd. to *Friends Over the Ocean: Andrew Lang's American Correspondents, 1881–1912.* n.p.: Gent. 5–18.

Devlin, Kimberly. 1985. 'The Romance Heroine Exposed: "Nausicaa" and *The Lamplighter.' James Joyce Quarterly* 22 (4): 383–96.

– 1999. 'Visible Shades and Shades of Visibility: The En-Gendering of Death in "Hades."' In Devlin and Reizbaum 1999, 67–85.

Devlin, Kimberly, and Marilyn Reizbaum, eds. 1999. *Ulysses: Engendered Perspectives.* Columbia: University of South Carolina Press.

Dick, Susan. 1992. Introd. and Notes to *To the Lighthouse,* by Virginia Woolf. Oxford: Blackwell.

Dickens, Charles. 1853. 'Frauds on the Fairies.' In Salway 1976, 111–18.

Donoghue, Emma. 1997. *Kissing the Witch: Old Tales in New Skins.* New York: Harper, 1999.

Dowling, Colette. 1981. *The Cinderella Complex: Women's Hidden Fear of Independence.* New York: Pocket.

Dundes, Alan, ed. 1982. *Cinderella: A Folklore Casebook.* New York: Garland.

– ed. 1989. *Little Red Riding Hood: A Casebook.* Madison: University of Wisconsin Press.

Dusinberre, Juliet. 1987. *Alice to the Lighthouse: Children's Books and Radical Experiments in Art.* London: Macmillan.

Dworkin, Andrea. 1974. *Women Hating.* New York: Dutton.

Eberhard, Wolfram. 1970. 'The Story of Grandaunt Tiger.' In Dundes 1989, 21–63.

Eglinton, John. 1916. *Bards and Saints*. Dublin: Maunsel.

Egoff, Sheila. 1980. 'Precepts, Pleasures, and Portents: Changing Emphases in Children's Literature.' In *Only Connect: Readings on Children's Literature*, 2nd ed., ed. Sheila Egoff, G.T. Stubbs, and L.F. Ashley, 405–33. Toronto: Oxford University Press.

Eliot, George. 1856. 'Silly Novels by Lady Novelists.' In *The Essays of George Eliot*, ed. Thomas Pinney, 300–24. London: Routledge, 1968.

Eliot, T.S. 1922a. 'Marie Lloyd.' In T.S. Eliot 1975, 172–4.

– 1922b. *The Waste Land*. In T.S. Eliot 1963, 61–86.

– 1923. '*Ulysses*, Order, and Myth.' In T.S. Eliot 1975, 175–8.

– 1930. 'Marina.' In T.S. Eliot 1963, 115–16.

– 1935. 'Burnt Norton.' In T.S. Eliot 1963, 189–95.

– 1937. Introd. to *Nightwood*, by Djuna Barnes. New York: New Directions, 1961.

– 1942. 'Little Gidding.' In T.S. Eliot 1963, 214–23.

– 1954. 'The Cultivation of Christmas Trees.' In T.S. Eliot 1963, 117–18.

– 1963. *Collected Poems: 1909–1962*. London: Faber, 1990.

– 1975. *Selected Prose of T.S. Eliot*. Ed. Frank Kermode. New York: Harcourt.

Elliott, Bridget, and Jo-Ann Wallace. 1994. *Women Artists and Writers: Modernist (im)positionings*. London: Routledge.

Ellmann, Richard. 1982. *James Joyce*. Rev. ed. New York: Oxford University Press.

Favat, André. 1977. *Child and Tale: The Origins of Interest*. Urbana, IL: NCTE.

Field, Andrew. 1983. *Djuna: The Life and Times of Djuna Barnes*. New York: Putnam's.

Fielding, Sarah. 1749. *The Governess, or Little Female Academy*. London: Oxford University Press, 1968.

Firbank, Ronald. 1916. *Odette: A Fairy Tale for Weary People*. London: Grant Richards.

Flanner, Janet. 1972. *Paris Was Yesterday: 1925–1939*. New York: Viking.

Follett, Beth. 2001. *Tell It Slant*. Toronto: Coach House.

Ford, Ford Madox. 1894. *The Queen Who Flew: A Fairy Tale*. New York: George Braziller, 1965.

Frazer, Sir James George. 1922. *The Golden Bough: A Study in Magic and Religion*. Abridged ed. New York: Simon, 1996.

Freud, Sigmund. 1958a. 'The Occurrence in Dreams of Material from Fairy Tales.' In vol. 12 of *The Standard Edition of the Complete Psychological Works of Sigmund Freud*, trans. James Strachey, 279–87. London: Hogarth.

– 1958b. 'The Theme of the Three Caskets.' In vol. 12 of *The Standard Edition of the Complete Psychological Works of Sigmund Freud*, trans. James Strachey, 289–301. London: Hogarth.

– 1959. 'From the History of an Infantile Neurosis.' In vol. 3 of *Collected Papers*, trans. Alix and James Strachey, 471–605. New York: Basic.

– 1973. 'The Uncanny.' In vol. 17 of *The Standard Edition of the Complete Psychological Works of Sigmund Freud*, trans. James Strachey, 219–52. London: Hogarth.

Friedan, Betty. 1963. *The Feminine Mystique*. New York: Dell.

Fuller, Hester Thackeray, and Violet Hammersley, eds. 1952. *Thackeray's Daughter*. 2nd ed. Dublin: Euphorian.

Fussell, Paul. 1975. *The Great War and Modern Memory*. London: Oxford University Press, 1977.

Gaiman, Neil. 1994. 'Snow, Glass, Apples.' *The Dreaming: The Neil Gaiman Page*. http://www.holycow.com/dreaming/stories/snow.html (accessed 9 July 2004).

Galef, David. 1991. 'The Fashion Show in *Ulysses*.' *Twentieth Century Literature* 37 (4): 420–31.

Gallop, Jane. 1985. *Reading Lacan*. Ithaca: Cornell University Press, 1996.

Garber, Marjorie. 1992. *Vested Interests: Cross-dressing and Cultural Anxiety*. New York: Routledge, 1997.

Garner, James Finn.1994. 'Little Red Riding Hood.' In *Politically Correct Bedtime Stories: Modern Tales for Our Life and Times*, 1–4. Toronto: Macmillan.

Gérin, Winifred. 1981. *Anne Thackeray Ritchie: A Biography*. Oxford: Oxford University Press.

Gerstenberger, Donna. 1989. 'The Radical Narrative of Djuna Barnes's *Nightwood*.' In *Breaking the Sequence*, ed. Ellen Friedman and Miriam Fuchs, 129–39. Princeton, NJ: Princeton University Press.

Giacosa, Giuseppe, and Luigi Illica. 1972. Libretto. *La Bohème*. Music by Giacomo Puccini. Orch. Berliner Philharmoniker. Cond. Herbert Von Karajan. Berlin.

Gibson, Andrew. 1991. '"History, All That": Revival Historiography and Literary Strategy in the "Cyclops" Episode in *Ulysses*.' *Essays and Studies* 44: 53–69.

Gifford, Don, with Robert J. Seidman. 1989. '*Ulysses*' Annotated: Notes for James Joyce's '*Ulysses*.' 2nd ed. Berkeley: University of California Press.

Gilbert, Sandra M., and Susan Gubar. 1979. *The Madwoman in the Attic: The Woman Writer and the Nineteenth-Century Literary Imagination*. New Haven, CT: Yale University Press.

– 1987. *The War of the Words*. Vol. 1 of *No Man's Land: The Place of the Woman Writer in the Twentieth Century*. New Haven, CT: Yale University Press.

– 1994. *Letters From the Front*. Vol. 3 of *No Man's Land: The Place of the Woman Writer in the Twentieth Century*. New Haven, CT: Yale University Press.

Gilbert, W.S. 1912. *Princess Ida, or Castle Adamant.* London: Bell.

Gilet, Peter. 1998. *Vladimir Propp and the Universal Folktale: Recommissioning an Old Paradigm – Story as Initiation.* New York: Lang.

Gillespie, Diane F. 1987. 'The Elusive Julia Stephen.' In *Stories for Children, Essays for Adults,* by Julia Duckworth Stephen, ed. Diane F. Gillespie and Elizabeth Steele, 1–27. Syracuse, NY: Syracuse University Press.

Gilmore, Leigh. 1994. 'Obscenity, Modernity, Identity: Legalizing *The Well of Loneliness* and *Nightwood.*' *Journal of the History of Sexuality* 4 (4): 603–24.

Gordon, Daphne. 2002. 'Makeovers: Why Women Bite.' *Toronto Star.* 28 Dec.: J3.

Gorman, Herbert. 1940. *James Joyce.* New York: Farrar, 1974.

Grahame, Kenneth. 1908. *The Wind in the Willows.* London: Methuen, 1971.

Graves, Robert. 1965. *Collected Poems, 1965.* London: Cassell.

Green, Martin, and John Swan. 1993. *The Triumph of Pierrot: The Commedia dell'Arte and the Modern Imagination.* Rev. ed. University Park: Pennsylvania State University Press.

Green, Percy. 1899. *A History of Nursery Rhymes.* Detroit: Singing Tree, 1968.

Green, Roger Lancelyn. 1946. *Andrew Lang: A Critical Biography.* Leicester, UK: Ward.

– 1969. *Tellers of Tales.* Rev. ed. London: Kaye & Ward.

Grey, Jill E. 1968. Introd. to *The Governess, or Little Female Academy,* by Sarah Fielding. London: Oxford University Press.

Grimm, Jacob, and Wilhelm Grimm. 1972. *The Complete Grimm's Fairy Tales.* Trans. Margaret Hunt and James Stern. New York: Random.

– 1992. *The Complete Fairy Tales of the Brothers Grimm.* Trans. and ed. Jack Zipes. New York: Bantam.

Halliwell-Phillipps, James Orchard. 1849. *Popular Rhymes and Nursery Tales.* Detroit: Singing Tree, 1968.

Hanscombe, Gillian, and Virginia L. Smyers. 1987. *Writing for Their Lives: The Modernist Women, 1910–1940.* London: Women's Press.

'Harlequin.' 1989. In *Oxford Reference Dictionary,* ed. Joyce M. Hawkins, 372. Oxford: Clarendon.

Harris, Janice H. 1986. 'Not Suffering and Not Still: Women Writers at the *Cornhill Magazine,* 1860–1900.' *Modern Language Quarterly* 47 (4): 382–92.

Hartland, Edwin Sidney. 1891. *The Science of Fairy Tales: An Inquiry Into Fairy Mythology.* Detroit: Singing Tree, 1968.

Helder, Jack. 1975. 'Fool Convention and Conrad's Hollow Harlequin.' *Studies in Short Fiction* 12: 361–8.

Henstra, Sarah. 2000. 'Looking the Part: Performative Narration in Djuna Barnes's *Nightwood* and Katherine Mansfield's "Je Ne Parle Pas Français."' *Twentieth Century Literature* 46 (2): 125–49.

Herr, Cheryl. 1986. *Joyce's Anatomy of Culture*. Urbana: University of Illinois Press.

– 1999. 'Old Wives' Tales as Portals of Discovery in 'Proteus.'' In Devlin and Reizbaum 1999, 30–41.

Herring, Phillip. 1993. 'Zadel Barnes: Journalist.' *Review of Contemporary Fiction* 13 (3): 107–16.

– 1995. *Djuna: The Life and Work of Djuna Barnes*. New York: Penguin, 1996.

Holland, Peter. 1997. 'The Play of Eros: Paradoxes of Gender in English Pantomime.' *New Theatre Quarterly* 13 (51): 195–204.

Holliss, Richard, and Brian Sibley. 1987. *Walt Disney's Snow White and the Seven Dwarfs & the Making of the Classic Film.'* New York: Hyperion, 1994.

Hopcke, Robert H. 1997. Foreword to *Fairy Tales: Traditional Stories Retold for Gay Men*, by Peter Cashorali. New York: Harper.

Horrall, Andrew. 2001. *Popular Culture in London c. 1890–1918: The Transformation of Entertainment*. Manchester: Manchester University Press.

Howes, Marjorie, and Derek Attridge. 2000. Introd. to *Semicolonial Joyce*, ed. Derek Attridge and Marjorie Howes, 1–20. Cambridge: Cambridge University Press.

Hunt, Peter, ed. 1995. *Children's Literature: An Illustrated History*. Oxford: Oxford University Press.

Hunter, Pamela. 1987. Introd. to *Façade* by Edith Sitwell, 9–18. London: Duckworth.

Hutcheon, Linda. 1994. *Irony's Edge: The Theory and Politics of Irony*. London: Routledge, 1995.

Hyde, Douglas, ed. and trans. 1890. *Beside the Fire: A Collection of Irish Gaelic Folk Stories*. New York: Lemma, 1973.

Irigaray, Luce. 1977. *This Sex Which Is Not One*. Trans. Catherine Porter and Carolyn Burke. Ithaca, NY: Cornell University Press, 1985.

Jackson, Mary. 1989. *Engines of Instruction, Mischief, and Magic: Children's Literature in England From Its Beginnings to 1839*. Lincoln: University of Nebraska Press.

Jackson, Tony E. 1991. '"Cyclops," "Nausicaa," and Joyce's Imaginary Irish Couple.' *James Joyce Quarterly* 29 (1): 63–83.

Jacobs, Joseph. 1890. *English Fairy Tales*. London: David Nutt.

Jarrell, Randall. 1956. *Selected Poems*. London: Faber.

Jay, Karla. 1990. 'The Outsider Among the Expatriates: Djuna Barnes's Satire on the Ladies of the *Almanack*.' In *Lesbian Texts and Contexts: Radical Revisions*, ed. Karla Jay, Joanne Glasgow, and Catharine Stimpson, 204–16. New York: New York University Press.

Jensen, Emily. 1983. 'Clarissa Dalloway's Respectable Suicide.' In *Virginia Woolf: A Feminist Slant,* ed. Jane Marcus, 162–79. Lincoln: University of Nebraska Press.

Jordan, Neil, dir. 1984. *The Company of Wolves.* Palace / ITC.

Joyce, James. 1900. 'Drama and Life.' In Joyce 1959, 38–46.

– 1901. 'The Day of the Rabblement.' In Joyce 1959, 68–72.

– 1904. 'The Holy Office.' *Poems and 'Exiles,'* ed. J.C.C. Mays, 103–6. London: Penguin, 1992.

– 1914. 'An Encounter.' In *Dubliners,* 11–20. London: Penguin, 1992.

– 1916. *A Portrait of the Artist as a Young Man.* New York: Penguin, 1999.

– 1939. *Finnegans Wake.* New York: Penguin, 1976.

– 1944. *Stephen Hero.* Ed. Theodore Spencer, John J. Slocum, and Herbert Cahoon. New York: New Directions, 1955.

– 1951. *Exiles.* Ed. Padraic Colum. New York: Viking, 1962.

– 1959. *The Critical Writings of James Joyce.* Ed. Ellsworth Mason and Richard Ellmann. Ithaca, NY: Cornell University Press, 1989.

– 1986. *Ulysses: The Corrected Text.* Ed. Hans Walter Gabler, Wolfhard Steppe, and Claus Melchior. New York: Vintage.

Jung, Carl. 1948. 'The Phenomenology of the Spirit in Fairytales.' In vol. 9 of *Collected Works,* trans. R.F.C. Hull, 207–54. New York: Pantheon, 1959.

Kaehele, Sharon, and Howard German. 1962. '"To the Lighthouse": Symbol and Vision.' In *Virginia Woolf 'To the Lighthouse': A Casebook,* ed. Morris Beja, 189–209. London: Macmillan, 1970.

Kearney, Richard. 1988. *Transitions: Narratives in Modern Irish Culture.* Manchester: Manchester University Press.

Kemp, Sandra. 1994. Introd. and Critical Commentary to *To the Lighthouse,* by Virginia Woolf, 1–27, 197–218. London: Routledge.

Kenner, Hugh. 1955. *Dublin's Joyce.* London: Chatto.

Kent, Kathryn R. 1993. '"Lullaby for a Lady's Lady': Lesbian Identity in *Ladies Almanack.'* *Review of Contemporary Fiction* 13 (3): 89–96.

Kershner, R.B. 1989. *Joyce, Bakhtin, and Popular Literature: Chronicles of Disorder.* Chapel Hill: University of North Carolina Press.

Kiberd, Declan. 1995. *Inventing Ireland.* London: Cape.

King, James. 1994. *Virginia Woolf.* London: Penguin, 1995.

Kinnell, Margaret. 1995. 'Publishing for Children, 1700–1780.' In Hunt 1995, 26–45.

Kipling, Rudyard. 1906. *Puck of Pook's Hill.* Ed. Sarah Wintle. London: Penguin, 1990.

Knoepflmacher, U.C. 1998. *Ventures into Childland: Victorians, Fairy Tales, and Femininity.* Chicago: University of Chicago Press.

Kolbenschlag, Madonna. 1979. *Goodbye Sleeping Beauty: Breaking the Spell of Feminine Myths and Models*. Dublin: Arlen House, 1983.

Lacan, Jacques. 1966. 'The Mirror Stage as Formative of the Function of the I as Revealed in Psychoanalytic Experience.' In *Écrits: A Selection*, trans. Alan Sheridan, 1–7. New York: Norton, 1977.

– 1981. 'The Quilting Point.' In *The Psychoses, 1955–1956*, trans. Russell Grigg, ed. Jacques-Alain Miller, 258–70. New York: Norton, 1993.

– 1975. 'Seminar of 21 January 1975.' *Feminine Sexuality: Jacques Lacan and the école freudienne*, trans. Jacqueline Rose, ed. Juliet Mitchell and Jacqueline Rose, 162–71. New York: Norton, 1985.

Lane, Marcia. 1994. *Picturing the Rose: A Way of Looking at Fairy Tales*. n.p.: Wilson.

Lang, Andrew. 1888. Introd. to *Perrault's Popular Tales*. Oxford: Clarendon.

– ed. 1889. 'Little Red Riding-Hood.' In *The Blue Fairy Book*, 51–3. New York: Dover, 1965.

– 1892. 'Modern Fairy Tales.' In Salway 1976, 133–6.

Lang, Fritz, dir. 1931. *M*. Janus.

Langstaff, Eleanor de Selms. 1978. *Andrew Lang*. Boston: Twayne.

Lanser, Susan Sniader. 1991. 'Speaking in Tongues: *Ladies Almanack* and the Discourse of Desire.' In Broe 1991, 156–68.

Law, Jules David. 1990. '"Pity They Can't See Themselves": Assessing the "Subject" of Pornography in "Nausicaa."' *James Joyce Quarterly* 27 (2): 219–39.

Leckie, Barbara. 1996–7. 'Reading Bodies, Reading Nerves: "Nausicaa" and the Discourse of Censorship.' *James Joyce Quarterly* 34 (1–2): 65–85.

Lee, Hermione. 1996. *Virginia Woolf*. London: Vintage, 1997.

Lee, Judith. 1991. '*Nightwood:* 'The Sweetest Lie."' In Broe 1991, 207–18.

Leonard, Garry. 1991. 'Women on the Market: Commodity Culture, "Femininity," and "Those Lovely Seaside Girls."' *Joyce Studies Annual* 2: 27–68.

– 1998. *Advertising and Commodity Culture in Joyce*. Gainesville: University Press of Florida.

– 1999. '"A Little Trouble about Those White Corpuscles": Mockery, Heresy, and the Transubstantiation of Masculinity in "Telemachus."' In Devlin and Reizbaum 1999, 1–19.

Lewis, Naomi. 1984. Introd. to *Hans Andersen's Fairy Tales: A Selection*. Oxford: Oxford University Press, 1998.

Lewis, Wyndham. 1927. *Time and Western Man*. Ed. Paul Edwards. Santa Rosa, CA: Black Sparrow, 1993.

Liukkonen, Petri. 2000. 'Alfred de Musset.' *Books and Writers*. http://www.kirjasto.sci.fi/demusset.htm (accessed 1 March 2002).

Locke, John. 1693. *Some Thoughts Concerning Education*. Ed. John W. and Jean S. Yolton. Oxford: Clarendon, 1989.

Lyon, George Ella. 1983. 'Virginia Woolf and the Problem of the Body.' In *Virginia Woolf: Centennial Essays*, ed. Elaine K. Ginsberg and Laura Moss Gottlieb, 111–25. Troy, NY: Whitston.

Lurie, Alison. 1990. *Not in Front of the Grown-Ups: Subversive Children's Literature*. London: Sphere, 1991.

Lüthi, Max. 1970. *Once Upon a Time: On the Nature of Fairy Tales*. Trans. Lee Chadeayne and Paul Gottwald. Bloomington: Indiana University Press.

MacDonald, Ruth K. 1982. *Literature for Children in England and America from 1646 to 1774*. Troy, NY: Whitston.

MacKay, Carol Hanbery. 1987. 'The Thackeray Connection: Virginia Woolf's Aunt Anny.' In *Virginia Woolf and Bloomsbury: A Centenary Celebration*, ed. Jane Marcus, 68–95. London: Macmillan.

Mander, Raymond, and Joe Mitchenson. 1973. *Pantomime: A Story in Pictures*. London: Peter Davies.

Manganaro, Marc. 2002. *Culture, 1922: The Emergence of a Concept*. Princeton, NJ: Princeton University Press.

Mansfield, Katherine. 1945. 'The Little Governess.' In *The Collected Stories of Katherine Mansfield*, 174–89. London: Penguin, 1981.

Mao, Douglas. 1998. *Solid Objects: Modernism and the Test of Production*. Princeton: Princeton University Press.

Marcus, Jane. 1980. 'Enchanted Organs, Magic Bells: *Night and Day* as Comic Opera.' In *Virginia Woolf: Revaluation and Continuity*, ed. Ralph Freedman, 97–122. Berkeley: University of California Press.

– 1988. *Art and Anger: Reading Like a Woman*. Columbus: Ohio State University Press.

– 1991. 'Laughing at Leviticus: *Nightwood* as Woman's Circus Epic.' In Broe 1991, 221–50.

Marshall, Peter. 1995. *Sex, Nursery Rhymes and Other Evils: A Look at the Bizarre, Amusing, Sometimes Shocking Advice of Victorian Childcare Experts*. Vancouver: Whitecap.

Martin, Ann. 2000. '"Sweet Dolly Sodam": The Politics of Narrative Drag in Djuna Barnes's *Ryder*.' *torquere: Journal of the Canadian Lesbian and Gay Studies Association* 2: 105–22.

Marx, Karl. 1995. *Capital: An Abridged Edition*. Ed. David McLellan. Oxford: Oxford University Press.

McGee, Patrick. 1987. 'Joyce's Nausea: Style and Representation in "Nausicaa."' *James Joyce Quarterly* 24 (3): 305–18.

McHugh, Roland. 1991. '*Annotations to Finnegans Wake.*' Rev. ed. Baltimore: Johns Hopkins University Press.

Mieder, Wolfgang. 1982. 'Survival Forms of "Little Red Riding Hood" in Modern Society.' *International Folklore Review* 2: 23–40.

Milne, A.A. 1971. *Winnie the Pooh: A Reproduction of the Original Manuscript.* London: Methuen.

Moch, Cheryl. 1989. *Cinderella, the Real True Story.* In *Lesbian Plays: Two,* ed. Jill Davis, 109–47. London: Methuen.

Montefiore, Jan. 1994. *Feminism and Poetry: Language, Experience, Identity in Women's Writing.* 2nd ed. London: Pandora.

Montgomery, L.M. 1997. *The Annotated Anne of Green Gables.* Ed. Wendy E. Barry, Margaret Anne Doody, and Mary E. Doody Jones. Oxford: Oxford University Press.

Moon, Kenneth. 1980. 'Where is Clarissa?: Doris Kilman in *Mrs. Dalloway.*' In *Clarissa Dalloway,* ed. Harold Bloom, 147–57. New York: Chelsea, 1990.

Moon, Michael, and Eve Kosofsky Sedgwick. 1993. 'Divinity: A Dossier, a Performance Piece, a Little-Understood Emotion.' In *Tendencies,* by Eve Kosofsky Sedgwick, 215–51. Durham, NC: Duke University Press, 1994.

Moore, Madeline. 1984. *The Short Season Between Silences.* Boston: George Allen & Unwin.

Murray, Heather. 1985. 'Frances Hoodgson Burnett's *The Secret Garden:* The Organ(ic)ized World.' In vol. 1 of *Touchstones: Reflections on the Best in Children's Literature,* ed. Perry Nodelman, 30–43. West Lafayette, IN: Children's Literature Assoc.

Neuberg, Victor E. 1968. *The Penny Histories: A Study of Chapbooks for Young Readers Over Two Centuries.* London: Oxford University Press.

– 1982. *The Batsford Companion to Popular Literature.* London: Batsford.

Nicoll, Allardyce. 1963. *The World of Harlequin: A Critical Study of the Commedia dell'Arte.* Cambridge: Cambridge University Press.

Nichols, Roger. 2002. *The Harlequin Years: Music in Paris, 1917–1929.* Berkeley: University of California Press.

Nicholls, Peter. 1995. *Modernisms: A Literary Guide.* Berkeley: University of California Press.

Nin, Anais. 1954. *A Spy in the House of Love.* New York: Pocket, 1994.

Norris, Margot. 1988. 'Modernism, Myth, and Desire in "Nausicaa."' *James Joyce Quarterly* 26 (1): 37–50.

Ochoa, Peggy. 1993. 'Joyce's 'Nausicaa': The Paradox of Advertising Narcissism.' *James Joyce Quarterly* 30–1 (4–1): 783–93.

O'Grady, Standish James. 1879. *Early Bardic Literature, Ireland.* New York: Lemma, 1970.

O'Leary, Philip. 1994. *The Prose Literature of the Gaelic Revival, 1881–1921: Ideology and Innovation.* University Park: Pennsylvania State University Press.

O'Neal, Hank. 1990. *'Life is Painful, Nasty and Short … In My Case It Has Only Been Painful and Nasty': Djuna Barnes, 1978–1981: An Informal Memoir.* New York: Paragon.

Opie, Iona, and Peter Opie. 1974. *The Classic Fairy Tales.* New York: Oxford University Press, 1980.

Orenstein, Catherine. 2002. *Little Red Riding Hood Uncloaked: Sex, Morality, and the Evolution of a Fairy Tale.* New York: Basic.

Parkes, Adam. 1997. '"Literature and instruments for abortion": "Nausicaa" and the *Little Review* Trial.' *James Joyce Quarterly* 34 (3): 283–301.

Paterakis, Deborah Tannen. 1972. 'Mananaan MacLir in *Ulysses.*' *Eire-Ireland: A Journal of Irish Studies* 7 (3): 29–35.

Patmore, Coventry. 1854–6. *The Angel in the House.* 2 vols. London: Parker.

Paul, Janis M. 1987. *The Victorian Heritage of Virginia Woolf: The External World in Her Novels.* Norman, OK: Pilgrim.

Pearson, Karl. 1897. *The Chances of Death and Other Studies in Evolution.* Vol. 2. London: Edward Arnold.

Perrault, Charles. 1969. *Perrault's Fairy Tales.* Trans. A.E. Johnson. New York: Dover.

– 1989. Preface to the Tales in Verse. In *Charles Perrault: Memoirs of My Life*, trans. and ed. Jeanne Morgan Zanuchi, 120–3. Columbia: University of Missouri Press.

Planché, James Robinson. 1986. *Plays by James Robinson Planché.* Ed. Donald Roy. Cambridge: Cambridge University Press.

Plumb, Cheryl. 1986. *Fancy's Craft: Art and Identity in the Early Works of Djuna Barnes.* Toronto: Associated University Presses.

Propp, Vladimir. 1968. *Morphology of the Folktale.* 2nd ed. Ed. Louis A. Wagner. Austin: University of Texas Press.

Rackham, Arthur and Edmund Gosse. 1916. *The Allies' Fairy Book / Fairy Tales from Many Lands.* London: Heineman, 1974.

Radford, F.L. 1987. 'Daedalus and the Bird Girl: Classical Text and Celtic Subtext in *A Portrait.*' *James Joyce Quarterly* 24 (3): 253–74.

Radway, Janice. 1984. *Reading the Romance: Women, Patriarchy, and Popular Literature.* Chapel Hill: University of North Carolina Press, 1991.

Rhys, Jean. 1939. *Good Morning, Midnight.* London: Penguin, 1969.

Richards, Thomas. 1990. *The Commodity Culture of Victorian England: Advertising and Spectacle, 1851–1914.* Stanford, CA: Stanford University Press.

Richter, Harvena. 1970. *Virginia Woolf: The Inward Voyage.* Princeton, NJ: Princeton University Press.

Riley, James Whitcomb. 1993. *The Complete Poetical Works of James Whitcomb Riley.* Bloomington: Indiana University Press.

Ritchie, Anne Thackeray. 1874. 'Toilers and Spinsters.' In *Toilers and Spinsters and Other Essays,* 1–35. London: Smith, 1890.

– 1902. *Bluebeard's Keys and Other Stories.* London: Smith.

– 1905. *Five Old Friends and a Young Prince.* London: Smith.

Rose, Jacqueline. 1984. *The Case of Peter Pan, or the Impossibility of Children's Fiction.* London: Macmillan.

– 1985. Introd. II to *Feminine Sexuality: Jacques Lacan and the école freudienne,* trans. Jacqueline Rose, ed. Juliet Mitchell and Jacqueline Rose, 27–57. New York: Norton.

Rosenman, Ellen Bayuk. 1986. *The Invisible Presence: Virginia Woolf and the Mother-Daughter Relationship.* Baton Rouge: Louisiana State University Press.

Rossetti, Christina. 1861. 'In an Artist's Studio.' In vol. 3 of *The Complete Poems of Christina Rossetti,* ed. R.W. Clump, 264. Baton Rouge: Louisiana State University Press, 1990.

Rousseau, Jean-Jacques. 1762. *Émile.* Trans. Barbara Foxley. London: Dent, 1955.

Rowe, Karen E. 1986. 'To Spin a Yarn: The Female Voice in Folklore and Fairy Tale.' In *Fairy Tales and Society: Illusion, Allusion, and Paradigm,* ed. Ruth B. Bottigheimer, 53–74. Philadelphia: University of Pennsylvania Press.

Rush, Florence. 1980. *The Best Kept Secret: Sexual Abuse of Children.* New York: McGraw-Hill.

Ruskin, John. 1841. *The King of the Golden River, or The Black Brothers: A Legend of Stiria.* Boston: Ginn, 1885.

– 1868. 'Fairy Stories.' In Salway 1976, 127–32.

Saki. 1914. 'The Storyteller.' In *Short Stories and the Unbearable Bassington,* ed. John Carey, 121–6. New York: Oxford University Press, 1994.

Sale, Roger. 1978. *Fairy Tales and After: From Snow White to E.B. White.* Cambridge: Harvard University Press.

Salway, Lance, ed. 1976. *A Peculiar Gift: Nineteenth-Century Writings on Books for Children.* Harmondsworth, UK: Kestrel.

Samber, Richard, trans. 1729. 'The Little Red Riding-Hood.' In *The Classic Fairy Tales,* ed. Iona Opie and Peter Opie, 122–5. New York: Oxford University Press.

Sayers, Dorothy L. 1933. *Murder Must Advertise.* London: New English, 1978.

– 1935. *Gaudy Night.* London: New English, 1978.

Schlack, Beverly Ann. 1979. *Continuing Presences: Virginia Woolf's Use of Literary Allusion.* University Park: Pennsylvania State University Press.

Scott, Bonnie Kime. 1987. *James Joyce*. Atlantic Highlands, NJ: Humanities.

– 1995. *Refiguring Modernism*. 2 vols. Bloomington: Indiana University Press.

Scott, James B. 1976. *Djuna Barnes*. Boston: Twayne.

Sedgwick, Eve Kosofsky. 1993. 'Queer and Now.' In *Tendencies*, 1–20. Durham: Duke University Press.

Senn, Fritz. 1971. 'Nausicaa.' In *Joyce's Dislocations: Essays on Reading as Translation*, ed. John Paul Riquelme, 160–87. Baltimore: Johns Hopkins University Press, 1984.

Sexton, Anne. 1971. *Transformations*. Boston: Houghton.

Shelton, Jen. 1996–7. 'Bad Girls: Gerty, Cissy, and the Erotics of Unruly Speech.' *James Joyce Quarterly* 34 (1–2): 87–102.

Sicker, Philip. 1999. '"Alone in the Hiding Twilight": Bloom's Cinematic Gaze in "Nausicaa."' *James Joyce Quarterly* 36 (4): 825–50.

Silver, Brenda R. 1983. Introd. to *Virginia Woolf's Reading Notebooks*, 3–31 Princeton, NJ: Princeton University Press.

Silver, Carole. 1994. 'When Rumpelstiltskin Ruled: Victorian Fairy Tales.' *Victorian Literature and Culture* 22: 327–36.

Simmel, Georg. 1903. 'The Metropolis and Mental Life.' In *The Sociology of Georg Simmel*, 409–24. London: Collier, 1950.

Sitwell, Edith. 1987. *Façade, with an interpretation by Pamela Hunter*. London: Duckworth.

Smith, Craig. 1991. 'Twilight in Dublin: A Look at Joyce's "Nausicaa."' *James Joyce Quarterly* 28 (3): 631–5.

Smith, Stevie. 1936. *Novel on Yellow Paper, or, Work it Out for Yourself*. London: Cape.

Smith, Victoria L. 1999. 'A Story beside(s) Itself: The Language of Loss in Djuna Barnes's *Nightwood*.' *PMLA* 114 (2): 194–206.

Sondheim, Stephen and James Lapine. 1987. *Into the Woods*. New York: Theatre Communications Group.

Spalding, Frances. 1983. *Vanessa Bell*. London: Weidenfeld.

Squier, Susan M. 1985. *Virginia Woolf and London: The Sexual Politics of the City*. Chapel Hill: University of North Carolina Press.

Stallybrass, Peter, and Allon White. 1986. *The Politics and Poetics of Transgression*. London: Methuen.

Steele, Elizabeth. 1987. 'Stories for Children.' In *Stories for Children, Essays for Adults*, by Julia Duckworth Stephen, ed. Diane F. Gillespie and Elizabeth Steele, 29–35. Syracuse, NY: Syracuse University Press.

Stephen, Julia Duckworth. 1987. *Stories for Children, Essays for Adults*. Ed. Diane F. Gillespie and Elizabeth Steele. Syracuse, NY: Syracuse University Press.

Stephen, Leslie. 1977. *Mausoleum Book.* Oxford: Clarendon.

Stephens, James. 1912. *The Charwoman's Daughter.* Dublin: Macmillan, 1972.

Stevenson, Sheryl. 1991. 'Writing the Grotesque Body: Djuna Barnes' Carnival Parody.' In Broe 1991, 81–91.

Summerfield, Geoffrey. 1984. *Fantasy and Reason: Children's Literature in the Eighteenth Century.* London: Methuen.

Tambling, Jeremy. 1989. 'Repression in Mrs Dalloway's London.' *Essays in Criticism* 39 (2): 137–55.

Tatar, Maria. 1992. *Off with Their Heads! Fairytales and the Culture of Childhood.* Princeton, NJ: Princeton University Press.

Taylor, Ronald. 1963. *Hoffmann.* London: Bowes.

'Thackeray (Anne Isabella).' 1986. In *Terju-Theve.* Vol. 323 of *The British Library General Catalogue of Printed Books to 1975,* 181–2. London: Saur.

Thackeray, William Makepeace. 1855. *The Rose and the Ring; or, the History of Prince Giglio and Prince Bulbo.* Vol. 8 of *Miscellanies,* 197–328. London: Smith, Elder, 1877.

Thurber, James. 1940. 'The Little Girl and the Wolf.' In Mieder 1982, 26.

Thwaite, Ann. 1984. *Edmund Gosse: A Literary Landscape 1849–1928.* London: Secker.

Tintner, Adeline R. 1989. *The Pop World of Henry James: From Fairy Tales to Science Fiction.* Ann Arbor, MI: UMI.

Tolkien, J.R.R. 1937. *The Hobbit.* London: Harper, 1993.

– 1955. *The Return of the King.* London: Harper, 1993.

– 1964. *Tree and Leaf.* London: George Allen & Unwin.

Townsend, John Rowe. 1974. *Written for Children: An Outline of English-Language Children's Literature.* New York: Penguin, 1977.

Tymoczko, Maria. 1989. 'Symbolic Structures in *Ulysses* from Early Irish Literature.' In Ben-Merre and Murphy 1989, 17–29.

Valente, Joseph. 1999. 'The Perils of Masculinity in "Scylla and Charybdis."' In Devlin and Reizbaum 1999, 111–35.

Vian, Boris. 1992. *Blues for a Black Cat and Other Stories.* Trans. and ed. Julia Older. Lincoln: University of Nebraska Press.

Vogler, Thomas A. 1970. Introd. to *Twentieth Century Interpretations of 'To the Lighthouse,'* 1–38. Englewood Cliffs, NJ: Prentice.

Walker, Barbara. 1996. *Feminist Fairy Tales.* New York: Harper.

Walkerdine, Valerie. 1984. 'Some Day my Prince Will Come: Young Girls and the Preparation for Adolescent Sexuality.' In *Gender and Generation,* ed. Angela McRobbie and Mina Nava, 162–84. London: Macmillan.

Warner, Marina. 1994a. *From the Beast to the Blonde: On Fairy Tales and Their Tellers.* London: Vintage, 1995.

– 1994b. Introd. to *Wonder Tales*, 1–17. New York: Ferrar, 1996.

Warner, Sylvia Townsend. 1940. *The Cat's Cradle-Book*. New York: Viking.

Watson, G.J. 1994. *Irish Identity and the Literary Revival: Synge, Yeats, Joyce and O'Casey*. 2nd ed. Washington: Catholic University of American Press.

Watt, Ian. 1957. *The Rise of the Novel*. London: Chatto, 1963.

Wicke, Jennifer. 1994a. 'Lingerie and (literary) History: Joyce's Ulysses and Fashionability.' *Critical Quarterly* 36 (2): 25–41.

– 1994b. 'Mrs. Dalloway Goes to Market: Woolf, Keynes, and Modern Markets.' *Novel: A Forum on Fiction* 28 (1): 5–23.

– 1994c. '"Who's She When She's at Home?": Molly Bloom and the Work of Consumption.' In *Molly Blooms: A Polylogue on 'Penelope' and Cultural Studies*, ed. Richard Pearce, 174–237. Madison: University of Wisconsin Press.

Wilde, Oscar. 1888. 'The Happy Prince.' In *The Happy Prince and Other Stories*, 11–24. Middlesex, UK: Penguin, 1968.

– 1902. *The Decay of Lying*. n.p.: Sunflower.

Wilde, W.R. 1852. *Irish Popular Superstitions*. Shannon: Irish University Press, 1972.

Williams, Raymond. 1973. *The Country and the City*. London: Chatto & Windus.

– 1983. *Keywords: A Vocabulary of Culture and Society*. Rev. ed. New York: Oxford University Press.

– 1989. *The Politics of Modernism*. London: Verso, 1996.

Wilson, A.E. 1949. *The Story of Pantomime*. London: Home.

Wilson, Edmund. 1931. *Axel's Castle: A Study in the Imaginative Literature of 1870–1930*. New York: Macmillan, 1991.

Winkiel, Laura. 1997. 'Circuses and Spectacles: Public Culture in Nightwood.' *Journal of Modern Literature* 21 (1): 7–28.

Winterson, Jeannette. 1989. *Sexing the Cherry*. Toronto: Vintage, 2000.

Wiser, William. 1983. *The Crazy Years: Paris in the Twenties*. London: Thames.

Wittig, Monique. 1980. 'The Point of View: Universal or Particular?' In *The Straight Mind and Other Essays*, 59–67. Boston: Beacon, 1992.

Woolf, Virginia. 1917. 'A Victorian Echo.' In Woolf 1987, 149–51.

– 1919a. 'Lady Ritchie.' In Woolf 1988, 13–20.

– 1919b. *Night and Day*. Ed. J.H. Stape. London: Blackwell, 1994.

– 1919c. 'Washington Irving.' In Woolf 1988, 28–30.

– 1920. 'Pure English.' In Woolf 1988, 235–8.

– 1924. 'The Enchanted Organ.' In Woolf 1988, 399–403.

– 1925a. '*David Copperfield*.' In Woolf 1947b, 65–9.

– 1925b. 'Jane Austen.' In *The Common Reader, First Series*, ed. Andrew McNeillie, 134–45. San Diego, CA: Harcourt, 1984.

- 1925c. *Mrs Dalloway*. Ed. Morris Beja. London: Blackwell, 1996.
- 1927a. 'The New Dress.' In Woolf 1989, 170–7.
- 1927b. *To the Lighthouse*. Ed. Susan Dick. London: Blackwell, 1992.
- 1928a. 'Moments of Being: Slater's Pins Have No Points.' In Woolf 1989, 215–20.
- 1928b. *Orlando*. Ed. J.H. Stape. London: Blackwell, 1998.
- 1929a. *A Room of One's Own*. In '*A Room of One's Own' and 'Three Guineas*,' ed. Michèle Barrett, 1–114. London: Penguin, 1993.
- 1929b. 'Women and Fiction.' In *Women and Writing*, ed. Michèle Barrett, 43–52. London: Women's Press, 1979.
- 1932. 'I am Christina Rossetti.' In *The Common Reader, Second Series*, 237–44. London: Hogarth, 1965.
- 1937. *The Years*. London: Grafton, 1990.
- 1939a. 'Lewis Carroll.' In Woolf 1947b, 70–1.
- 1939b. 'Reviewing.' In *The Crowded Dance of Modern Life: Selected Essays, Volume Two*, ed. Rachel Bowlby, 152–63. New York: Penguin, 1993.
- 1939c. *Three Guineas*. In '*A Room of One's Own' and 'Three Guineas*,' ed. Michèle Barrett, 115–334. London: Penguin, 1993.
- 1941. *Between the Acts*. Ed. Stella McNichol. London: Penguin, 1992.
- 1942. 'Professions for Women.' In *The Crowded Dance of Modern Life*. Ed. Rachel Bowlby, 101–6. London: Penguin, 1993.
- 1947a. 'Edmund Gosse.' In Woolf 1947b, 72–8.
- 1947b. *The Moment and Other Essays*. London: Hogarth, 1952.
- 1950. 'Ruskin.' In *The Captain's Death Bed and Other Essays*, 49–52. London: Hogarth.
- 1976a. *Freshwater: A Comedy*. Ed. Lucio P. Ruotolo. New York: Harcourt.
- 1976b. *Moments of Being: Unpublished Autobiographical Writings*. Ed. Jeanne Schulkind. Sussex, UK: Sussex University Press.
- 1976c. *The Question of Things Happening*. Vol. 2 of *The Letters of Virginia Woolf*. Ed. Nigel Nicolson and Joanne Trautmann. London: Hogarth.
- 1977. *The Diary of Virginia Woolf*. Vol. 1. Ed. Anne Olivier Bell and Andrew McNeillie. New York: Harcourt.
- 1978. *The Diary of Virginia Woolf*. Vol. 2. Ed. Anne Olivier Bell and Andrew McNeillie. New York: Harcourt.
- 1980. *The Diary of Virginia Woolf*. Vol. 3. Ed. Anne Olivier Bell and Andrew McNeillie. New York: Harcourt.
- 1982a. *The Diary of Virginia Woolf*. Vol. 4. Ed. Anne Olivier Bell and Andrew McNeillie. New York: Harcourt.
- 1982b. *The Widow and the Parrot*. Illus. Julian Bell. New York: Harcourt, 1988.
- 1984. *The Diary of Virginia Woolf*. Vol. 5. Ed. Anne Olivier Bell and Andrew

McNeillie. New York: Harcourt.

– 1986. *The Essays of Virginia Woolf.* Vol. 1. Ed. Andrew McNeillie. London: Hogarth.

– 1987. *The Essays of Virginia Woolf.* Vol. 2. Ed. Andrew McNeillie. London: Hogarth.

– 1988. *The Essays of Virginia Woolf.* Vol. 3. Ed. Andrew McNeillie. London: Hogarth.

– 1989. *The Complete Shorter Fiction of Virginia Woolf.* Rev. ed. Ed. Susan Dick. London: Hogarth.

– 1990. *A Passionate Apprentice: The Early Journals, 1897–1909.* Ed. Mitchell A. Leaska. San Diego, CA: Harcourt.

– 1991. *Nurse Lugton's Curtain.* Illus. Julie Vivas. London: Bodley Head.

– 1994. *The Essays of Virginia Woolf.* Vol. 4. Ed. Andrew McNeillie. London: Hogarth.

– 1999. *Flush: A Biography.* Ed. Elizabeth Steele. Oxford: Blackwell.

Wordsworth, William. 1965. 'Written in London, September, 1802.' In *Selected Poems and Prefaces,* ed. Jack Stillinger, 172. Boston: Houghton.

Yeats, W.B. 1888. Introd. to *Fairy and Folk Tales of the Irish Peasantry.* In Yeats 1993, 1–7.

– 1892. Introd. to *Irish Fairy Tales.* In *Fairy and Folk Tales of Ireland,* ed. Kathleen Raine, 301–3. Gerrards Cross, UK: Smythe, 1977.

– 1898. 'The Celtic Element in Literature.' In Yeats 1993, 189–200.

– 1902. *The Celtic Twilight.* Rev. ed. Gerrards Cross, UK: Smythe, 1981.

– 1955. *Autobiographies.* London: Macmillan, 1991.

– 1993. *Writings on Irish Folklore, Legend and Myth.* Ed. Robert Welch. London: Penguin.

Yoder, Emily K. 1980. 'The Demon Harlequin in Conrad's Hell.' *Conradiana* 12: 88–92.

Yolen, Jane. 1982. 'America's Cinderella.' In Dundes 1982, 294–306.

Zipes, Jack. 1983. *Fairy Tales and the Art of Subversion: The Classic Genre for Children and the Process of Civilization.* New York: Routledge, 1991.

– 1992. Notes to *The Complete Fairy Tales of the Brothers Grimm,* ed. and trans. Jack Zipes, 728–43. New York: Bantam.

– 1999. *When Dreams Came True: Classical Fairy Tales and Their Tradition.* New York: Routledge.

Zwerdling, Alex. 1986. *Virginia Woolf and the Real World.* Berkeley: University of California Press.

Index

DATE DUE